The Wisdom Way of Teaching: Educating for Social Conscience and Inner Awakening in the High School Classroom

A Volume in:
Transforming Education for the Future

Series Editors:
Jing Lin
Rebecca L. Oxford
Vachel W. Miller

Transforming Education for the Future

Series Editors:
Jing Lin
University of Maryland

Rebecca L. Oxford
University of Maryland

Vachel W. Miller
Appalachian State University

Books in This Series:

Contemplative Pedagogies for Transformative Teaching, Learning, and Being (2019)
Jing Lin, Tom E. Culham, & Sachi Edwards

*Apocalyptic Leadership in Education:
Facing an Unsustainable World from Where We Stand* (2017)
Vachel W. Miller

*Critical Conversations about Religion:
Promises and Pitfalls of a Social Justice Approach to Interfaith Dialogue* (2016)
Sachi Edwards

*Toward a Spiritual Research Paradigm:
Exploring New Ways of Knowing, Researching and Being* (2016)
Jing Lin, Rebecca L. Oxford, & Tom E. Culham

*Re-Envisioning Higher Education:
Embodied Pathways to Wisdom and Social Transformation* (2013)
Jing Lin, Rebecca L. Oxford, & Edward J. Brantmeier

*Ethics Education of Business Leaders:
Emotional Intelligence, Virtues, and Contemplative Learning* (2013)
Tom E. Culham

Transformative Eco-Education for Human and Planetary Survival (2011)
Jing Lin & Rebecca L. Oxford

The Wisdom Way of Teaching: Educating for Social Conscience and Inner Awakening in the High School Classroom

Martin E. Schmidt

INFORMATION AGE PUBLISHING, INC.
Charlotte, NC • www.infoagepub.com

Library of Congress Cataloging-In-Publication Data

The CIP data for this book can be found on the Library of Congress website (loc.gov).

Paperback: 978-1-64802-847-2
Hardcover: 978-1-64802-848-9
E-Book: 978-1-64802-849-6

Copyright © 2022 Information Age Publishing Inc.

All rights reserved. No part of this publication may be reproduced, stored in a retrieval system, or transmitted, in any form or by any means, electronic, mechanical, photocopying, microfilming, recording or otherwise, without written permission from the publisher.

Printed in the United States of America

CONTENTS

Dedication and Acknowledgements ix

Foreword xi
Cynthia Bourgeault

Introducing the Wisdom Way of Teaching xv

Introduction to Hong Kong International School xxv
Jim Handrich

PART I
TEACHING FOR SOCIAL CONSCIENCE

1. My Journey of Teaching for Social Conscience 3
2. Humanities I in Action Curriculum and the Impact of Social Conscience Education 11
3. Is Ignorance Bliss? Teaching About Chocolate Slavery on Day One 37
4. The Heroic Journey from Self-Focus to Compassion: Mentoring Students Through an Orphanage Trip Experience 51
5. The Elixir Project: Initiating a Path Towards Meaningful Adulthood 63
6. Principles of Social Conscience Curriculum Design 73
7. The Four Essential Roles of Social Conscience Teachers 83

v

PART II
TEACHING FOR INNER AWAKENING

8. My Journey of Teaching for Inner Awakening 93
9. The Essentials of a Curriculum for Self-Understanding: The Body-Mind-Heart Framework in Service, Society, and the Sacred 103
10. Balancing Body, Mind, and Heart: Introducing the Wisdom Tradition in a World Religions Class 117
11. Waking Up to the Vertical Dimension: Student Reflections on a Practice-Based Religion Curriculum in Spiritual Explorations 125
12. Teaching Toward Inner Awakening Through a Spiritual Practices Project in SPEX 141
13. The Wisdom Way of Knowing and Teaching: The Epistemological Foundations of SPEX Teachers 153

PART III
SPECIAL TOPICS IN INNER AWAKENING

14. Teaching Consciousness of the Body: Two Practitioners in Dialogue 161
    Sangeeta Bansal and Martin E. Schmidt
15. Non-Reactivity: The Supreme Practice of Everyday Life 169
16. Dealing With the Accuser: Befriending Your Inner Critic 177
    Sangeeta Bansal and Martin E. Schmidt

PART IV
REFLECTIONS ON THE WISDOM WAY OF TEACHING

17. Teacher Perspectives 191
18. Student Voices 203
19. My Wisdom Way of Teaching Philosophy 219
    Appendix A.   Interview about Humanities I in Action 231

Appendix B. Exemplary "Service, Society, and the Sacred" Final Essays	235
Appendix C. My Worldview: Do I Believe in a Vertical Dimension?	243
Appendix D. Overview of the SPEX Curriculum	247
References	257

Truly I tell you, whatever you did for one of the least of these brothers and sisters of mine, you did for me.

Blessed are the pure in heart, for they shall see God.
—Jesus, Matthew 25:40 and 5:8

Those who are mine love to teach and to serve. They long for an opportunity of service as a hungry man longs for food, and they are always watching for it. Their hearts are so full of divine Love that it must be always overflowing in love for those around them. Only such are fit to be teachers—those to whom teaching is not only a holy and imperative duty, but also the greatest of pleasures.

—- Jiddu Krishnamurti, Education as Service

DEDICATION AND ACKNOWLEDGEMENTS

In a book drawing on material spanning three decades, including hundreds of colleagues and students, where does one start in expressing appreciation for the many contributions that compose this text? Before recognizing those in my immediate proximity, however, I would first like to offer my most profound gratitude to my spiritual teacher Cynthia Bourgeault as the torchbearer in my life and for so many others around the world of the mysterious wellspring of Wisdom that runs through the centuries. Her own journey has changed mine, and so it is my great joy to offer back to her and the global Wisdom network how these teachings have reverberated through one school community—with the hope of fruitful experimentation in other settings across the planet as a result.

I also want to offer my deepest appreciation to the two institutions, the Lutheran Church Missouri Synod (LCMS) and Hong Kong International School, which have offered me and my colleagues the spaciousness for these ideas and practices to slowly take root over many years. I am particularly indebted to Chuck Dull, Jim Handrich, and Ted Engelbrecht, all of whom personally supported combining my school and church roles beginning in 1999 for 15 years—without which there would have been far fewer service opportunities, no research and no book—as well as the World Mission Department of the LCMS, which generously supported me throughout those years.

Those closest to the work here, of course, have been my inimitable colleagues in the Humanities Department of Hong Kong International School that has been the incubator of all the courses and experiences described here. Conversations about social justice, service, and spirituality mix easily with the daily antics of 25 people in the same office who have dedicated their professional lives to collective values of the highest order. Special thanks to those colleagues past and present who have contributed to the teacher reflections in Chapter 17, and to my co-author of two of the inner awakening chapters, Sangeeta Bansal.

To the hundreds of students who have contributed here and whom we have taught, you have led the way. I've always said that my best ideas come from students, so for your wisdom and compassion that are palpable throughout this text, this is all for you and for future students.

I also want to extend my deep gratitude to my doctoral advisor Alan Pritchard, who surehandedly guided my research on social conscience education. Special notes of thanks as well to Andy Donlan, Nancy Kroonenberg, and Shobha Nihalani, all of whom provided not only their linguistic skills, but also invested themselves personally to improve the quality of the writing. I also want to thank alum Katie Lam (class of 2020) for her graphic design expertise that can be seen in the figures throughout the text as well as my colleague Geoff Ballard for patiently creating a cover design that I'm very happy with.

Finally, I would like to offer my love and respect to my parents, Allan and Sandy Schmidt, who dedicated their marital partnership as loving service to people stretching from Baltimore and Nebraska to Shanghai and Hanoi for 60 years. I also happily offer my heartfelt thanks to my wife and partner in so much of this work, Zella, and our dear children, Christa and Micah, for not only encouraging me to write this book, but also participating in so much of what is described in these pages. Christa Ming (明), may you be the "light of Christ," and Micah, may you "do justice, love mercy, and walk humbly with your God."

The last word is to dedicate this book to Wisdom itself, which in Cynthia's lineage is not some inert abstraction, but rather an inner aliveness that moves the planets and the stars, but seems most pleased to take up residence in the human heart.

FOREWORD

Cynthia Bourgeault

It is an honor to introduce this wonderful new book by master teacher and Wisdom trailblazer Martin E. Schmidt.

Almost every time I give a retreat or a Wisdom teaching day, the question will inevitably come up, "What can we do to share this with younger people?" The concern is real and heartfelt. My audiences are filled primarily with grey-heads like myself, who appreciate the transformative impact of the contemplative and Wisdom practices they are learning and wish sincerely to share them with the younger generation, their children and grandchildren. "If I only had known this when I was growing up!" "If I had only learned these skills and insights in my formative years, what a difference it would have made in my life." These are the invariable refrains.

I know this personally to be true, because I had one such teacher who did exactly that: a gifted high school religion teacher when I was sixteen, who encouraged us to ask the real questions and pointed us toward what is deep and universal in the heart of humanity. Moving beyond stock doctrinal questions and clichéd answers, he encouraged us to think, to feel, and to trust the intuitive wisdom that lay coiled in our own souls. The depth of his imprint on my being reverberates to this day; he literally lit the inner lamp by which I would make my way through life. Such is the difference that one teacher, one powerful teaching, can make.

The Wisdom Way of Teaching: Educating for Social Conscience and Inner Awakening in the High School Classroom, pages xi–xiii.
Copyright © 2022 by Information Age Publishing
www.infoagepub.com
All rights of reproduction in any form reserved.

We need this kind of educational innovation, for we know that the old moral roadmap is not working anymore, at least not in the modern secular high school. Isolation and competition, alienation from one's body, peer pressure, academic pressure, a constant backdrop of social anxiety and anxiety-related disorders all betoken that beneath the shiny surface, something, indeed "is rotten in the state of Denmark." Disorientation and depression run sky high in a culture where the real things that give meaning and purpose to human life cannot be pursued or even talked about—and as always, our children are the canaries in the mine shaft. It is to this malady that the beautiful Wisdom Way of Teaching outlined in this book seeks to address.

What Marty is up to here is bringing overall coherence to two educational reforms—service learning and mindfulness—that have demonstrated real staying power. He neatly conjoins the two through the yin-yang symbol, making explicit the need to bring together social justice and inner work under the same directive of transformation. The myriad of student testimonials in this volume provide striking evidence of the transformative potential of service experiences, which brings them proximate to my primary interest of Wisdom.

Over the past decade now, riding the crest of the hugely successful mindfulness movement, we are seeing traditional spiritual practices such as meditation, conscious listening and speaking, and embodied awareness gently creeping into high school and even elementary school programs, largely under the auspices of emotional self-regulation, stress reduction, and personal wellness. This is a very encouraging first step, for all these practices can indeed go a long way toward restoring a sense of spaciousness and balance in an educational environment which—mirroring the cultural climate—finds itself increasingly dominated by dysfunctional levels of competition, stress, and a background anxiety that just won't quit. The sense of selfhood one touches, sometimes without knowing it, in those moments of quiet opening to some other depth of reality can go a long way toward establishing an inner "anchor to windward" against the continuing ravages of peer group definition, helicopter parenting, and the unremitting pressure to achieve. So if for no other reason than the wellness benefits they provide, the recovery of these practices is an eminently sane first step in a world grown increasingly hostile to the psyche, particularly the young psyche.

But these ancient Wisdom practices, held in common by all the sacred traditions worldwide, are more than simply therapeutic countermeasures. They contain a vision, an implicit anthropology of a human being: our real purposes and accountability, the web of interconnectedness that subtly holds us and our planet together. These are not doctrinal statements, applicable only within a specific tradition. They are a universal legacy of what it means and feels to be human, to live our lives with dignity, authenticity, and a true sense of purpose and connection. Without these roots and teachings, we default to secular society, where the goals are ruthlessly materialistic and self-referential: compete, get into a top college, be successful. This is the subtext churning relentlessly beneath the surface, ironically at its most destructive fever pitch in some of our most privileged schools.

I know Martin E. Schmidt first and foremost because I am a grandmother. I met him nearly a decade ago, when my three grandchildren were attending Hong Kong International School during a seven-year overseas career posting. Marty taught my oldest grandson, Jack; how I wish that the younger two could have been so blessed! Even factoring in differences of temperament and type, I can still see the clear and healthy traces of Marty's extraordinary touch with questing young minds in my now college-age firstborn. You will see that same extraordinary touch at work here in the pages of this book. I can personally validate Marty's pull-no-punches analysis of the impact of academic pressure and a pervasive sense of cultural isolation ("living in a bubble") even on children one would normally identify as "privileged." But far more important, we read the subtext of how deeply these young human consciences are intact and yearning to be reconnected to authentic purpose in their lives, a genuine connection with the rest of humanity and with our planet itself.

Marty's curriculum takes the powerful next step beyond Wisdom-practice-as-wellness to Wisdom-practice-as vision-and-purpose. With feedback at each step from the students who are fully his co-creators in this enterprise, he lays before us a teaching model for a collective deep dive into the practices and understandings that can open a heart and redirect a life. It takes an impartial and gifted educator to weave vision and practices into curricula, and this is what you will see here: a practical, wise, and thoroughly ground-tested roadmap for the path to inner awakening, specifically designed for the 13–18 year age group, the time when organic spiritual awakening most powerfully begins in a human being.

What you see unfolding on these pages is a courageous, compassionate, imaginative, well balanced curriculum to engage the hearts and minds of that next generation in our essential and common humanity, while we still can. It is truly Wisdom work, and to you, Martin E. Schmidt, I offer my gratitude and a deep grandmotherly bow.

INTRODUCING THE WISDOM WAY OF TEACHING

The whole secret of the teacher's force lies in the conviction that [humans] are convertible, and they are. They want awakening, to get the soul out of bed, out of [its] habitual sleep, out into God's universe, to a perception of its beauty, and hearing of its call.[1]

—*Emerson cited in Lothstein (2008, p. 88)*

A truly integrative education engages students in the systematic exploration of the relationship between their studies of the "objective" world and the purpose, meaning, limits, and aspirations of their lives. The greatest divide of all is often between the inner and the outer . . . The healing of this divide is at the heart of education.

—*Palmer et al. (2010, p. 10)*

---

[1] In this book, when quoting authors or sources from previous eras which use traditionally gendered language, I have updated such language to modern writing standards, which attempt to honor all people rather than excluding half of the population. Examples include changing the word "man" to [person] if referring to a generic individual and changing "he" to the generic plural [they] when necessary. No changes are made to gendered pronouns if referring to a specific person.

The Wisdom Way of Teaching: Educating for Social Conscience and Inner Awakening in the High School Classroom, pages xv–xxiv.
Copyright © 2022 by Information Age Publishing
www.infoagepub.com
All rights of reproduction in any form reserved.

> The way I imagined it was by picturing myself as a cocoon. Humanities I in Action [in grade 9] had effectively cracked the hard outer shell, but I still needed a final blow to completely eradicate the inner shell, allowing me to grow into a beautiful butterfly. SSS [in grade 12] was that final blow.
> —*Rohan, grade 12 male student*

When I first began teaching, I wanted to find the power of education. The root of this allurement was the Lutheran education of my youth that I received in Baltimore, Maryland. So many of my teachers from kindergarten to college were simply good, "salt of the earth" human beings who served others through their teaching and their lives. Although as a Lutheran community we did not use such elevated terms as "transformation" or "breaking of the ego," these messages were encoded in the sacred Christian story that formed the basis of our community. Stories like Jesus changing water into wine, the raising of Lazarus from the dead, the walk to Emmaus, or Paul's "Damascus Road" experience—all spoke in their rich narrative symbolism of the tradition's *raison d'être* as a catalyst of transformation. Of particular importance in my youth was the bold, plain speaking of II Corinthians 5:17: "If anyone is in Christ, [that person] is a new creation; the old has passed away, and the new has come." These teachings, received as God's Word, imprinted upon me the implicit understanding that human existence was all about some rupture from ordinary, temporal consciousness and entering into a new life of the Spirit, transforming the self in some fundamental, mysterious, and yet discernible way.

Now 30 years later, I still think that working with the power of transformation in education is the most important vocation that I can dedicate my life to. I have been on a quest in these years to work out for myself how power in education is fully and most holistically expressed, especially in the international school setting in which I teach in Hong Kong. The relatively small parochial community of my formative years in the 1970s and 1980s in which church, school, and family all adhered to the same sacred story contrasts dramatically with teaching affluent Western expatriate and Chinese international school students in 21st century Hong Kong. While the echo of a theistic belief system remains an important source of sustenance and hope for those who believe—assuring adherents that the human story ultimately culminates in a happy ending—most of my students find this traditional worldview of my youth to be bewildering and even contradictory. For most students, it simply does not speak to their personal and spiritual concerns.

In traditional cultures, a unified understanding of how the universe worked was taught hand-in-hand with rituals and practices to enable a seeker to find the Wisdom[2] path (Armstrong, 2019). However, in this age of scientific critique of all metanarra-

---

[2] Capitalizing "Wisdom" in this text indicates a reference to the "Wisdom tradition," a term my spiritual teacher Cynthia Bourgeault uses to denote the universal teachings about the inner work of transformation that runs through all world cultures and religions. Using the lower case—"wisdom"—suggests a more generic sense of insight found in human life.

tives, traditional cosmologies and their accompanying practices are often dismissed or simply unnoticed. Furthermore, the wealthy international students whom I teach, simply by their exposure to a world of travel, multiple perspectives, and high levels of affluence, assume a posture of superiority towards those limited by their nationalistic horizons and middle class incomes, further severing the link between traditional worldviews that, at their best, inculcate community-based values embedded in a sacred story and my students' attempts to create a cohesive belief system. The administrators and teachers, for their part, lack the commonly accepted certainty of previous eras, so the task of working out a fully integrated worldview falls to students to discern for themselves. This has left our students with highly attuned critical reasoning skills, but bereft of other ways of knowing. They can tell you what they don't believe, but find little guidance to stake their fidelity in anything beyond what appeals to their situational needs and values. For all of their achievements, my students seem adrift about the really big questions.

Given that the majority of our students are not typically dedicating their professional lives to serving the common good, most aim for conventional markers of success that one would expect to find in an affluent community.[3] A recent graduate spoke to me a few months ago describing the "HKIS narrative," which I then shared with all my classes to determine if students in fact agreed with its description: "Study hard, go to college, work crazy hours for some 'soul-sucking' job, make enough money to be 'comfortable,' and eventually find a way to retire early and live the good life, which is all about three-star Michelin restaurants, yachts, and 5-star+ vacations." And indeed, in my grade 9 Humanities I in Action class, 15 of the 21 students agreed that this was their basic narrative. Consulting with all my classes, I estimate that for more than 75% of students, this speaks to their guiding life philosophy.

Yet revealing a previously unacknowledged narrative opens up the possibility of change. I challenged one of my high-achieving students in the Humanities I in Action class, Anita,[4] to think beyond that story and consider using her abilities to create a more meaningful life. Some weeks later she wrote in her final essay:

> Prior to this class, my entire life had already been planned out according to society's norms of success, to get perfect grades, into an Ivy League school then a six-figure job. However, this class opened my eyes to a world outside of this selfish bubble of money and power . . . One guest speaker that spoke to me most was Liz Lo,[5] a graduated HKIS student. Although she grew up in an Asian household similar to mine, where grades are significantly valued, she was able to escape from the story that HKIS stu-

---
[3] I want to make clear that I note this as a matter of fact to be acknowledged and considered rather than any kind of judgment of my students, whom I respect deeply and enjoy working with immensely.
[4] I have chosen to generally use students' real names in the text because personal connections are an important part of the story I want to tell.
[5] Elizabeth Lo, graduate of HKIS in 2005, is an award-winning filmmaker who has recently completed her first feature film called "Stray," which unconventionally follows three dogs around on their daily experiences in Istanbul.

dents are captive to and instead created her own story by pursuing her passions and raising awareness about something she cares about. Her speech made me realize that it was more than possible to stray away from the story I was captive to, and from there I was able to start thinking about a new narrative . . . Because of Humanities I in Action, my worldview has changed radically, and I have walked out of this course determined to use my passion to make a difference in the world and live in my own story.

It is to encourage such moments of challenge and insight that the *Wisdom Way of Teaching* exists.

Two more pieces of my educational context are needed before the goals of this book can be stated directly. First, for all of our efforts to prepare students academically and for personal growth, a macro-micro paradox characteristic of affluent international educational systems is evident here as well: such communities simultaneously indulge in considerable ecological destruction while driving many students to personal exhaustion. Thus, any educational innovation that does not have one eye on the global environment and another on the mental well-being of students is incomplete. Put into an affirmative, agrarian pacifist Wendell Berry (1981) advises that we need to "solve for pattern" (pp. 137–138). To begin such a process, education first needs to help students connect their inner work with the great socio-political issues of our time. It was this linkage that propelled Anita to claim that her life narrative had "changed radically."

The final contextual element is the place of spirituality in this story. Fifteen years ago in a moment of curiosity I did a short exercise in my Humanities I in Action class—a social justice-oriented curriculum that only very occasionally ventures into topics that would be considered "spiritual"—asking students how they would define a spiritual person. I took their individual written responses and compiled them into a statement: "From the self-understanding that comes from an exploration of the heart, the spiritual person develops an inner state of contentment and an alertness to the world, which leads to new connections with others and service to society.[6]" Intuitively, these 14-year-olds understood that the quest to make the world a better place originates within the human heart.

For years, then, I had been seeking how to integrate students' inner and outer worlds in curricula. However, in spite of encouraging intimations that I was on the right path, I lacked the right match of satisfying theoretical understandings along with effective pedagogical methods to realize this holistic vision in the lives of my students.

Meeting Episcopalian priest, scholar, and mystic Cynthia Bourgeault in October, 2010, then, was a personal watershed moment. Listening to Cynthia[7] and reading her books opened a whole new world of Wisdom perspectives and prac-

---

[6] When we give students in our religion courses a variety of definitions of spirituality, this student-generated option is always the most popular choice.

[7] I have opted in most cases to simply refer to my spiritual teacher as "Cynthia" rather than the common protocol of including her last name or full name in an academic text. Having taught her grandson at HKIS some years ago when I knew her first as "Jack's grandmother" and participating

Introducing the Wisdom Way of Teaching • xix

The Author With Cynthia Bourgeault at a Wisdom School Spiritual Retreat at Lake Cowichan, British Columbia, Canada in April, 2019. Photo credit: Richard Friedericks

tices for me. Working deeply with her teachings offered me the clarity, depth, precision and confidence to take these intuitions and turn them into curricula for inner awakening. The impact of two of her works—*The Wisdom Way of Knowing: Reclaiming an Ancient Tradition to Awaken the Heart* (Bourgeault, 2003) and *Centering Prayer and Inner Awakening* (Bourgeault, 2004)—can be seen explicitly in the title of this book .

Along with the joy of discovery, however, came a sobering and saddening realization about teaching for Wisdom in the contemporary world. Early in *The Wisdom Way of Knowing* Cynthia writes:

> Wisdom lost its charter in the Christian West [in the late 5th century CE] . . . The vision that in virtually every other spiritual tradition of the world is regarded as not only possible but the whole point of the undertaking—namely, the transformation of the person into the perfected (complete, full, and whole) image of the divine—was now theologically off limits to Christians. It was a crushing defeat, the consequences of which are still being played out in the West. From that point almost until our own times, the Christian Wisdom tradition went underground in the West. (p. 18)

Having given many years of my teaching career searching for the transformative power of education, I can only hope that what I share here contributes in some way to the reversal of this long and tragic trend.

---

in five week-long retreats with her in various parts of the world, referring to her in this more casual sense feels most natural.

Thus, with this historical backdrop in mind as well as the contemporary challenges of rising worldview unmooring, environmental degradation, and mental distress among students, I offer *The Wisdom Way of Teaching* as my personal journey of discovering how to teach for what is most essential in today's 21st century world. The primary claim here is that it is possible to teach Wisdom to high school students. But what do I actually mean by this term? My working definition of Wisdom comes from Cynthia's description in her *Wisdom Way of Knowing*: a "precise and comprehensive science of spiritual transformation that has existed since the headwaters of the great world religions and is in fact their common ground" (Bourgeault, 2003, pp. xvi–xvii). Cynthia continues:

> Wisdom fundamentally describes a higher level of human consciousness characterized by a supple and alert awareness, compassionate intelligence, a substantial reduction in the "internal dialogue," and the capacity to engage reality directly, without the superimposition of mental constructs and categories. It is the original Integral Knowing. Wisdom is not about knowing more, but about knowing deeper, with more of you participating. It is fundamentally accessed through spiritual practice. (Bourgeault, n.d.)

Cynthia's statements encapsulate the most important aspects of my argument about teaching for Wisdom, which I summarize in this way:

- Wisdom is a higher state of consciousness grounded in a universal tradition.
- Wisdom involves integrating the body, mind, and heart in order to perceive/experience reality more directly.
- Wisdom requires spiritual practice to quiet the overactive mind that veils perception.
- Wisdom results in compassionate action.

Wisdom, in short, is the world's accumulated understanding of how to educate for transformation, which necessitates a reconceptualization, or perhaps more accurately a "re-experiencing," of the intersubjective relationship between self and world. Parks (2000) describes in more detail this self-world reorientation process by stating in *Big Questions, Worthy Dreams* that the central task of adolescence is to engage in the "dissolution and recomposition of the meaning of self, other, world, and 'God'" (p. 5). Thus, educating for Wisdom involves a continuous waterwheel of self-relinquishing and self-realizing. Welwood (2000) succinctly describes this dual, reciprocal movement as an inherently psychospiritual process: "If psychological work helps us find ourselves, spiritual work takes a step further, helping us let go of ourselves" (p. 97). My experience is that it's possible to educate students towards such psychospiritual transformation that they consider at some depth what kind of person they want to grow into and how they can make a positive impact on the world.

While Cynthia associates Wisdom primarily with contemplative practices, I have taken license to broaden her use of the concept to also include my emphasis on social conscience education.[8] Emerging from many years of observing and contributing to the developmental needs of adolescents, my colleagues and I have become convinced that another critical element besides teaching for spiritual growth is needed: inviting and empowering students to make a difference in society. Wisdom work, guiding students on a path towards wholeness and fulfillment, is all about awakening, and we have found that it's oftentimes easier to make an initial psychic breakthrough for many high school students through service learning, as stated in Rohan's epigraph, rather than spiritual practices. Recently one of my students Antoinette reflected in an essay, "In Humanities I in Action we went to the Jungsing[9] orphanage and that has changed my life. I love to be connected to people, so the idea of being connected to God wasn't a big surprise to me." Once students have experienced the power of living for someone or something besides themselves, they are more open to the spiritual dimension.

This book brings together my two big takeaways of more than 30 years of teaching in one international school in Hong Kong. Part I, which draws primarily from the first two decades of my teaching experience, explores the social conscience aspect of teaching for Wisdom: breaking the outer shell of the ego, destabilizing the cloud of self-centeredness that is the natural default of ordinary life. My colleagues and I teach towards such self-expansion in a course called "Humanities I in Action," which engages students in a curriculum that enlarges their thoughts, feelings, and actions beyond their immediate circle of family and friends by addressing great contemporary issues of our time, such as genocide, globalization, and the environment. Such a journey considering the suffering of others can be utterly transformative for students, akin to the Buddha who left his protective gates and ventured into the world in order to face social realities. The ultimate goal of Humanities I in Action is to sensitize students' minds and hearts to the plight of others and to empower them to ease this suffering.

However, in the last ten years I have found that a second domain of growth is equally necessary for truly transformative education. This approach might go by the terms *character education, moral education,* or *religious education.* Drawing upon Cynthia's *Centering Prayer* book, however, I prefer the more descriptive and edgier term *inner awakening* (Bourgeault, 2004). Like social conscience, this approach also involves transformation of students' thoughts, feelings, and actions, but, intriguingly, the process of development of these three dimensions is distinctly different than what occurs in a course like Humanities I in Action. Each aspect needs to be redirected and retrained towards letting go and letting be, requiring a delicate touch.

---

[8] In my doctoral research with HKIS teachers and students, I define the term social conscience as "a personal consideration of one's role and responsibility in society in the context of an emotionally-engaged understanding of the world" (Schmidt, 2009, p. 124).

[9] Jungsing is a pseudonym for the town and name of the orphanage that we visit in China.

FIGURE 1. The Yang of Social Conscience and the Yin of Inner Awakening

Thus, the case I'm presenting is that the Wisdom needed in a world of existential confusion, environmental deterioration, and unprecedented levels of anxiety is a yin-yang process. The first cracking of the ego is elicited by the *yang of social conscience*, which can be described in a shorthand sense as an *emotionally engaged understanding of the world* (Schmidt, 2009). However, as my students have conveyed to me for years, such a powerful change is not completely satisfying, nor fully sustainable. The fire of social justice does not necessarily light an inner flame. A second complementary step, what I call the *yin of inner awakening*, requires a gradual dissolution of the ego's inner shell as well, offering students the opportunity to find an aliveness felt within one's being.

The yin-yang symbol is an elegant representation of this hybrid service learning-spiritual practice educational approach. The apparent duality of action and contemplation is not only portrayed in dynamic interplay, but, as indicated by the eye contained at the heart of each force, the core of each polarity contains its opposite. The implication in terms of transformative education is that action responses require a reflective and even contemplative dimension in order to purify motives of self-interest and egoic attachment. Conversely, spiritual practices are not acts of escape from the world, but aim to influence it in a more pervasive, if perhaps more subtle, manner. Understood properly, it can be the desire to serve the world, to alleviate suffering, that motivates spiritual practices.

The *Wisdom Way of Teaching* emerges out of a worldview that is explicitly religious and/or spiritual in nature. As a Christian teacher in a pluralistic setting, my teaching of social conscience and inner awakening has been deeply shaped and immeasurably enriched by my Christian faith and the faith traditions of many other religions and spiritualities. Indeed, it's no secret that, even as countless of our daily actions are increasingly dominated by science and technology, and usefully so, the most crucial domains of life are ones that they do not oversee. The

Introducing the Wisdom Way of Teaching • **xxiii**

Rachel Putting the Last Piece of A Yin-Yang Symbol in Place in a World Religions Class Project Preparing for an All-School Assembly. Photo Credit: Author.

vast majority of the world continues to define life's intrinsic meaning and even Wisdom itself in terms of religious and spiritual traditions.

I draw upon these traditions in this book, as I do in my multicultural setting at an international school in the East-meets-West city of Hong Kong, for the simple reason that to avoid them would result in a more superficial and less effective approach, presuming a needlessly reductive vision of human nature, one that does not integrate the depth and breadth of our inner and outer worlds. It would also not be true to the lessons that have been offered through the course of my experience. Students' intrinsic pursuit of wholeness seems to impel them to explore the interwoven aims of social conscience and inner awakening that form the basis of this book; I've come to believe that these noble goals can best be realized in an interspiritual milieu such as HKIS, which describes itself as a school "grounded in the Christian faith and respecting the spiritual lives of all."

While this holistic vision has arisen naturally from my particular school context which advocates for development of a student's spiritual identity, it is at the same time situated within a vibrant international setting characterized by a wide variety of beliefs, including nonbelief as well. Thus, if spiritual references are a stumbling block, then the aims of social conscience and inner awakening can also be easily conveyed in secular educational language. Put in more widely recognized terms, then, this book explores why *service learning* and *mindfulness* continue to inspire so many teachers and students. Regardless of the reader's personal belief system, the findings and practices in this book can be used in markedly different multicultural settings and in schools of all types, from parochial to secular.

Despite vast cultural differences there was—in the Lutheran upbringing of my past—and certainly is—in the international school of my present—an underlying yearning for the same imperatives of human selfhood: meaning, authenticity, service to something beyond oneself, and understanding one's place in the universe. The belief system, culture, language, and socio-economic level are markedly different, but the quest for purpose, integration, and wholeness remains. Teaching for Wisdom aims at these perennial values, attempting to transform both the world and the self, or in the terms of this book, joining the yang of social conscience with the yin of inner awakening. This is the education that is needed to simultaneously heal both the planet and the psyches of students who study in our classrooms.

INTRODUCTION TO HONG KONG INTERNATIONAL SCHOOL

Jim Handrich

The Wisdom Way of Teaching has emerged from more than thirty years of teaching in one particular setting, Hong Kong International School, so some background about the school seems useful as a backdrop to the story I am telling. HKIS was established in 1966 as the result of a partnership between Lutheran (Lutheran Church-Missouri Synod) missionaries and Hong Kong businessmen, who together wanted to bring an American-style education to expatriates, especially Americans, living in the British colony, which already had an established British school system. Situated picturesquely on two well-maintained campuses on the south side of Hong Kong island—lower and upper primary in Repulse Bay and middle school and high school in Tai Tam— the school is nestled amongst mountainous greenery, yet located only a short 25-minute drive from the Central business district.

Personally, Hong Kong has been a brilliant East-meets-West crossroads for me to develop, reconsider and revise my own Western and Christian heritage in dialogue with the cultural riches and spiritual resources of a burgeoning Asia, particularly from Chinese and Indian influences. I have had the opportunity to learn from many sources, including colleagues and friends, about the ancient teachings

---

The Wisdom Way of Teaching: Educating for Social Conscience and Inner Awakening in the High School Classroom, pages xxv–xxx.
Copyright © 2022 by Information Age Publishing
www.infoagepub.com
All rights of reproduction in any form reserved.

This Photo Was Taken During the 50th Anniversary of HKIS in December, 2016. The "50" and the HKIS emblem are composed of HKIS students, faculty, and staff who all gathered on the field to mark the occasion. The high school is in the right foreground. My classroom is at the bottom of the rectangular block on the right that is closest to and faces the field. A visiting speaker from Australia recently likened the campus setting to a Zen monastery, an image that reflects not only its beauty, but also speaks to me of the sacred nature of our vocation. Photo credit: Hong Kong International School.

and practices of Confucianism, Taoism, Classical Chinese Medicine, Hinduism, Buddhism, and Tibetan Buddhism. I have led perhaps 80 school-related service trips to China, 7 to India, 6 to Thailand, 5 to Vietnam, and 1 to Bhutan. I have also learned to speak Cantonese with some level of proficiency. Teaching at HKIS for all of these years in one of the world's great cities has offered me a rich and diverse laboratory in which to experiment with the various pedagogies and practices that are contained in this volume. I will be forever grateful.

The school serves wealthy expatriate families as well as local Hong Kong and mainland Chinese families who want to send their children to American, Canadian, British, or Australian tertiary institutions—with the vast majority going to the U.S. Many of these students set their sights on Ivy League admissions and work diligently to achieve this goal. At present there are more than 2800 students attending the school, most of whom are of Chinese descent and who speak English fluently.

Early on in the school's history, many of the administrators and teachers came from the Lutheran Church. When I arrived in 1990, I remember perhaps as many as 50 teachers from the Lutheran school system. Now thirty years later, I am one of only about 5 teachers out of a faculty of 250 who come from this heritage. Despite the loss of the Lutheran presence, the school has maintained a commitment to the spiritual dimension of life that would be considered impossible in an affluent U.S.—based public school setting. While very few parents send their children to HKIS because of its spiritual commitment, at the same time there seems to be wide acceptance of the school's drawing upon Christianity and other religions and spiritualities to support the development of values and student well-being.

Whenever anyone asks why I have stayed so long at HKIS, the answer for me is very simple. I have had the curricular freedom, support, and resources to teach from my heart. I have been able to create courses and experiences that meet the school's guiding curricular principles while at the same time feeding my own inner fire for self-cultivation and even transformation. I will always be grateful for the school and church's strong support for the classes and programs which facilitated my rich intellectual and spiritual explorations over the past three decades.

In particular, the two main themes of this book, social conscience and inner awakening, are in my view a clear application of our school's mission statement:

> Dedicating our minds to inquiry, our hearts to compassion, and our lives to service and global understanding—an American-style education, grounded in the Christian faith, and respecting the spiritual lives of all.

Emerging from this mission statement are the HKIS Student Learning Results (SLRs), the bedrock guideposts that represent the lived curriculum in our classrooms. There is an obvious connection between the development of social conscience and inner awakening and our SLRs.

1. Academic Excellence;
2. Self-Motivated Learning;
3. Character Development;
4. Chinese Culture;
5. Spirituality; and
6. Contributing to Society.

With these key formulations in place, I have asked Jim Handrich, a much-loved and former long-serving administrator at HKIS, to provide an institutional perspective of the school's commitment to service learning and spiritual development. When Jim retired in 2007, several alumni created the "James A. Handrich Service Leadership Endowment Fund" that annually provides financial support to current students who request seed money to start service initiatives.

Jim Handrich, High School Principal, 1990–2004

What an amazing journey HKIS humanities teachers are on, led by Martin E. Schmidt, along with students who are determined to make a difference in the lives

Jim Handrich With Two Recipients of the James A. Handrich Service Leadership Endowment Fund, Caroline Scown (l) and Brittany Fried (r), During the 50th Anniversary Celebrations. Learn More About the Girls' "Teaching for Empowerment" Curriculum Project in Chapter 5 and in Brittany's Reflections in Chapter 18. Photo credit: Hong Kong International School.

of others. Permit me a few observations from a former high school principal's perspective. HKIS students, faculty and administrators have always had a heart for service, an ethic of care, and a desire to make the world a better place. From my perspective, this commitment flows out of the school's Lutheran and Christian heritage, endeavoring to grow into having the mind of Christ and heeding the call to love our neighbor, regardless of any differences in our neighbor's beliefs or circumstances.

In the early 90s, HKIS was selected by the Association for Supervision and Curriculum Development as one of 25 high schools in the US to design and implement the best high school education for the future. The other 24 schools were in the US, but since HKIS has an American-style education and most graduates went on to US universities, HKIS applied and was accepted to be a part of this consortium to design the high school of the future. Out of that initial work came our guiding mission statement, which surely undergirds the journey and curricular changes that Marty so vividly describes in this book. The HKIS mission, developed from our work with the high school consortium, has now been embraced by the whole pre-K–12 school, which reads: "Dedicating our minds to **inquiry**, our hearts to **compassion**, and our lives to service and **global understanding**—an American-style education, grounded in the Christian faith, and **respecting the spiritual lives of all.**" (Bold added for emphasis.)

My first piece of advice, then, to any teacher, leader or school that wants to begin replicating the curriculum and teaching work about which Marty, the teachers, and the students write about so convincingly here, is to spend time developing and examining your own school's mission statement. The curriculum design and pedagogy have to support the school's mission. As you read this book, do you see in these new courses a penchant for *inquiry?* In chronicling the journey from Interact fundraising[1] for those in need during the early 90s, to beginning Service on Saturday[2] with groups of teachers and students spending their Saturday mornings at orphanages and homes for the elderly in Hong Kong in the mid-90s, can you see how these activities reflect the *compassion* in the mission statement? In the '90s, our Interim program[3] saw the number of service trips increase from just 1 to over 15 opportunities for students to be involved in countries, communities and cultures across Asia. Does that not lead to increased *global understanding?* And in the new Spiritual Explorations course, do you see how that *respects the spiritual lives of all?* By designing courses that dynamically fit the HKIS Mission and Student Learning Results, Marty and his Humanities Department colleagues ensure that these new courses, which are so needed by youth in our 21st century, would easily be supported and passed by the department heads and the administration. In some schools it's not always easy to implement new courses, but if they fit so closely with the school's mission and student learning results, how could this direction and these courses ever be rejected? This was masterful planning and implementation!

A second piece of advice for those reading this book is that it is critical to hire humanities teachers who believe in interdisciplinary learning, have a heart for service, are willing to lead student travel for week-long service Interims, and are enthusiastically supportive of this curriculum and pedagogy. And, in the case of HKIS, new teachers also have to be happy and willing to live and teach in Hong Kong. In my responsibility for hiring teachers, I always consulted with the Humanities Department leaders during the recruitment process. Because HKIS is an excellent school with talented educators and high-achieving students, we often

---

[1] Interact is a school club at HKIS initiated by Rotary International, a business group that fosters school-community engagement opportunities. The Interact Club was most well-known at the school for performing an annual charity fashion show that involved over a hundred students in its production. Some years the show would raise approximately $50,000 USD for a selected charity organization.

[2] In 1996, my wife Zella, Jim, and myself created a Service on Saturday (SOS) program, which organized service activities in the local Hong Kong community for approximately 8–10 Saturdays in a given year.

[3] HKIS has a long-standing program of week-long overseas field trips called "Interim," which occurs every year in March.

had numerous applications for any individual opening in the Humanities Department. However, while it was possible to find the right candidate who had the curiosity or passion for inquiry-based teaching, along with a heart for service and a willingness to take students on overseas service Interims, we still rarely found teachers who had experience teaching such courses that you will read about. From interviewing and dialogue, we had to determine which candidates had an understanding or even some previous service learning experience and who could also see the amazing value of this particular curriculum for the 21st century learner. We also liked to hire a diverse HKIS faculty that matched our student body. As the Humanities Department continues on this journey and more students and families see the wisdom of these courses for developing whole and healthy adults, HKIS will need even more teachers who are learners themselves and who also want to seize this opportunity for a different kind of education in spiritual development, the social sciences, English and communication.

Now that I am retired and back in the US, so far I have not found university education departments that are developing educators who would be willing and able to teach this curriculum. HKIS should perhaps partner with at least one university that might be interested in student learning of this quality and direction, and who then might prepare graduates to teach these amazing courses that have the potential to make a significant difference in students' perspectives and lives. Such a university might also see the potential for significant research on the short-term and long-term effects of this unique curriculum.

A third and final observation relates to the junior and senior courses yet to be developed in understanding the Christian faith. Indeed, writing and developing that new course that seeks to have students understand who Jesus is and what is the place of the gospel in our 21st century world, will be another challenge for a school that is owned and operated by the Lutheran Church Missouri Synod. Though not an easy assignment for future curriculum development, I have every confidence that Marty and his humanities, health, and counseling colleagues can successfully meet that challenge. I'll be looking forward to reading the syllabus for that course.[4]

Oh, how I wish in my student days I could have taken courses like these! In my teaching days, I would have wanted the opportunity and privilege to create and teach Humanities I in Action, or Service, Society and the Sacred. And now with the new unique interdisciplinary courses of spiritual development being jointly designed and taught by teachers of religion, humanities, health and counseling, I am filled with such gratitude for these teachers at HKIS and for the difference they are and will be making in their students' learning and lives.

---

[4] Now that we have completed the creation and implementation of the four-year SPEX curriculum for the first time, our sights are set on this goal. Teaching the Christian story is a high priority at HKIS, and the humanities teachers who teach SPEX are in full accord with this important aim. Robust conversations about not only the content and structure of such a course(s), but the logistics of implementation into the high school curriculum, continue.

PART I

TEACHING FOR SOCIAL CONSCIENCE

CHAPTER 1

MY JOURNEY OF TEACHING FOR SOCIAL CONSCIENCE

[Human beings] experiences[themselves], [their] thoughts and feelings as something separated from the rest—a kind of optical delusion of our consciousness. This delusion is a kind of prison for us, restricting us to our personal desires and to affection for a few persons nearest to us. Our task must be to free ourselves from this prison by widening our circle of compassion to embrace all living creatures and the whole of nature in its beauty.
—*Einstein cited in Eves (2003, p. 60)*

The reason I chose this worldview of separateness may be because of my ten years of education in local school. When I discussed this matter with my friends in my old school, they all agreed with my thoughts. In a local school, everyone is in their small glass marble, caring only about their tests and exam grades. We do not walk out of our bubbles and connect to the world. This is how life is: everyone is separated.
—*Chloe, grade 9 female student, reflecting in her Humanities I in Action class on her transition from a local school to HKIS*

In 1990 when I began teaching as a first-year humanities teacher at Hong Kong International School, I wanted to make a difference in students' lives. Although

---

The Wisdom Way of Teaching: Educating for Social Conscience and Inner Awakening in the High School Classroom, pages 3–9.
Copyright © 2022 by Information Age Publishing
www.infoagepub.com
All rights of reproduction in any form reserved.

I couldn't have articulated it at that point, I believed that the heart of education was about transformation of the human person—and that such a change would have real bearing on the world. However, my first several years of teaching were a struggle. Having been trained to teach in American middle class Lutheran schools, I was painfully unprepared to teach affluent, success-oriented Western expatriate and Chinese students anything that could make a difference in their lives. My most memorable moment in those early years came in a meeting for Lutheran teachers when I inadvertently blurted out, as a young, inexperienced teacher attempting to teach Christian-based religion courses at the school, that I felt "alienated" and "shot at." I felt lost in my quest to understand the power of education, especially in relationship to the school's Christian vision.

FROM COMMUNITY SERVICE TO SERVICE LEARNING

However, later in that second year I was assigned to co-lead a weeklong service trip to an orphanage in Thailand. The trip was a success, and much to my surprise, students started talking about the deep impact that the experience had made on them in terms that were transformative in nature. The sought-after power I had labored fruitlessly to realize in my classroom seemed, by comparison, tantalizingly within reach by the relatively simple task of taking students to play with orphans for a week.

Several years later I began taking students to an orphanage in the Chinese city of Jungsing, and these experiences affirmed that I was indeed onto something. One of my students, Bethany, wrote on one of those first trips, "Service scars you in the most beautiful way possible." Bethany's powerful paradoxical statement

Bethany at the Jungsing Orphanage. Reflecting on experience these many years later, Bethany commented, "That trip forever changed me."

George Coombs and I visiting Ateneo High School in Manila, Philippines in April, 1997." Photo credit: George Coombs.

inspired me to pursue the mysterious alchemy of love, service, and transformation that seemed available not far beyond our school gates. The next year my wife and I started a "Service on Saturday" program at HKIS. On about ten Saturdays a year, groups of students would, for example, teach English at local Chinese schools, visit the elderly, or teach horseback riding to special needs students. At the same time, the number of service Interims[1] grew rapidly. By the mid-1990s, extracurricular service experiences, typically referred to as *community service*, were becoming an increasingly visible element of school life. Again, students spoke of the deep impact that these experiences had far beyond that of conventional instruction.

The next big jump in my understanding of the role service can play in transformative education occurred in 1997 when a colleague, George Coombs, and I visited Ateneo High School, a prestigious Jesuit prep school outside of Manila, Philippines. We were very impressed with a required Senior economics, sociology, and theology course that prepared Filipinos to give back to those most in need in their country. The interdisciplinary vision presented in the course, which included an experiential component of living with a family in a Manila slum for a week, was so appealing that I returned to HKIS feeling called to start such a course at our school. Based on Ateneo's model, three years later George and I initiated a senior religion elective called "Service, Society, and the Sacred" that attempted to integrate service and spirituality in one course. Building on this foundation, in 2003 my wife and I implemented a core grade 9, interdisciplin-

---

[1] HKIS has a long-standing program of week-long overseas field trips called "Interim," which occurs every year in March.

ary course entitled "Humanities I in Action," a service-oriented curriculum that explores, among other topics, human nature and behavior, genocide, the environment, and globalization, and does so within a framework of working to make a difference in society. The course includes approximately six or more service or experiential outings in Hong Kong, the highlight of which is a powerful weekend in November caring for young children at the Jungsing orphanage. Whereas community service seemed eye-opening to many students, joining service experiences with the study of pressing contemporary issues—together called *service learning* (Eyler & Giles, 1999)—initiated a far deeper transformative process.

RESEARCH ON SOCIAL CONSCIENCE EDUCATION

In 2005 I began a qualitative research study of students and teachers who had experienced community service and service learning activities at HKIS. My first step was to understand what prevented students from feeling bonded to and caring for society. My interviews with HKIS students made clear that the intense focus on achievement was the primary culprit, which appeared in various guises in their lives: social expectations of affluent parents and peers; the exam-driven culture of local Chinese schools; the competitive, profit-driven values of entrepreneurial Hong Kong; and the normalization of the disparity between rich and poor in Hong Kong and other Asian cities. Students frequently referred to this sense of separateness from social issues by employing the metaphor of "living in a bubble," which described their disconnectedness from the realities of life that most Asian people face, including our home city of Hong Kong, which is known for its marked gap between the rich and poor.

Through my research I found persuasive evidence that this fundamental challenge of disconnectedness could be addressed through creating courses that aimed to develop students' social conscience. The goal of such instruction is to burst students' bubbles of isolation and re-connect them to social reality. At its best, social conscience education challenges students to embark upon a personal journey to consider their "role and responsibility in society in the context of an emotionally-engaged understanding of the world" (Schmidt, 2009, p. 124).

In my research I discovered that a social conscience curriculum aims to not only raise awareness, but also engage students at an emotional level. When cognitive awareness and emotional engagement are combined, students experience an intrinsic desire to act. Thus, service learning experiences serve the dual purpose of bursting students' bubbles of indifference, while also providing them with the opportunity to act upon their burgeoning emotionally-engaged understanding of the world. Through all of these various dimensions of social conscience education, the research indicated a growing sense of relatedness between students and "invisible others" in society that permeates the levels of increasing awareness, emotional engagement, and action. The research can be represented graphically as depicted in Figure 1.1.

My Journey of Teaching for Social Conscience • 7

FIGURE 1.1. The Short-Term Impact of Social Conscience Education

When social conscience education is done intentionally over the course of one or more years, the impact upon some students can truly be transformative, cultivating new dimensions of the self, as illustrated in a second triangle in Figure 1.2.

As social conscience education unfolds over time, student awareness grows into "perspective transformation," indicating that students see the world in a whole new way. Their initial emotional responses, much of what we might call negative emotions (e.g., disillusionment, guilt, anger, etc.), become transformed into empathy for others. And finally, their initial action responses mature into self-efficacy, which means that they have gained the skills, confidence, and will to make a difference in the world.

In practice, then, I regularly have conversations with students or read student writings that speak to the impact of social conscience education. Here is a late-night note from one of my students, Ava:

> I know it is really late but I feel like I had an epiphany. I see how a lot of the units connect now! It's about how we can make a difference! One person who has the courage can change the group script. One person can blow the whistle on something

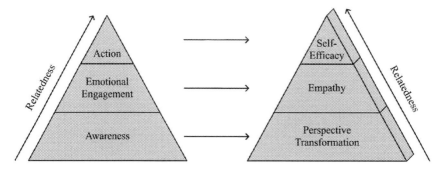

FIGURE 1.2. The Short and Long-Term Impact of Social Conscience Education

inhumane, one person can help the orphanage in Jungsing, one person can stay civil when the island is turning into savages, and one person can help those in need like Crossroads [a local charity]. You are teaching us that we can be those people. That we can be better people morally. We as kids can make a difference! I'm sorry to email so late, but I was afraid that I would forget it in the morning.

Ava's note speaks to the deep impact that the combination of emotive class materials coupled with experiential learning can make on students. This is the power of education that I intuitively yearned for in my early years of teaching.

Since 2003 when my colleagues and I began teaching Humanities I in Action, this course has served to wake students up to the reality of suffering in the world and their role in taking action steps to make a difference in people's lives. It has also led to the creation of new courses with this focus on service learning. We have had elective courses that focus on particular locations—Cambodia, Philippines, and Hong Kong—and in 2018 added a Humanities II in Action course. In addition, Service on Saturday and our service Interims continue to impact our students.

What impels us as teachers to continually strive to raise the quality of our work are the students themselves. I took Tiffany to the Jungsing orphanage in both her freshman year in Humanities I in Action and her senior year in Service, Society, and the Sacred. Following that second trip, she penned what I still consider the single most eloquent student reflection on social conscience education:

Before a journey begins, there is a moment . . . when a darker side of the world is thrust upon us. The journey begins when the blindfolds are untied and fall away from our vision; it is when we see. When we went to Jungsing in my freshman year, I saw. When I went to Mongolia that same year, I saw. It was a slow stirring of my soul, an insistent urging to go further out, to see more, to do more, feel more, give

Tiffany at the Jungsing Orphanage in November, 2004. Photo Credit: Author.

more, empathize more with the rest of the world. My journey began at the draw of a window curtain, at the flick of a light switch, at the light of a matchstick. It was ultimately, the ignition of a fire that I hope will never cease to burn.

Every year students like Tiffany have shared with me what social conscience education means to them, its power to awaken them to the world, to diminish their sense of self-focus in the context of a previously veiled world of suffering. Recently one of my 9th grade students, Camilla, pulled me aside during class, "Mr. Schmidt, I have to talk to you. I'm so disappointed in myself." She went on to relate how after visiting the orphanage she vowed to be a different person, but just that morning she had descended into tears upon receiving a low mark on a geometry test. The stark disparity between her old and new self, which had been our topic of discussion in class that day, drove her to seek advice. I suggested to her that she was in the process of "waking up," but to change those habits of reactivity to a relatively trivial grade in contrast to the lives of orphans in China, would require spiritual practice, which she would be doing in her Spiritual Explorations class. Another perceptive student, Nicole, who had listened intently to our impromptu conversation commented as we closed, "Wow, I've never eavesdropped on a conversation like that!"

This anecdote illustrates the innate need for wholeness that invites students like Camilla to seek out that which challenges their preconceptions. Like the Buddha leaving the palace walls, it takes courage and curiosity for our students to escape their affluent bubbles. This difficult, even painful, process of student growth requires that Wisdom teachers serve as patient and perceptive mentors who can guide young people along the journey. But in order to provide such support, instructors must attend to the trajectory of students' social conscience growth, which is the focus of Chapter 2.

CHAPTER 2

HUMANITIES I IN ACTION CURRICULUM AND THE IMPACT OF SOCIAL CONSCIENCE EDUCATION

Occasions of . . . revelatory insight are the motivating purpose of all truly liberal education.
—*Sharon Parks (2000, p. 119)*

I believe that in a decade's time, the only high school course that I will remember vividly is the Humanities I in Action course. It was an eye-opening, unique experience that touched my heart. It allowed me to be connected with the abandoned orphans, the neglected elderly, the unwanted addicts, and the helpless disabled. Not only did it open my eyes to the sufferings of those who are less fortunate, it also moved me deeply into appreciating what a wonderful life I had been leading, and how I should share my love and care with those who have nothing. The course sparked my eagerness to be a committed volunteer at Riding for Disabled and sacrifice every Saturday to help young handicapped children to regain their sense of mobility and confidence; and it prompted me to take an interest in other social enterprises and take part in launching a new charity that provides school meals to schools in China and Africa. I believe that it is the overwhelming sense of gratitude and love towards what my parents, teachers and friends had provided me that enabled me to share what I can with others. And I do believe that the insights that I have gained from Humanities I in Action will always remain in my heart and mind, and become part of my core values, steering the way I feel and act towards others.

— *Jacqui, grade 12 female student, in Service, Society, and the Sacred class, reflecting on her 9th grade experience in Humanities I in Action*

INTRODUCTION

If I had one gift to offer the world, it would be the Humanities I in Action curriculum, for no other course has so powerfully served as a wake-up call for students to the beauty and intensity of a meaningful life. Its impact could not be more crucial in our time in light of the dual external and internal crises that societies confront today. On one hand, we face harrowing environmental and social problems that have critical implications for life on this planet. On the other hand, students also confront what seems to be almost unprecedented inner challenges of disconnectedness and purposelessness, manifesting for many as pervasive anxiety or even depression. What I have found in nearly two decades of teaching Humanities I in Action is that it is possible to engage high school freshmen in curricular materials of social injustice, genocide, and the environment that serve as a personal call to each student to develop understanding, empathy, and self-efficacy on behalf of a world in need; the drawing forth of these inner qualities simultaneously begins to heal the second crisis, young people's melancholy about their own personal future. This dual pedagogical strategy of studying issues that involve suffering as a call to action strikes an ennobling internal resonance in students' hearts: "You are needed in the world!," which offers to lift them above the pessimistic instrumentalist rhetoric, implicit in much of 21st century education, of economic survival in an increasingly competitive world. Responding to the world's suffering by helping others can serve to alleviate the anxiety evident among many adolescents.

THE BIRTH OF HUMANITIES I IN ACTION

Before sharing the Humanities I in Action curriculum, it seems useful to share the context of our high school Humanities Department out of which this course emerged. After more than a decade of experimenting with interdisciplinary classes taught by members of our English and Social Studies departments, in 1997 the school administration decided to combine English, Social Studies, and Religion disciplines into a single, interdisciplinary Humanities Department. Today the 25 department members share a large office space that facilitates an unusually high level of collaboration and esprit de corps.

The HKIS Humanities Department. Photo credit: Sarah Wheatley.

"Humanities I in Action" originally emerged out of the "Humanities I" curriculum, a required interdisciplinary course for incoming grade 9 students (14- and 15-year-olds) that focused on various cultures and regions, such as China, India, Africa, and the Middle East. The course was rigorously academic, developing cognitive outcomes of critical reading and writing, but did not explicitly aim to improve society or inspire action.

In 2003 I proposed Humanities I in Action as an alternative to the regular course. The "in Action" affixture indicated that students would commit themselves to at least six Saturday service or experiential learning activities,[1] including a four-day, three-night trip to a Chinese orphanage. This meant that students could choose a course from day one of their high school career aimed at social change.

When Humanities I in Action was first implemented, the curricula of the two courses had substantial overlap, with the main difference being the service experiences. However, through an organic process of responding to student feedback, the "in Action" curriculum evolved into a thematic psychosocial journey, which ventured into new territory not envisioned in the Humanities I course.

From the start we have been sensitive to anticipate concerns about the new "action" format, specifically, fears that the new course might sacrifice rigor or represent a departure from a strong academic focus. Maintaining the same high

---

[1] In the early years, we often had 10 or more outings, but that level of involvement has been hard to sustain for both teachers and students. Also, with the addition of the Elixir Project (Chapter 5), a community-based project undertaken during second semester, students need more individual time for their projects.

educational standards as the regular course has always been a priority for the "in Action" teachers. Although at times the course has had to fend off perceptions of being more "hands-on" and therefore less rigorous, today neither one is seen as the more academically challenging. Indeed many of the "in Action" teachers and students feel that the implicit sense of meaning in the course materials and activities inspires strong intellectual growth along with the development of students' social consciences.

While this academic emphasis is built into the course design and supported by the commitment of the instructors, it is also necessitated by parent needs and demands. Since students "vote" when they enroll in classes, continuation of the course depends on student and parent satisfaction with the overall experience.

Since its inception, a number of further critical factors have proved essential to the school community's receptivity to the course. Most important has been the presence of strong buy-in and commitment to the class from both students and the school. The course benefits from student openness and interest from day one; since students select the class, it is not subject to the ambivalence or even resistance that might arise were the class mandatory. In addition, the course has benefitted from a remarkable degree of administrative support. As long as the class aligns with the mission of the school, instructors are given wide latitude to form the curriculum around whatever works best. A final factor that has contributed to the course's success has been the substantial amount of time of active student engagement, which includes nearly 300 contact hours of in-class instruction and out-of-class experiences.

HUMANITIES I IN ACTION CURRICULUM

It took about 15 years of developing the Humanities I in Action curriculum before our teaching team reached the point of feeling quite confident about the effectiveness of its core structure and distinct narrative flow. At the same time, however, there remains a commitment to innovation in the finer-grained elements of the framework. New teachers of the course value the balance we strike between an established curriculum and the flexibility to introduce new materials or even whole units, if we see fit. For example, the past-present-future progression of the second semester was implemented four years ago, and Pinker's (2018) materials in the present unit were added even more recently. Thus, the curriculum is considered a living document, which keeps teachers engaged in its ongoing development.

Students experience the unique nature of the class from day one. The first lesson is an exploration of the issue of fair trade chocolate (Chapter 3), challenging students with the question "Is ignorance bliss?," which becomes a main throughline of the first semester as we confront students with distressing social issues and disturbing human behavior. This "shock and awe" assault is necessary, students tell us, to burst their bubbles of ignorance and apathy about the world. The most impactful experience of the course is the trip to the Jungsing orphanage (Chapter 4).

The two semesters work in tandem such that the first is an extensive journey into problems and needs, while the second explores how a student can express hopeful agency in such a world. The first semester's day 1 question "Is ignorance bliss?" becomes "Can I make a difference?" at the beginning of the second semester. While the second semester does continue to offer additional content about challenges in the present moment, including a focus on humans' troubled relationship with the earth, the emphasis in the second half of the course is on students taking action, which is most clearly seen in the semester-long Elixir Project (Chapter 5).

With this general overview in place, the following describes the major units of the course and their core assessments:

1. **Worldview Matters**: In our initial unit, we suggest that every action emerges from a certain belief system, or what we call a *worldview*. We introduce the concept by using set of ten worldview questions, posted in our classrooms, to stimulate deep reflection about the philosophical beliefs that underpin any effort to effect change in society. We study many examples—featuring the movie *Rabbit-Proof Fence* about Australia's Stolen Generations—that demonstrate how even well-intentioned change makers can implement decisions that have disastrous consequences. This caveat necessitates, then, a deeply reflective study of human nature and human behavior—the key components of worldview formation—as a precursor to any attempt to "take action."

    Humanities I in Action Worldview Questions
    1. Is human nature fundamentally good or evil?
    2. What is humanity's relationship to nature, ruler or part?
    3. Is humankind progressing or declining?
    4. What's more important, the group or the individual?
    5. Which value should society emphasize more, hierarchy or equality?
    6. Does the pursuit of wealth do more to improve or harm society?
    7. Which determines our identity to a greater extent, nature or nature?
    8. Which philosophy, essentialism or existentialism, best explains where meaning comes from?
    9. What is more fundamental to the universe, matter or consciousness?
    10. Are gender roles biologically or socially constructed?

    Assessments: Summary writing of a *New York Times* op-ed piece; an in-class essay which students explain why it is important to study worldview in a class that aims to make a difference in the world.

2. **Human Nature and Human Behavior**: We read William Golding's (1954) novel *Lord of the Flies*, watch Philip Zimbardo's 3-part BBC series *The Human Zoo*, and study the Milgram Experiment and the

Stanford Prison Experiment to consider the dark side of human nature.[2] Along with Simon in *Lord of the Flies* who struggles "in his effort to express [human]kind's essential illness" (p. 89) or Ralph who wants to know "what makes things break up like they do?" (p. 139), we seek as a class to explain human depravity. This disturbing exploration of the psychology of evil along with the sociology of the "group script"[3] are necessary to burst students' bubbles of complacency. This intense focus on "real life" is something that students have time and again characterized as an element necessary for their growth.

Assessment: Literary analysis of *Lord of the Flies*.

3. **Genocide and Modern Conflict:** We then explore a set of worst-case scenarios of human nature and behavior gone awry, studying the Rwandan genocide and watching the heart-wrenching film, *Shooting Dogs*, the single most moving curricular material in the course. Students also read a memoir by someone who has survived a genocide or some other modern conflict. In terms of student impact, this is the most powerful unit of the year.

Genocide and Modern Conflict Memoirs

- *A Long Way Gone* by Ishmael Beah (Beah, 2007) about Sierra Leone.
- *First They Killed My Father* by Loung Ung (Loung, 2006) about the Cambodian genocide.
- *In Order to Live* by Yeonmi Park (Park & Vollers, 2015) about North Korea.
- *Left to Tell* by Immaculee Ilibagiza (Ilibagiza & Irwin, 2006) about the Rwandan genocide.
- *Slave: My True Story* by Mende Nazer (Nazer & Lewis, 2010) about slavery in Sudan and the UK.
- *The Road to Lost Innocence* by Somaly Mam (Mam, 2009) about sex trafficking in Cambodia.

---

[2] In the school year that this book was undergoing final revisions, the Humanities I in Action team used for the first time excerpts of Rutger Bregman's (2020) *Humankind: A Hopeful History*, which re-interprets most of the materials in this unit. Incorporating his perspectives provided a powerful counter-argument to the decidedly negative view of human nature and human behavior portrayed throughout the entire first semester materials, deepening student reflection on perhaps the most pivotal worldview question: is human nature fundamentally good or evil? Given our very positive experience with Bregman's argument in reframing these materials and engaging students' critical thinking, we enthusiastically recommend using this student-friendly resource early on in the course. I comment more on Bregman's book in Chapter 6.

[3] The term "group script" is introduced in *The Human Zoo* to explain how social situations create group-induced behavioral norms. This psychosocial construct is illustrated by an experiment in the video in which research participants will not leave a room filling with smoke and violate the "group script," if none of the confederates (i.e., those on the research team) remain seated and continue their assigned task.

Assessments: Students document their reading of a genocide/conflict memoir through a personal response journal; group presentation of their book.

4. **Chinese Orphanage:** Usually in November we take students to two orphanages in the Chinese city of Jungsing to explore both the consequences of a particular government policy—the one-child policy—as well as give students both individually and as a class an experience of providing care for someone in obvious need. Time and again students have explained that this trip, more than any single material or experience, was their wake-up call to suffering in the world. As one student stated, "Somehow the orphans made it [the course content] all true." On the other hand, coming back from the orphanage gives us the opportunity to talk about not only what's wrong with humanity, but also what's right, as they see the natural empathy that emerges from themselves and their classmates for total strangers. Upon our return we read the Chinese novel *To Live* by Yu Hua (1993). Despite the tragic events that are recounted from World War II through the Cultural Revolution, Yu Hua's poignant narrative describes a rich young man's transformative journey from arrogance to virtue through the suffering he and his family endure. We hope that the students, too, in imitation of the lead character Fugui, can successfully cross over the metaphorical river from ignorance and hubris to wisdom and compassion.

Assessment: Personal narrative about the orphanage experience (or another life experience).

Semester 1 Assessment: Following reading *To Live*, students write an end-of-semester essay in which they respond to the core question of the year: "Given your study in Humanities I in Action, how has your worldview been expanded, challenged, deepened or influenced by the content and experiences in this course?"

It's important at this point to emphasize that the "negative" tone of the first semester is a deliberate choice to achieve the goals of cultivating in students a realistic understanding of the world and awakening in them a sense of empathy. We have found that this requires content marked by a high degree of seriousness and intensity, at times bordering on despair, culminating in our study of the Rwandan genocide. Whenever I have asked students, "Do you want the tough stuff or the *really* tough stuff?," they always opt for the latter. Sometimes I speak quite candidly to the class during study of the most challenging materials and ask them if it ever becomes too much, please speak to me. What gives me the assurance to press forward is that when I have asked students after the course if we should lighten the hard-hitting impact of the materials, they unequivocally state that this approach is necessary to penetrate their veneer of indifference. Thus, it would be a mistake to presume that pessimism is in any sense an intent of the course. We have found, however, that in order to reach our ultimate aim—to inspire deep understanding, empathy, and action responses to make the world a better place—students need a concentrated engagement with painful realities that all of us would prefer to avoid.

Thus, we pay careful attention to calibrate elements of the course to achieve the right overall tone. In order to counterbalance the curricular elements that highlight human suffering, the content also includes direct examination of good news, signs in the historical record that offer clear evidence of progress and positive change (Bregman, 2020; Pinker, 2018; Rosling, 2018; Wright, 2001). This careful choice of materials illustrates the Wisdom way of teaching's approach of integrating the right mix of despair, hope, and inspiration for our students.

The second semester, beginning right after the new year holidays, offers the opportunity to begin anew after surviving the difficult issues of the first semester. Following introduction of the Elixir Project, a semester-long assignment aimed at positively impacting the community, the remainder of the semester directs students to consider major issues of the 21st century, including economic development, environmental destruction, and human well-being, through provocative materials that offer interpretations of our past, present, and future.

5. **Elixir Project:** The second semester's key question is, "Can I make a difference?" We begin by having students read about the inspirational advocacy of 12-year old activist Craig Kielburger in his book *Free the Children* (Kielburger & Major, 1998), which serves as a strong lead-in to the Elixir Project, our semester-long project that aims to bring about positive change in the community. On the first weekend after the Christmas break, we host a half-day mini-conference called the "Service Summit," which features former "in Action" students' projects as well as off-campus community speakers to inspire their Elixir choices. They work on their project throughout the semester and present it at the end of the school year. The major academic task during this unit is writing a research paper in an area related to their Elixir Project.

    Assessments: Research paper; end-of-year Elixir project presentation.

6. **The Past:** We read the novel *Ishmael* by Daniel Quinn (1992), the most impactful book of second semester, which prompts students to consider the underlying causes of planetary destruction. Students wrestle with Quinn's accusation that 10,000 years ago a cultural shift occurred in which so-called Leaver societies—best represented by aboriginal cultures—were overtaken by those with a Taker mentality, which prioritizes growth of the human species without limits. During our reading of *Ishmael*, we also look at a variety of pertinent modern issues related to the environment and globalization, such as population growth, loss of aboriginal cultures, advertising, corporate sustainability initiatives, and climate change.

Assessment: Content-based objective test with some short and long answer questions on concepts in *Ishmael*.

7. **The Present:** In contrast to *Ishmael's* critique, we then read portions of Steven Pinker's (2018) *Enlightenment Now*, which argues that rather than haranguing ourselves over our missteps and overreach, it is more useful and true to the historical record to celebrate the tremendous progress in nearly all areas of human development in the last several centuries. Rather than raising an alarm about contemporary society—our more common pedagogical strategy—Pinker's data-laden counterargument suggests that we need to appreciate how far we have come and trust the trajectory of progress that we are riding rather than scolding students into action. This is an uplifting change after *Ishmael's* dire cautions, although which is the more accurate reading of the contemporary moment is left to students' personal interpretations.

    Assessment: Speech or video presentation based on a chapter in *Enlightenment Now*.

8. **The Future:** We finish the year having students read dystopian novels which extrapolate current trends into the future. Most recently, we have opted to read *Scythe* by Neil Shusterman (2018). At the same time, we watch the documentary *Transcendent Man* about inventor Ray Kurzweil, who believes he can defy death through technological development. We bring in guest speakers, too, who alternately excite and caution students about technology in the future. Once again, students see the relationship between worldview beliefs and the actions people take, especially with regard to humans' relationship with nature and the cosmos.

    Assessments: Read a dystopian novel, keep a personal journal response, and write a dystopian short story.

    End-of-Year Assessments: The conclusion of the course asks students to share their Elixir Projects. Have they truly been able to make a difference, as we asked at the beginning of the second semester? We also have them write the worldview essay again. The final weeks reinforce that the key ideas in this course are making sense of the world, developing empathy, and taking action.

For all of the far-reaching personal changes that we aim for, perhaps it's helpful to note that a visit on most days would reveal what feels like a normal English or Social Studies class. The tone is far more academic than one might imagine; it is not a support group for or a laboratory of social activism. That being said, the emotion-laden nature of the material and the explicit expectation from day one that our goal is to "make a difference" creates an underlying sense that somehow this course really matters far beyond the common educational outcomes of building students' academic skills or remembering a specific body of content.

20 • THE WISDOM WAY OF TEACHING

Humanities I in Action Students Sell "Flags" in Exchange for a Small Donation to a Specific Charity. Student reflections on this very first service outing are always surprisingly deep as they reflect on not only their own feelings of trying to make a positive social impact, but also how people on Hong Kong streets respond to their attempts. Photo Credit: Author.

OUTINGS

Humanities I in Action students participate in at least six outings in a given year, with the specific format dependent on the teacher's time and interests. The following are a list of current core experiences shared by all the "in Action" classes:

- Flag Day (September): a Hong Kong fundraiser in which students sell "flags" or stickers to people on the streets in exchange for a small donation to a government-approved charity. ("Flag Days" are a well-established program in the Hong Kong community that many schools participate in.)
- Refugee Kitchen (October): Students pay for a lunch hosted by Rwandan refugees and engage in associated activities to learn about the plight of asylum seekers in Hong Kong and to prepare for studying the Rwandan genocide.
- China Orphanage trip (November): A three-night trip to two orphanages in Jungsing.

- Refugee Run (December): During our genocide unit, students experience a powerful refugee simulation created by a local NGO called Crossroads, a charity established by an HKIS family in the mid-1990s.
- Service Summit (January): A 2.5 hour mini-conference to kick off students' Elixir Projects.
- Beach Clean-Up (May): A two-hour clean-up of a local beach.

We have fewer activities during second semester because students need time to work on their Elixir Projects.

Some classes have also engaged in additional activities:

- Teaching English in local Cantonese-speaking schools;
- Visiting a special needs facility in preparation for the China orphanage trip;
- Participating in a "blind simulation" with a social business called "Dialogue in the Dark" to understand the challenges faced by the visually impaired;
- Visiting homes for the elderly; and
- Visiting people in Hong Kong who live in substandard housing.

We attempt to link specific service events or experiences to relevant units, although given the complexity of schedules and venues, the connections are not always as clear as we would like. Even when the curricular resonances aren't pitch perfect, the out-of-the-classroom experiences build class spirit and again remind students that this course involves real-world issues.

IMPACT OF SOCIAL CONSCIENCE EDUCATION

The big question for teachers, of course, is what difference does this kind of curriculum make in the lives of students. Drawing upon focus group interviews with students and analysis of their essays and other writings, I developed the two figures introduced in Chapter 1, which describe student growth from awareness to perspective transformation; emotional engagement to empathy; and action to self-efficacy—all in terms of an increasing sense of relatedness between themselves and the world.

Now in the context of describing Humanities I in Action, I share this student impact with a finer brush, breaking down these two triangles into an 18-step narrative of the journey of social conscience. First, I lay out the entire trajectory in Table 2.1 so that the reader can easily grasp the overall trajectory of transformation. Secondly, I explore each step, providing a representative quote as well as my own commentary as a teacher who is supporting students through the various stages of this process. It was the neat and comprehendible journey that emerged as well as the depth and quality of the comments that have inspired my passion and confidence to teach for social conscience in Humanities I in Action year after year.

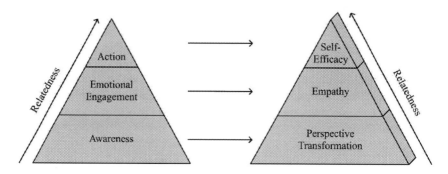

The Short-Term and Long-Term Impact of Social Conscience Education

TABLE 2.1. A Model of the Journey of Social Conscience

Awakening in the Bubble of Ignorance and Disconnectedness
1. While living in a bubble of affluence, there is a vague understanding that another world exists in which others suffer and have much less.
2. The most common way to awaken is through first-hand experiences with those who suffer outside of the bubble. These experiences cause students to question many basic assumptions about life.
3. A realization emerges that one is trapped in a bubble of ignorance and self-centeredness.
Connecting through Awareness and Emotional Engagement
4. Learning about the world requires a consideration of the suffering of others. This new orientation in turn causes a range of disorienting and at times overwhelming feelings including shock, anger, sadness, compassion, helplessness, and hopelessness.
5. A feeling of guilt develops around the sense that materially privileged persons inside the bubble have so much and so many others outside the bubble have so little.
6. These intense feelings and questions prompt varied reactions. Some resist this knowledge and its implications, while others feel energized to make a difference in the world.
7. At some point the challenge of studying the world's problems is regarded less as a burden and more as an opportunity, as helping others gives rise to a deep sense of meaningfulness.
8. Making sense of the world occurs through the formation of new physical, emotional and spiritual connections. The new links which form serve to help bring otherwise dissociated life experiences into a more interconnected whole.
9. One of the most important parts of personal growth is the formation of opinions, values, and beliefs about human nature, human behavior, and social issues.
10. A feeling develops of an expanded world and a sense of the "big picture."
11. An important part of this personal journey is its social dimension. Dialogue with friends, development of deeper friendships, and experiences of the growth process together with peers are all important components of this journey.
12. A feeling develops of being on a personal journey of growth. At the same time, there is a recognition that transformation is far from complete.

TABLE 2.1. Continued

13.	Upon reflection, there is a realization that the pathway out of the bubble has involved a new sense of identity and interconnected relationship with the world.
Acting on Social Conscience	
14.	Often the first way that action motivated by social conscience occurs is talking to family and friends about ideas, concerns, and issues. This sometimes causes tension, especially with parents.
15.	Social conscience frequently brings new ideas, attitudes, and choices into daily life.
16.	A new awareness develops that at some point a decision to act needs to be made or a stand needs to be taken.
17.	Acts of caring and of making a difference in the lives of others, especially ones that involve the exercise of leadership, facilitate greater appreciation of one's ability to effect positive change in the world.
18.	A commitment is made to continue the journey of social conscience through further self-exploration for the purpose of benefiting society.

Now I share a representative quote or quotes from students for each of the 18 steps and add my own commentary about each. The tone here is more informal, which allows me to share my own pedagogical reflections on my work with students that does not fall so easily in the other chapters.

AWAKENING IN THE BUBBLE OF IGNORANCE AND DISCONNECTEDNESS

1. **While living in a bubble of affluence, there is a vague understanding that another world exists in which others suffer and have much less.**

   As a kid growing up in an international school, almost everyone I knew had a pretty well-off financial background . . . In a way, I had subconsciously divided the world's population into two worlds. One was the one I and many others lived in, while the other was the one that the 'unfortunate people' lived in; the kind of people that you see on the news every day, struck by some tragedy. They were 'different' from us.

   My Comment (MC): This comment describes in very clear language the sense of separation that our students' socioeconomic position causes many of them to experience. While they initially seem blissfully unaware of their mental boundaries that separate the world into "my good life" and "unfortunate others," as the class progresses, the psychic cost of maintaining this division reveals itself.

   I have always led what most people would deem as a sheltered life. Living in the bubble of my home and school, I only had contact with sides of the world that were positive and uplifting. My parents were protectors who would try to prevent me from seeing the sometimes more horrific, but sadly more realistic aspects of life. They took my hand and led me away from 'that person' on the MTR [Hong Kong subway system] who might have had some horrible skin condition, or away from the walking stick of a blind person . . . My parents were, I found out later, like many other Hong Kong parents in that they didn't want me to have too much contact with the more marginal parts of society.

MC: A surprising finding in my research was that many Chinese students and teachers explained that the traditional Chinese worldview[4] was a barrier to social conscience. As this student explains, Hong Kong parents often steer their children away from those who appear sick or weak. In a culture that prioritizes family, expressing sympathy for non-family members may be met with the reply 唔關你事, which means "it's not your business." Students used this phrase in my research to explain their perceptions that traditional Chinese culture resists doing service work to support "strangers." Surfacing these questions of culture for students who come from more conservative Chinese families provides an opportunity to discuss the implicit values of varying worldviews.

2. **The most common way to awaken is through first-hand experiences with those who suffer outside of the bubble. These experiences cause students to question many basic assumptions about life.**

   For me it was the Jungsing trip. It brought out all the emotions like happy, sad, scared, guilty I guess. So before [the trip] people [would] say poor people are happier than you rich people and I was going along with that. Then I went to the orphanage and I actually experienced it. I saw the kids—they don't have much but they're really happy. I realized when I looked into myself [and asked] am I actually happy and that just brought a lot of questions. Honestly, I still don't know what the definition of happiness is.

   MC: While I am fully aware that taking students to an orphanage runs the risk of voluntourism[5] and that our visits in no way change the socio-

---

[4] Space does not allow me to deal with cultural issues, which was a major focus of my dissertation research. Suffice it to say on a personal note that despite what students in interviews said about the traditional Chinese worldview, I have deep respect for Chinese culture, especially the indigenous teachings of Taoism, which are a world treasure. Not only has Taoism provided humanity with the universal concept of yin-yang, my fundamental metaphor in this book, but it has bequeathed to the global community Classical Chinese Medicine (Fruehauf, 1999), which has become a recent area of great personal interest to me.

[5] Voluntourism is a term which describes students from wealthier Westernized countries who make short visits to the "disadvantaged," usually in Asia and Africa, take pictures, and pat themselves on the back as they reflect on their "noble" efforts to reach out to the poor. Such tokenism may very well exacerbate the distance between "us" and "them" rather than overcoming these barriers. In its worst form, such orphanages profit from the visits of volunteers, using children as props to make money on gullible visitors. By contrast, we have made a long-term commitment to the Jungsing Orphanage, having visited perhaps 50 times with students since 1995.

political factors that gave rise to institutional care of orphans, the reason I have taken students to the Jungsing Orphanage since 1995 is because pedagogically I have never had an experience that helps students to pierce through their self-described bubbles any more effectively than these visits.

Somehow the orphans made it all true. All the other things I'd heard about or read about —genocide, child labor, refugees—turned suddenly real. It was like realizing that people weren't lying to me, activists weren't making things up; the terrible things were really there.

MC: While the most perceptive students in Humanities I in Action will "get" what we are trying to teach through the content itself, for most students the direct confrontation with suffering is what makes "it all true."

In sophomore year, I went on a service trip to Mongolia. It was the most eye-opening experience I have ever had. What stayed with me the most . . . was coming into contact with street families that gave me the biggest paradigm shift. We had the chance to go down manholes where many street families lived . . . When I emerged from that hole and smelled the brisk, fresh air, I felt relieved to be out. At the same time, I felt so guilty because I do not deserve to be better off than they do, yet our fates turned out so differently. This experience shattered conceptions that my parents instilled in me as a child. All along, I believed that poor people are poor because they are lazy, and the government should not help them; otherwise, they would just leech off the country's wealth without doing anything. Now I am ashamed I ever felt that way because the homeless I met in Mongolia were trying their hardest, picking up bottles and whatever trash they could find on the streets to sell.

MC: The writer of this reflection, Jasmine Lau, started her own NGO eight years ago in Beijing that she told me is trying to pass onto local Chinese people the lessons about social conscience that she first learned about in Humanities I in Action. You may read Jasmine's self-reflection in Chapter 18.

3. **A realization emerges that one is trapped in a bubble of ignorance and self-centeredness.**

The bubble indicates the separation that I sometimes feel from the rest of the world. The 'before' picture is of a person being blindfolded, unaware, and ignorant. The 'after' picture is the same person without the blindfold, but still in the bubble, indicating the fact that I can still feel that I am trapped in the bubble, but no longer unaware.

MC: Many students become fully aware that the values implicit in Humanities I in Action run counter to those espoused by the culture at large, leaving students feeling quite stuck. Such cognitive dissonance seems to be a necessary part of the "suffering" that must be endured to grow along the trajectory of social conscience education.

> Before the Jungsing trip, I felt like I had two solid, continuous walls on each side of my face, giving me a straight, narrow outlook of the world. Caught in my own selfishness, . . . I focused too much on myself. I can honestly say that I never seriously considered the unfortunate vast majority of the world. Once I experienced spending time with orphan children who are just like you and me, and who have not felt proper love and compassion before, I slowly began to realize truths. I felt the walls barring my knowledge crumbling away, and I was able to wake up and broaden my span of vision to the world around me.

MC: When students begin studying in a social conscience course, many begin to realize that they have been totally pre-occupied by their own academic and personal concerns, oblivious to the suffering of others. As this young Japanese student alludes to in her comment, the most effective way to break down these walls of self-centeredness comes from the experience of love that comes most readily in our context in the orphanage visits.

Connecting through Awareness and Emotional Engagement

4. **Learning about the world requires a consideration of the suffering of others. This new orientation in turn causes a range of disorienting and at times overwhelming feelings including shock, anger, sadness, compassion, helplessness, and hopelessness.**

> I went into this course thinking that I already knew there was suffering in the world, I already knew life was unfair and people were dying, but that knowledge was tucked away, deep in my heart where I could avoid it at all costs and pull it out only when it was necessary. This course literally pulled that knowledge out of me and with it came compassion, sadness, sometimes anger, and for the first time in my life I felt motivation to do something about it.

MC: One of the lessons I've had to learn as a teacher of this course is to simply assume that many students feel far more than they ever give away. Deep processes are at work in the confrontation with suffering and I simply need to be ever-aware that these feelings might surface at any time for students. Many times I only recognize the impact of certain experiences years later.

> Yes, in complete honesty, this class made me so depressed. At one point, I always found myself crying in the middle of the night . . . Maybe yes, I'm still depressed because this class had left me feeling so hopeless. We see all the problems of the world, yet we can't do anything about it.

MC: There have been a few times where I've even had distraught students talk to school counselors or parents about the hard-hitting nature of the content. Because of these experiences, sometimes I will speak to the class candidly and say, "I show you difficult things in this class because students have always said it's necessary for their growth. But if at any time, it's too much, please talk to me. You have to be able to handle what I'm sharing with you. If that's a problem, we'll change it." The key is sensitivity and always checking in with students to make sure everyone is fine with the challenging materials.

5. **A feeling of guilt develops around the sense that materially privileged persons inside the bubble have so much and so many others outside the bubble have so little.**

   While I was living a materialistic life for the past thirteen to fourteen years . . . . I realized that living that kind of life places a lot of guilt on me. I felt guilty for everything I took for granted, as well as my superficial way of living. I could see that I am destroying my inner self and well-being with this guilt . . . . I feel that my old desire to lead a materialistic life is destroying the animals' happiness and I feel guilty for this. I feel even more guilty when I realize that not only am I hurting the animal species, but I am also destroying my own kind too—human beings. My superficial meaning of happiness is destroying other less fortunate human beings' happiness. When I buy a bar of chocolate, I am supporting slavery in the modern world. When I get a new carpet, I am encouraging child labor.

   MC: The reality of guilt that nearly all of our students face studying in this course or doing service work in general was the single most revealing aspect of my interviews with students. I simply had no idea the burden of guilt that our wealthy students feel when they are confronted with the reality of people's lives who have so much less than they do. I raise this question directly with them in class, offering that guilt is perhaps the best of the "negative" emotions in that if its energy is used to fuel actions on behalf of others, those feelings can be mitigated. This is one of main reasons we include experiential learning in the curriculum, including the Elixir Project: students need to *do something* to work with and through these powerful emotions.

6. **These intense feelings and questions prompt varied reactions. Some resist this knowledge and its implications, while others feel energized to make a difference in the world.**

   Student A: I chose a wild horse [to represent this course] because as it lives, it encounters different situations and runs. Just like how I acknowledge the world's crisis problems, but I simply just run away from them, not wanting to face them.

Student B: If I feel a deep connection with a child in Darfur at the moment, I would feel very sad and undeserving. However, almost as a defense mechanism I have to insulate myself to some degree so I can go about my normal business.

Student C: I have become a bigger part in the global community . . . more motivated to do service and have really understood the incredible impact and reward of helping others. I have grown a better sense of identity and where I stand on various political, economic, and worldview issues. I have grown so much that it would take forever to write it all down . . . [I] feel excited to bring hope to the hopeless situation from my knowledge attained in this class.

MC: Each student processes studying the world's problems differently, so I am extremely cautious in dealing with students' emotional responses to the material, especially given that they are only 14-year olds. I resist passing judgment on whether students respond "properly" or not, allowing them to work through their journey at their own pace.

7. **At some point the challenge of studying the world's problems is regarded less as a burden and more as an opportunity, as helping others gives rise to a deep sense of meaningfulness.**

    As I continued learning about everything that was wrong in the world, there were moments I wanted to close my eyes forever, to forget and erase and not care. The crisis in Myanmar had not abated, but no one was talking about it anymore. In Darfur, people were being burned to death, cut to pieces and shot. I was doing nothing about it, and the world did not seem to care about it, and the little they were doing wasn't enough. I was the little child trying to plug up holes in a bursting dam of world disasters . . . I felt utterly alone and wanted to stop. Relief didn't come until December when I went to Jungsing . . . As I sat in the hotel conference room, I had a lot to say about hope and love and caring for people, but I still wasn't sure if I meant it. In fact, it wasn't until I walked into the nursery and saw a small, quiet baby reach for me that I began to feel some sort of peace . . . In all my previous experiences with service, I've always had specific goals to help the community. I had never considered that the people I helped could give to me that inexplicable something that I was so hungry for . . . With genuine love for them and not just a mechanical mission . . . my work could have a soul and I could go on.

    MC: Early on in the course we read a version (Powers, 2008) of the famous Loren Eiseley (1978) story about two men walking on a beach who see thousands of marooned starfish dying in front of them. One friend laments the situation, while the other begins heaving starfish into the sea. Seeing the reflexive response to help, the one man says, "The numbers are so vast. Nothing we do could make a difference" (p. 4). The other friend continues rescuing starfish, and then responds, "It makes a difference to this one" (p. 4). "The Star Thrower" story communicates the dual truth that students come to understand in the course. First, global needs are overwhelming. And yet secondly, there can be something satisfying in helping even one person or one issue at a time. Again, this is why actual service experiences are essential to social conscience education.

8. **Making sense of the world occurs through the formation of new physical, emotional and spiritual connections. The new links which form serve to help bring otherwise dissociated life experiences into a more interconnected whole.**

Student A: When I went back to visit [the Jungsing orphanage], my baby . . . could tell when I walked through [the door] that she recognized me. I guess it's not like you have to do something huge to change the world. We learned about interconnectedness last year and so we are all connected . . . the butterfly effect. If you change one little thing, it's going to change another thing.

Student B: Through my service experiences, I not only realized (rationally) but felt, deep in my core, that we human beings are ultimately not separate from the world and each other, but are interdependent and interconnected. We have the same fundamental needs and wants, hopes and dreams, and hence we should recognize and appreciate the sacredness and beauty in the other.

MC: If the fundamental problem is that students are disconnected from social reality, then it is through connections that students find relief from their angst. This is a challenge to what they perceive as their primary adolescent task—to get into a highly regarded university through individual achievement. This dilemma forces them to weigh the relative merits of the various life narratives that have been given to them by their parents, community, and school. Referring to student B's comment, we have found—and even more so in our SPEX classes— that many students are existentially curious about the claim of both spiritual traditions and quantum physics that, on some level of reality, we are all indeed interconnected.

9. **One of the most important parts of personal growth is the formation of opinions, values, and beliefs about human nature, human behavior, and social issues.**

You realize the answers you had were other people's answers, not your own . . . You need to come up with your own answers. When I think of Humanities I in Action, I think of . . . how you see sheep being herded and . . . I see this one lone sheep. He's going the other way . . . Humanities would teach us how to break the shackles when you're in the cave . . . and go out and see the sun . . . Humanities I in Action . . . was about finding truth as in the sense of once again breaking away from the herd mentality. Finding what you think is right, not what other people think is right.

MC: The semester and final exam essay question about worldview underscores that the most important assessments ask students to explain their opinion about the course materials. While they listen to many voices throughout the year, ultimately they need to articulate their own personal life philosophy with regard to the curriculum.

10. **A feeling develops of an expanded world and a sense of the "big picture."**

Everybody plays a role in the elaborate domino set up of the world. When you zoom in, you can only see yourself, your own life, with nothing attached. However, when you look at the big picture, when you know more about the world, you see that if you fall, the whole also eventually collapses and falls. In this class, I have learned a lot more about the big picture. Now, I do not only see the small dominos, but the whole.

MC: Because of the careful selection of both current and historical topics across various human cultures framed within the overall construct of worldview, students often speak of seeing the "big picture." Coming into the course, most students don't know what a worldview is, yet they quickly come to understand how this concept can be applied to human civilizations across time and space. This school year I had a number of students who had spent quite a few years in local Hong Kong schools in which critical thinking was not highly developed; the cognitive growth they went through in Humanities I in Action was akin to stepping from a 2-D world into 3-D. Even if students struggle to articulate this shift, I believe it's this expanded epistemological vantage point that lies behind their expression of seeing the "big picture."

11. **An important part of this personal journey is its social dimension. Dialogue with friends, development of deeper friendships, and experiences of the growth process together with peers are all important components of this journey.**

I think that doing a service course, what you gain from it personally or spiritually is not so much the service you do, but it's the service you do in the company of your classmates . . . When we went to Jungsing [taking care of] the babies . . . it's not like the actual event that really changes my life but it's more like seeing how my classmates act in an orphanage and seeing how they take care of others and how that motivates me, and gives me hope and changes me.

MC: One of the reasons for including service outings together as a class is to break down the school-life divide. Friendships and conversations flow on fields trips in a way that cannot happen inside the classroom. Oftentimes it is out of this sense of authentic community that students' deepest learning emerges. It's worth mentioning that all of our experiential and service outings in Humanities I in Action include the classroom teachers, which enhances the sense these activities and the conversations that inevitably emerge are integral to the course outcomes.

12. **A feeling develops of being on a personal journey of growth. At the same time, there is a recognition that transformation is far from complete.**

I feel like I was a caterpillar when I began this course, and the more I learned and understood what the world was really going through, I started wrapping myself in a cocoon. I don't think I have accomplished 'metamorphosis' yet where I am completely . . . transformed into a butterfly, but I believe I am in the process of doing so.

MC: When students read about the example of 12-year old Craig Kielburger (Kielburger & Major, 1998), whose life was changed by the reality of child labor, students realize that they too could do so much more to benefit others. They understand that the world's needs call upon them, especially as highly privileged students, to do something for others, yet they are also quite well-aware of the personal, social, and cultural barriers that question how much time and energy they should invest in the needs of others. Genuine personal struggle lies at the center of social conscience education.

13. **Upon reflection, there is a realization that the pathway out of the bubble has involved a new sense of identity and an interconnected relationship with the world.**

I have been through a journey of self-awareness, a road to recognize the interconnectedness between each and every one of us, and further, how we are all connected to the world.

MC: I often feel that Humanities I in Action, taught to high school freshman, is offered at the perfect developmental level, because, first, students' ability to think abstractly phases in around this age. They are also in their first year of high school when, for the first time, their grades "count" towards future college placement. For these reasons, they are more aware of their own life path than ever before. It's at this point of heightened self-awareness regarding their *own* future that we take them on another journey: the future prospects of other people and the planet. It is this collision of narratives that fuels their "journey of self-awareness."

Acting on Social Conscience

14. **Often the first way that action motivated by social conscience occurs is talking to family and friends about ideas, concerns, and issues. This sometimes causes tension, especially with parents.**

   I talked to my parents and they started getting a bit mad because they thought that I wasn't learning anything because I was talking like nonsense. My Dad asked why am I paying for this school if you're not really learning . . . Then he was always getting mad because he was like I don't want to buy you any more organic eggs . . . Then I talked to my Mom about things like the group pressure and about situational ethics, especially about genocide and I made my Dad read Ishmael and I actually thought he wouldn't read it . . . I said, you have to read this book. So, it was cool to be able to communicate with someone who wasn't taking the course . . . He read the book and I think both of my parents ended up loving the course.

   MC: Even if students feel they have done little in terms of their Elixir Projects or the "in Action" elements, I pick up quickly anytime that they mention they have spoken to those in their social sphere about the class. I recognized through my research that the seemingly mundane act of speaking to family and friends about the course materials is *the* primary way that grade 9 students express their social conscience growth.

15. **Social conscience frequently brings new ideas, attitudes, and choices into daily life.**

   We were talking about sweatshops and we . . . asked how connected are we to a sweatshop worker? Through that I kind of realized . . . every purchase that I make dictates . . . the flow of supply and demand—basic economics . . . You just think a lot more about simple decisions like that and how it might affect someone else's life . . . Do we eat chocolate? Should I research it before I eat it? And clothes—should I be buying that? It's hard because I was so interested in fashion and it's like, oh, what do I do now? Do I have to stop everything? You get really stressed out I think and it's really difficult.

   MC: Very few pedagogical strategies work better than asking students to make practical ethical decisions. For affluent students whose very comfortable lifestyle may depend on factory work in China or other parts of Asia, to consider that their consumer habits may be leading to suffering can be a cause for substantial cognitive dissonance or even alarm. This is the premise of our very effective day 1 chocolate experience (Chapter 3), which asks students to consider that perhaps a slave harvested the cocoa in their inexpensive chocolate bar.

16. **A new awareness develops that at some point a decision to act needs to be made or a stand needs to be taken.**

Last week I was in the country park and I saw a couple of men like smoking away . . . This whole year I've been in this class called A.P. Environmental Science and one of the biggest topics is pollution . . . So I just got mad because I was working out and . . . they were just in front of me so. . . I actually went up to them and I was like, hey mister, can you not smoke in the country park because it is against the law . . . Before telling them, I was debating in my head whether or not to . . . One part of me was saying you know that's kind of rude [to correct them], but another part of me was saying it's morally right to because as a citizen of Hong Kong and the world I want to preserve [our natural world] . . . I thought I should tell them because even though they might get mad at that moment, I believe in the long run I'm doing a good cause for the environment and the society.

MC: As a teacher I forget how difficult it is for most students to take a stand on an issue and to act on that position. Yet this is what it means to be an adult: to make judgments on behalf of society and take steps to bring about change, even if that act is as small as making ethical food choices or conserving energy. Most students see themselves as observers of society rather than participants, so taking an action step based on their beliefs is an important indication that students are growing in self-efficacy.

17. **Acts of caring and of making a difference in the lives of others, especially ones that involve the exercise of leadership, facilitate greater appreciation of one's ability to effect positive change in the world.**

    When I went to Jungsing, I was so shocked and wanted to do something to help, but I really couldn't adopt every single baby, so it made me want to help, but I really couldn't. That's the feeling . . . [But] this course teaches you that even one person, one child, can make a difference in this world, so it taught me that I have the power to change, like impact the world. For example, we went to Deqing [a trip after the Jungsing trip] and I felt very accomplished when I taught the girls English and they gained something from my visit . . . I was like emotionally connected to the students and then after we left, we saw them crying . . . Those tears meant that we actually impacted and changed [them].

    MC: This student shows the cumulative effect over time that can happen with successive service experiences. In this case, a female student, who had a powerful but ultimately unsatisfying experience in Jungsing, decided to devote herself to a girls scholarship trip with clear intention to benefit her students and bring about a more fulfilling experience than the orphanage. The takeaway for teachers is that they need to deeply engage students in this action-reflection cycle on service outings.

18. **A commitment is made to continue the journey of social conscience through further self-exploration for the purpose of benefiting society.**

   Given my belief to always seek out the beautiful, positive things in people and my general love for others, I plan to further explore the area of positive psychology in college and use my gifts and passion in this field to understand humanity better and give all that I am back to people in need. Additionally and most importantly, I promise to be a person of integrity, that my work may be completely in line with my actions, my actions completely congruous with my thoughts, and that my thoughts may always reflect my unwavering faith in an all-loving God.

   MC: I frequently tell students that their greatest challenge will be once they leave the supportive confines of the Humanities I in Action classroom. Statements like the one above, written by a senior whom I taught in both her freshman and senior year, usually come about as a result of nurturance over some years. I always try to offer students ways to stay in touch, such as extending their Elixir Project into a four-year commitment. Fortunately, the Humanities curriculum now also offers a Humanities II in Action course for students to continue developing their vision of social impact. For schools wanting to develop students' social conscience, it's not enough to have only one course. Developing social conscience involves fostering a lifelong ethic towards the whole of one's existence. In the best-case scenario, institutions provide manifold opportunities at every year of high school for students to renew their commitment to the common good.

* * *

Year after year students share aspects of this journey as they make their way through the Humanities I in Action course. Knowing the arc of their trajectory allows me to guide them through various stages. Of course, this does not mean that transformation will be permanently imprinted on all students. While some are irreversibly changed, others lose their conviction once they return to more conventional classrooms in years to come. But all students are given the opportunity to take a journey that offers them a fundamental reorientation of their relationship to the world.

CONCLUSION

Many years ago, I set out to find the power of education for myself and my students. At the time I didn't know what I was looking for; I didn't have words or even concepts to frame something that I intuitively yearned for in my life as well as in my teaching. Only through personal and curricular experimentation did some kind of gradual resolution present itself in the form of social conscience education in the Humanities I in Action course.

To now put this understanding into words, social conscience education is a potentially transformative path offering students an integrated curriculum that engages their minds (awareness), hearts (emotional engagement), and hands (action). For teachers called to this educational approach, it is helpful to understand and trust the deep psychological impact that a social conscience curriculum can make as they mentor students through this transformative process.

CHAPTER 3

IS IGNORANCE BLISS?

Teaching About Chocolate Slavery on Day One

Many young adults . . . are often being cheated . . . They are not being asked big-enough questions. They are not being invited to entertain the greatest questions of their own lives or their own times.
—*Sharon Parks (2000, p. 138)*

I think what has stuck to me the most was the exercise on the very first day of class where you talked about chocolate and how cocoa beans were really sourced. You asked us the question "Is ignorance bliss?," and I think that that was the most important concept that I learned and what really led me to realize my interest in world affairs and social change.
—*Bea, female student, senior at University of Toronto majoring in political science, commenting on her experience in Humanities I in Action seven years earlier*[1]

---

[1] See Bea's full comments on Humanities I in Action in Chapter 18.

The Wisdom Way of Teaching: Educating for Social Conscience and Inner Awakening in the High School Classroom, pages 37–48.
Copyright © 2022 by Information Age Publishing
www.infoagepub.com
All rights of reproduction in any form reserved.

INTRODUCTION

Having offered an overview of the Humanities I in Action class and its impact upon students in Chapter 2, this chapter hones in on my classroom on the first day of school to show how the process of social conscience growth begins from the very first moment. Several years ago my colleagues and I designed a classroom activity to kick off Humanities I in Action that would not only be a valuable lesson in its own right, but would also represent in microcosm our approach to student learning and growth throughout the year. We based the lesson on the awareness-emotional engagement-action model presented in Chapter 1 (Figure 1.1). It has proven to be a remarkably memorable lesson, and sets the tone for all that is to follow.

For some years we had used the issue of slave-produced chocolate in our globalization unit. Because many students almost obsessively consume chocolate, this issue hits home with them. In the lesson, chocolate itself serves as a seed for consideration of its broader social implications, including child trafficking, challenging students to think more deeply about the impact of their consumption patterns. In moving this topic to the initial activity of the year, we were able to provide an exercise that prepares students for the central question of our first semester of study, "Is ignorance bliss?"

TEACHING DAY ONE

A palpable nervous energy permeates the school corridors as all 760 students and 90 faculty members exit the assembly in the gym and move towards their very first class of the year.[2] I race ahead to make sure I'm the first in the door before the rest of the timid and tentative freshmen arrive, taking one last glance at the room set-up. Five sets of four-person rectangular desk pods are neatly arranged with each student's name written on brightly colored 3 x 5 cards at each seat. Located in what we unflatteringly call "the dungeons—the below-ground segment of our eight-floor, white-textured "in-the-round" school campus that won an architectural design award—my spacious classroom has a full bank of windows looking out on the artificial turf below with the red "HKIS" insignia emblazoned at the center. Behind the sports field are a verdant row of green hills, the likes of which dominate most of southern Hong Kong island. The only truly conspicuous classroom prop is situated at the front of the room: a bulletin board of images representing various course topics constellated around a blue eye that boldly asks "What is your Worldview?"

I take a last deep breath and open the door to welcome the students to their very first period of their high school career. I greet these slightly overgrown middle schoolers with a friendly hello and thank them for choosing Humanities I in Ac-

---

[2] The descriptions of these first two class periods, including the student responses, come from the first year in which I did the chocolate activity on the first day of class.

Humanities I in Action Bulletin Board. Photo Credit: Author.

tion, but what animates my energy is not primarily first-day jitters but the conviction that the next 60 minutes are actually the most teachable day of the entire school year.

Following the taking of names, I ask students to choose one of the following questions and to free write a response on a 4 × 6 notecard:

1. Describe your favorite chocolate treat.
2. What is a good memory you have of eating chocolate?
3. What would be an ideal time and place for you to eat chocolate?

As they write, I walk around the room with a plateful of Ghana chocolate broken into bite-sized pieces. I ask them if they would like a whiff of the chocolate for inspiration, promising that by the end of the class they would have a chance to consume it.

We share some of our stories afterwards. One student talks about how she would cut fresh fruit and put the fruit and a piece of chocolate in a zodiac-like circle, almost ritualistically, before eating them. She also mentions that whenever she was upset as a child, her mother would comfort her with chocolate. Reflecting on pleasurable experiences with chocolate is an upbeat icebreaker for the first day of class.

Then I change the focus by asking them to do a second free write: "Share an experience in which you learned something about society that was disturbing. How did you feel?" The tone shifts from pleasure to purpose, as students talked of traveling in Asia and seeing poor people, meeting refugees in Hong Kong, the question of shark fin soup, and more.

I then ask them to consider the question, "Is ignorance bliss? Are you glad that you learned about these disturbing experiences or not?" We had a wide-ranging conversation about whether ignorance of these issues was truly blissful or not.

I explain that I want to put this question to the test and show them the opening segments of the BBC production, *Chocolate: The Bitter Truth* (Buchanan, 2015). Journalist Paul Kenyon takes viewers to the West African rainforest to trace the origins of chocolate production. First, we meet a group of mothers in a poor village in Burkina Faso who were tricked into sending off their sons to work as slaves in the cocoa fields of neighboring Ghana, the world's second largest producer of cocoa. Kenyon then travels to these fields, and, acting as a cocoa trader, meets trafficked children who harvest the cocoa beans. They do not get paid, nor go to school, but need to handle dangerous tools in doing their work, all violations of guidelines established by the International Labor Organization.

THE MOMENT OF DECISION

After about 10 minutes, I stop the video, and announce: "You have signed up for Humanities I *in Action*. And from day one I want you to understand that this class is about making decisions, about acting on what you learn. And so I have a choice for you. I have two plates of chocolate here. Both were produced in Ghana. This Ghana brand, one can assume, is produced by children like you see in the video. It is slave-produced. You may eat this chocolate at no cost to yourself. On the other hand, this second plate of Divine chocolate, which also uses Ghanaian cocoa beans, claims to be a fair trade product. It is significantly more expensive than the free trade chocolate, so if you would like some, you need to pay to eat it. So, you have three choices: eat the free trade chocolate at no cost, pay for the fair trade chocolate, or you can choose to abstain from the whole exercise."

The Remains of the First Day's Chocolate Experiment. Photo Credit: Author.

Then I explain the final twist in this social experiment: "However, to make your choice as free as possible of my influence as a teacher, I am going to leave the room. There is about 5 minutes left in class, and you cannot leave until the bell rings. I will come by after school and collect the chocolate and, if there is any, the money contributed for the fair trade chocolate. Do you have any questions?"

And with that, I place the two chocolate bars on a table in the back of the room, put a donation cup next to the fair trade chocolate, tell them I will see them tomorrow, and walk out of the room.

I come back 15 minutes later to pick up the chocolate and the money in the cup. I find two empty plates, and $130 HK dollars [about US $16.50] in the cup.

FOUR THEMES FROM STUDENT REFLECTION

As a follow-up to the day one chocolate activity, I ask students to comment on an online forum before the next class. The following is my prompt:

> Hello everyone,
>
> Day one was a great success! I appreciated all the great comments, and the way you listened to each other. Discussion of opinions about current issues, about human nature, and about what we can do are all key components of the course. These are all part of what we will call a "worldview," or a system of beliefs. American philosopher Ralph Waldo Emerson's quote is helpful here: "The ancestor of every action is a thought." For us to have right action in the world, we need right thought.
>
> So, your homework this weekend is to reflect on today's class and write a response. For full credit, you need to answer the three questions below in 15 lines or more by 9 PM on Sunday night. Look at all three items and plan your answers ahead of time so that you don't repeat the same ideas in different questions. Make sure you address all three.
> 1. What was your biggest insight from today's class?
> 2. What action did you take at the end of the class regarding the free trade (possibly slave-produced) vs. fair trade chocolate and why? Also think about: what went through your mind regarding what action you took, and how much/how little were you influenced by your peers?
> 3. I chose this activity because it represents in one class what I hope to do all year with you. Take a guess, then, what is my method for teaching you?

I read the homework and was so impressed with their responses that I decided to do an analysis of the critical thinking of this group of "in Action" students on their very first day of class.

However, before turning directly to the students responses, let me set the stage by expressing our intentions in carefully designing this initial activity and linking these to the four themes that did emerge. We want students to see that something as commonplace as a chocolate bar involves consideration of a myriad of ethical questions (theme 1) that connects them to people and places far distant from the grocery store standing across from our school gate. Reminiscent of the famous course at Harvard, "Justice," in which Michael Sandel's (2010) simple question "What's the right thing to do?" plunges students into complex moral introspection, we want students to know from day one that the blithely offered hope to "make the world a better place" requires, to students' surprise, a deep dialogue involving many considerations and perspectives about what truly is helpful action (theme 2). As I learned in my research, students' most common action steps[3] are making personal connections between a complex web of philosophical questions and lifestyle choices involving their families and friends (theme 3). Ensconced as our students are in HKIS' safe and affluent environs, the overarching philosophical question we want them to consider during the first semester—"is ignorance bliss" (theme 4)—is introduced on day one so that they understand from the very first minutes of the course that even though most of us would prefer not to face these realities, we paradoxically feel at the same time driven to understand the suffering of others and to ease the burdens of our fellow human beings.

Theme 1: Students reflected deeply about the ethics of their actions, especially in the context of their peer relations.

Shiv: When the fair trade and free trade chocolate was offered and the terms were set, my initial thought was no matter what, I was only going to eat the fair trade chocolate. I went and gave my donation and ate the fair trade chocolate. But as I saw my peers freely take the free trade chocolate, I began to get badly tempted, so much so I even picked up a piece of the free trade chocolate. As I was about to eat the free trade chocolate the video flashed through my head. I started thinking about the parents who have lost their children to cocoa farming and I thought how my parents would feel if that happened to them. As I let those thoughts mull over in my head, I made a decision. I dropped the chocolate back onto the plate, got my stuff, and walked out of the class with my head held high.

Ananya: I actually spent a lot of time thinking about what I should do. I also observed what other people did. Some made a donation and didn't eat any chocolate at all, which I thought was kind of fruitless. Some didn't donate and chose to eat the Ghana chocolate, possibly made by slaves. And all the others donated and ate the factory-made chocolate. Everyone had different opinions, but mine stood alone. My personal action was donating, but eating the Ghana chocolate instead. I felt the need to do this, because a lot of effort and time has been put in by children to make that chocolate bar. The children have given up their childhood and an education to make that chocolate bar, then why put their efforts to waste? . . . I think my action made sense.

---

[3] Step 14 in "A Model of the Journey of Social Conscience"

Jonathan: I picked the one that wasn't made by the trafficked children and donated my spare change to them. When I put the change in the cup the first thing I thought of was the children, not what my classmates thought of me. I was not as concerned about "face" as I was about following what my gut said, and if given another chance, I would do it in an instant because it's simply the right thing to do. I may not be able to save the world by myself, but making good ethical choices in such instances gives me a good feeling that I did something.

Theme 2: Students found the multiple perspectives expressed in the class discussion to be thought provoking.

Jessica: Through the class discussions, I got an insight into the different views that people had about the troubles of today's society. While talking about our opinions, I found that many people had contrasting views of each matter, and I found that intriguing.

Taina: The biggest insight for me during class was how everyone is so opinionated . . . In particular, everybody had a different perspective on the child trafficking topic so it did open eyes and doors to different viewpoints. I love hearing varied beliefs, it helps me realize and understand what others are thinking. I love debating so when everyone is opinionated it gets me worked up and it will go on for hours!!

Jonathan: I learned a lot from Friday's class. On that day I saw the world from different perspectives, all of which I agree with . . . I also learned that even simple pleasures like chocolate have a negative side. Students who don't take this class may never hear about the trafficked children who work day and night in the cocoa fields to bring us this great treat. I will remember this class the next time I buy chocolate.

Theme 3: Students made personal connections between this issue and their daily lives with family members and friends.

Jonathan: I recall my father bringing back chocolate from the US last year. He purchased it at Whole Foods, a US-based grocery store that not only focuses on healthier foods, but also the stories behind those foods and where they came from, and how they were harvested or brought to market. I believe more stores should take more responsibility to let consumers know the origin of our foods.

Matt: Many of us complain about parents being too strict or not getting the newest iPhone, but the reality is while you may be complaining about phones and parents, most kids in other places that aren't Hong Kong may not even have those things (parents included). The reason this was my biggest insight is because this will probably stick with me for a long time. When I complain about my brother getting something better than me, I'll remember that what I have is better than a lot of the kids and try to be more grateful for what I have.

Chris: The thing that really took me aback was not the child labor (though that surprised me too), but the number of people that didn't know how most chocolates are being produced. When I asked my siblings on their chocolate, they told me quite confidently "from chocolate factories" (they're both younger than me). Then after a few minutes, they came back to me and asked, "Right?" This shows me that they actually had no idea if their chocolate was made through child labor or sweat-free chocolate industries. As mentioned in class, Ghana owns one of the world's largest chocolate industries. I know a few friends who are fans of that brand, and out of curiosity, I asked them if they knew the process of their chocolate being made. They all guessed factories. This just simply shows me how oblivious most people are of what's going on in the world. Because I took the Humanities in Action course, I knew that taking action was not only part of my duty, but also the right thing. After watching the video, I successfully persuaded my siblings and some friends to not worry about the price when buying chocolate, but instead, buy what they think is made legally.

Theme 4: Students wrestled with the statement "ignorance is bliss" and began to define their own values in response.

Ananya: Though our class had a lot of insights from Friday's class, the one phrase that stuck with me throughout the discussion was "Is ignorance bliss?" I really had to process this, and upon hearing all the perspectives in the class, I came up with my own opinion: ignorance is not bliss. People like us know about what is going on in the world, but they choose not to take action towards it. Some say it's unavoidable, and some are just too lazy. But somewhere in the back of their mind, they know someone's dying of malnutrition, an animal is being skinned, and a beggar is trying to make a living. Ignoring the facts is not making us any happier, but instead it's making us feel guilty about who we are as a person. At least I know it's making me feel guilty, and appreciate whatever I have. I'm not saying that action needs to be taken, but a little appreciation would be nice.

Shiv: From my first class in Humanities in Action I came away with many new insights. Despite having those insights there was one question I couldn't get out of my mind. Is ignorance really bliss? At first glance during class I thought I had an idea of what my answer was to the question, but as class continued, I realized that I didn't know what my answer was. Throughout the class I felt like I was at a loss, till I came to a conclusion at the end of the class. I realized that ignorance is bliss until you are exposed to what you are ignoring.

Even though I had taught this course for many years, I was deeply impressed by how much insight these 14-year-old students had to offer on their very first day of high school. Two factors account for such depth, one involving teacher perception and the other teacher preparation. With regard to the former, one of my fundamental beliefs about teaching for social conscience is that the biggest impediment to student growth seems to be a teacher's limited vision of the vast potential of the students who sit before them. By contrast, if I can assume that every class of students has the potential from day one to enter into considerable moral complexity, my spacious expectations are oftentimes met or exceeded. As I raise the bar on "what's possible" in my own thinking, students then seem to clear the bar with ease.

However, a commitment to the latter is necessary as well: teachers need to consider truly significant questions, and then do the hard work of systematic design of lessons to engage learners' deeper potential. Like a rock climber finding a crevice that provides just the right handhold, social conscience teachers need to find just the right questions that open up students' minds and hearts. All of our Humanities curriculum planning attempts to identify these large exploratory questions around which we build our courses and units.

TEACHING DAY TWO

Having read students' blog comments, I am hoping to have a rich discussion on day two about the many topics raised on day one. To begin the period, I show the class a clip from a video made in the late 1990s about a related issue: *Slavery: A Global Investigation* (Real Stories, 2017). In one scene, a young man who worked for more than five years without pay on a cocoa plantation in the Ivory Coast is asked by the investigative reporter what message he has for the millions of people around the world who eat chocolate. He responds, "If I had to say something to them, it would not be nice words. They enjoy something I suffered to make; I worked hard for them, but saw no benefit." I pause the video to let this articulate former slave's provocative statements sink in. Then I hit play to let him deliver his parting shot, one of the most memorable lines of the year: "They are eating my flesh."

Then we begin to discuss the previous day's activity. What followed was a highly engaging conversation about the activity, which I have summarized for the sake of brevity.

1. How did you feel when I walked out of class and left you alone?

    Surprised and even shocked.

2. What new "group script"[4] emerged once I, the authority figure, left?

---

[4] As introduced in Chapter 2, the term "group script" describes how social situations create group-induced behavioral norms.

One quiet boy oversaw the students paying to eat the fair trade chocolate. When I asked how he felt about taking on the role of "The Enforcer" in the class, he said with a mix of pride and embarrassment that he felt "a little important."

3. Who was the first person to eat the free chocolate?

    One boy ate it and at least one other followed suit because of the first boy; soon the rest of the bar was consumed.

4. Do you feel guilty about eating the free chocolate?

    Some did, while others claimed they had guilt-free rationales for their choice.

5. How do you as wealthy students feel when you see poor children being taken advantage of?

    Guilty, even though we're not sure why.

6. Yet sometimes when we visit poor people in developing countries, they seem happier than we do. Why?

    Their lives are simpler and less stressful.

7. Would anyone be willing to switch your life for poor people's "simpler and less stressful" existence?

    One said definitely yes; the rest preferred their present lives.

8. Would the boy in the documentary approve of the decision some of you made "not to waste" the chocolate slaves' efforts and eat the free trade chocolate?

    No.

9. To what degree did you act on your own personal/moral values and to what degree were you influenced by the new norms of student behavior that emerged once I left?

    A mix of inner-directed and outer-directed behaviors.

10. Is ignorance of the chocolate labor issue bliss?

    It's blissful until exposure punctures the ignorance.

This hour-long discussion set up many themes for the year:

1. What are the motivations and values that undergird our actions?

2. Is individual participation in harmful patterns of consumption morally acceptable?
3. How do we in our own classroom relationships act out sociological concepts such as following a group script, diffusion of responsibility, loss of authority figures, and bystander apathy, which we will study about later during the semester?
4. How can individuals with a social conscience challenge harmful group norms?

MICROCOSM OF SOCIAL CONSCIENCE PEDAGOGY

The chocolate slavery activity demonstrates the pedagogical approach (Figure 3.1) that Humanities I in Action teachers employ to select and process particular class materials.

With respect to content selection, we look for current issues that touch the lives of our students. This factor is a powerful ingredient in truly engaging student interest. Next, we select issues that are easily accessible and contain relevant psychological and sociological aspects for student consideration. In these lessons, the psychological layer is addressed, for example, through student reflection on the feelings of the trafficked children and their parents as well as their own indirect connection to the chocolate slave trade through their consumption habits.

The sociological dimension is engaged, for example, through consideration of how global markets operate to drive the chocolate demand and its insidious side effects. It is also addressed when students contemplate how their peers influenced them when the teacher left the room. Finally, the content is also approached through underlying "big questions," which guide reflection on the issues through a more expansive or macro vantage point. Examples of big questions in the chocolate slavery lesson include: Is ignorance bliss? Can we live happy lives enjoying

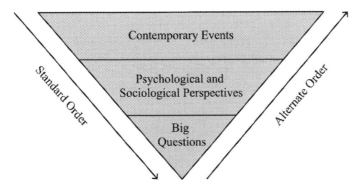

FIGURE 3.1. A Model for Teaching Social Conscience Curriculum

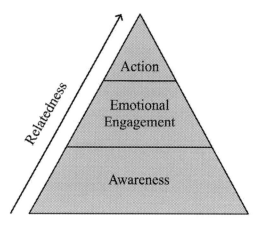

FIGURE 3.2. The Short-Term Impact of Social Conscience Education

commodities produced at the expense of others? In short, this model, which is explained in greater detail in Chapter 6, illustrates how the three levels work simultaneously to develop greater depth in students' social conscience.

While the chocolate slavery lesson illustrates a specific curricular approach, it also suggests the short-term impact that such lessons aim for. Figure 3.2 illustrates the three short-term student processes that compose a socially conscious lesson: awareness, emotional engagement, and action. First, students gained an awareness of the issue of slave-produced chocolate production. Second, students' emotions were engaged through their own memories of eating chocolate as well as dramatic video footage depicting the lives of chocolate labor slaves. Third, students were expected to make an action response to the cognitive and affective elements of the lesson at the end of the period by eating and paying for the fair trade chocolate, eating the free trade chocolate or abstaining. All three components are necessary in order to realize the goal of social conscience education, which is to provide students the opportunity to actively consider their role and responsibility in society in light of an emotionally-engaged understanding of the world (Schmidt, 2009).

CONCLUSION

Studying and acting upon a compelling issue such as chocolate slavery has proven to be a highly engaging and memorable lesson to start the school year. In addition, this two-day introduction to the basic pedagogical approaches of the class helps students better understand the holistic and potentially transformative nature of the learning methods used in Humanities I in Action. Through this model of social conscience instruction, Humanities I in Action students are systematically guided on a path that invites them to relate to the world in a new way.

During the Jungsing Orphanage Trip, the Class Visits the Chinese Goddess of Compassion to Help Students Consider Their Own Journey Towards Loving Kindness. Photo Credit: Author.

CHAPTER 4

THE HEROIC JOURNEY FROM SELF-FOCUS TO COMPASSION

Mentoring Students Through an Orphanage Trip Experience

> Profoundly attuned to the Other—to everything that is not ourselves—the right hemisphere is alert to relationships. It is the seat of empathy, pathos, and our sense of justice. Because it can see an-other point of view, it inhibits our natural selfishness . . . The best way of achieving this transcendence of self is to cultivate habits of empathy and compassion.
> —*Karen Armstrong, (2019, p. 6, 13)*

> My old self would have continued being oblivious to the real world and the suffering. On my journey to becoming my new self, I realized [the importance of] showing compassion and that I could make a huge difference in the lives of the less fortunate. I believe that I have changed because of this trip and that I am one step closer to becoming my Larger Self. All I need to do is step out of my bubble and listen to people in need.
> —*Annika, grade 9 female student, a week after her trip to the Jungsing Orphanages*

INTRODUCTION

By the time November arrives in Humanities I in Action, students have internalized an array of hard-hitting materials: chocolate slavery, Australia's Stolen Generations, Abu Ghraib prison torture, *Lord of the Flies*, the Milgram and Stanford Prison experiments, the Rwandan genocide, and memoirs from various modern conflicts. Every student who undergoes this barrage of disturbing topics becomes aware of human depravity in a new way. An accurate summary of students' worldview at this point in the year would be: humans are shockingly self-centered and in desperate need of a remedy. It is at this low point, however, the focus makes a 180 degree change. We take our classes to two orphanages in the Chinese city of Jungsing for a weekend of caring for children who are living in vastly different circumstances than ourselves.

My dramatic intentions—to offer students the experiential opportunity to pivot from melancholy to benevolence—go mostly unspoken, however, because I want such a turn to be discovered by the students themselves rather than as a result of my priming their imaginations. In line with this more prosaic approach, I proceed with the trip logistics before addressing the deeper aspects of the experience.

CROSSING FROM THE ORDINARY WORLD TO THE SPECIAL WORLD

Usually classes go two at a time on the trip, typically leaving after school on Thursday afternoon and returning home Sunday evening. The trip is quite simple in its design: Friday, Saturday, and Sunday mornings are spent at the orphanages, while Saturday afternoon we visit a statue of Kuan Yin, the Chinese goddess of compassion, about an hour outside of Jungsing. We have meetings every evening for journal writing and sharing.

We visit two orphanages, which differ markedly in their resources and atmosphere. One has abundant financial support as well as professionally-trained and caring nurses. The arts and crafts projects we join them in are well-organized and use excellent materials. All the children are happy to be with us. On the other hand, the second orphanage has fewer resources and is stuck, it seems, in a "basics only" mode of providing attention, food, and clothing. The nurses show kindness and care—we have known some of them for decades—but they are short-staffed and at times overwhelmed. The children are noticeably sadder than those in the other orphanage, leaving us in no doubt about the human cost of an under-resourced institution.[1]

In the hotel the night before we go to the orphanages for the first time, I prepare the students for their visit. To make the transition from the giddy excitement of being on a school trip to the quite different worlds we will enter, we congregate

---

[1] Most of our students, the majority of whom are of Chinese descent, speak some Mandarin and/or Cantonese—and some are fluent— so communication between our classes and the orphanage staff and others on the trip is easily managed.

in the hotel's conference room and watch portions of *China's Lost Girls* (Myers, 2004), a National Geographic documentary which poignantly covers key issues related to Chinese orphanages, such as the cultural preference for males over females and the one-child policy (which came to an end January 1, 2016). However, we don't overprepare them for their visit, for the open curiosity that they carry with them seems to leave space for indelible memories that are vital to their learning. So many essays over the years have detailed the intensity of the short, 10-minute bus ride from the hotel to the first orphanage, the ride up the elevator, and their first entry through the metallic doors behind which are the children they will spend their weekend with.

On that first night I also introduce Joseph Campbell's (2008) "Heroic Journey," which serves as a metaphor for not only the China trip, but the entire course as well. I explain that Campbell studied myths around the world and uncovered a common journey motif: a hero leaves his/her ordinary world of existence; travels to a special world filled with great tests and trials but also containing human and divine helpers; and perseveres in that special world until he/she finds an elixir, a healing balm with which to return and make the ordinary world a better place. Campbell's Heroic Journey makes clear, I explain, why we need to physically leave our ordinary world of Hong Kong, cross into a very different space and experience the "special world" with the orphans, and then journey home. Without explicitly stating it, the students begin to sense that this weekend is likely to entail challenges to their perception of "normal" reality.

Then I tell stories about my 25 years of bringing students to Jungsing, focusing on the lives of four children whom I met on my first trip in 1995. One baby girl with a cleft palate was adopted by an HKIS family, became the valedictorian of her high school in the US, and went on to study at a top U.S. university; a second was a mixed gender child who received surgery, and later was taken in by a local foster family; a third one with hemophilia—and a friend of the mixed gender child—had an accident one day at school and passed away suddenly at a local hospital; and a fourth child, who banged her head on concrete walls and floors in a repetitive motion 25 years ago when I first met her, now lives on one of the floors with other special needs adults. Finally, I mention my own daughter, who was born about the same time and who visited these children on countless occasions. She, like other HKIS students, received a high-quality international school education and then attended a prestigious university in the US. The life we all lead at HKIS, I explain, is not "real Asia." With this sobering thought, these stories, and Campbell's Heroic Journey in mind, we all head to our rooms, awaiting tomorrow's first visit to the orphanages.

VISITING KUAN YIN IN THE SPECIAL WORLD

The next morning we make the short but—in the minds of the students—dramatic trip to the two orphanages where we play with the children for about two hours. At the first, well-organized orphanage, we do arts and crafts with the children or take them to the playground or basketball court. The atmosphere is upbeat and child-friendly. At the other minimal care institution, students move between two floors, one for younger children and the other for older ones, including some in their teens. Although we bring balls to play with and paper to draw on, there are no organized activities at the second orphanage. There is a positive vibe to the floor with younger children, while the floor for the older children is initially intimidating and oftentimes chaotic.

As the morning comes to a close, we board the bus and take our students for their one outing of the weekend—to the temple of Kuan Yin, the goddess of compassion on top of a large volcanic mound that springs up from the flat river plain of Jungsing. As we enter the temple grounds, I remind them of the previous night's discussion of Campbell's Heroic Journey: each of us is called to leave our ordinary world of experience, enter into a special world to find some new insight, and return with an elixir to re-enliven our original world. Temples make this mythic pattern explicit, asking followers to leave the "profane" (literally "out in front of the temple") world behind, enter into a sacred dimension, and bring back some salve to assuage the discontent of daily existence.

Inside the temple complex, we glance upwards and take in the presence of the massive bronze statue of Kuan Yin, and consider her own heroic pathway. Kuan Yin's story of commitment to humanity and transformation is significant here. Originally, Kuan Yin took the form of male Indian god Avalokitesvara, who desired to help all who suffered. But these attempts left Avalokitesvara so heart-broken by his encounters that he shattered into a thousand pieces. From these broken fragments, the gods reconstituted the deity. Not only did he become transformed into a female goddess, but now she was reborn with a thousand outstretched arms, each with an open eye inside each palm, "a manifestation of nearly unimaginable compassion, reaching out to all beings in need" (Levine, 2013, p. 46). She is frequently pictured as long-eared, signifying that she can hear the cries of all who call on her aid. Suffering, I note, heightened Kuan Yin's capacity to see, hear, feel, and "lend a hand" to those in desperate need. This is the great teaching of Buddhism, I explain, that a heart shattered by crippling suffering can transform into a source of even deeper compassionate action.

In the shadow of Kuan Yin, we gather in a circle to put this teaching into practice. I ask the students to write down three examples of suffering that they observed today at the orphanages. We assume a meditation posture, and, in imitation of the Tibetan Buddhist practice of *tonglen*, we breathe in pain and breathe out compassion, seeking to encompass the suffering we have witnessed this morning in a more expansive flow.[2]

I tell them not to underestimate the challenges in this special world. I relate that some years ago we encountered a baby born only a few months earlier whose

---

[2] Most of our students at HKIS have had experiences with mindfulness practices by the time they enter grade 9.

The Heroic Journey from Self-Focus to Compassion • 55

Kuan Yin, the Chinese Goddess of Compassion, Symbolizes the Unconditional Love That We Are Seeking To Understand, Feel, and Enact During Our Trip to Jungsing. Photo Credit: Author.

face was extremely drawn as if in a permanent grimace. When we asked what was wrong, we were told that the baby had not eaten for about ten days and that nothing could be done. Stunned and unsure how to respond, we simply stayed. A teacher came to the room and played acoustic guitar, and then several girls intuitively began a vigil accompanying the suffering child into his premature final days. Kuan Yin's shattering is an apt metaphor for what those students experienced; the suffering we observe is real.

Kuan Yin is known as a bodhisattva, one who has accumulated sufficient spiritual sensitivity and maturity to reach enlightenment, but who chooses to stay on earth for the sake of all sentient beings. In her left hand she holds a vase of holy water that she sprinkles on all who cry for help, while the open right hand mudra symbolizes bestowing the blessing of patience. Sitting atop a mountain looking down across the plain, she is herself a benevolent bridge for all between heaven and earth. Kuan Yin models what Mahayana Buddhism's millennia-long search has come to understand about the path of compassionate action, which involves habitually setting aside the natural human tendency to seek pleasure and avoid pain and instead open up patiently to suffering, even that which might shatter the self, trusting that something deeper will still hold.

CHOICES IN THE SPECIAL WORLD

The next morning we give students a choice. They may return to the orphanage that is very well-resourced, or the under-resourced one with the more severe conditions. Reflecting on all they have seen, the vast majority of students opt for the latter institution where suffering is clearly visible and at times shockingly raw.

It is at this orphanage that we encounter what we are told is a 17-year-old boy—but who appears to be 10—lying flat on a bed, as he did four years ago when I first remember meeting him, wearing nothing but a diaper. Some thick brown growth lies like a partial beard on both sides of his face, and even more unnaturally appears across areas of his bare chest near his armpits. His arms are splayed behind him. He speaks and responds with an ever-present smile, but repeats the same simple phrases over and over again. A small group of students sits next to him and engages with him in Chinese. We help him do the one activity we can think of: we put a piece of paper behind and below his head where his right arm unnaturally falls, ask him to choose a color, place a crayon in his hand, and help him draw. Every few minutes the students hold up his piece of art for his approval, and then continue. On the last day we honor his one repeated request for a piece of cake. I tell the students that four years ago the students nicknamed him Simon—after the most spiritual boy on the island in *Lord of the Flies*—because of his unflagging positivity amidst sadness.

When we leave on the last day, students are fully engaged with children to the last minute. We take our one group picture of the weekend and then say goodbye. Tears erupt from the children who so crave our attention; our students, too, find it difficult to leave, some fighting back their own tears. A range of profoundly deep feelings—sadness, guilt, and anger as well as joy, gratefulness, and warmth—mark our departure. Their experience of the pathos of suffering echoes Kuan Yin's story.

RETURNING TO THE ORDINARY WORLD OF HONG KONG

Returning to our ordinary world of Hong Kong, we begin to process the experience back in school. Monday is a catch up day for homework in their other classes, but on Tuesday we start to debrief the trip. I use the first five steps of Mezirow's (2000) Adult Transformative Learning Theory as a guide to help students make sense of their experience:

1. *A disorienting dilemma*: What was disturbing, disorienting, maybe even shocking to you as you think about the weekend? What moved you out of your comfort zone?
2. *Self-examination with feelings of guilt or shame*: Do you feel these emotions or any others now that you're back in the ordinary world?
3. *A critical assessment of assumptions*: Have you started to think about any "big questions" in your life as a result of the trip?
4. *Recognition that one's discontent and process of transformation are shared*: Do you have anyone to share your experience with? Have you had valuable conversations with students/teachers on the trip that have helped you make sense of your experience?
5. *Exploration of options for new roles, relationships, and actions*: Have any of you gotten beyond simply asking "big questions" (#3) and started exploring new ways of acting or living as a result of the trip?

Most significantly, when I ask about their emotional responses, the vast majority report what are considered to be "negative" feelings: sadness, guilt, helplessness, anger, confusion, and disorientation. I know that these are the crucial points 4 and 5 in the Journey of Social Conscience Model (Table 2.1) that I need to guide them through as they move towards compassion.

RETURNING WITH THE ELIXIR

By the middle of the week, we begin reading the Chinese novel *To Live*, which chronicles the sudden fall from wealth of a rich landlord's son named Fugui (福貴, which means "blessed wealth") in the 1940s and how his life as a peasant farmer unfolds through the travails of modern Chinese history until the Cultural Revolution in the 1960s. Through this tale by author Yu Hua (1993), we further explore how to deal with suffering so that one can become a wise person "rich" in life experience, self-understanding, and empathy. We explore the difference between the son's ordinary self before losing his wealth and the Larger Self that emerges out of a series of tragedies. A couple of days into the book, then, I use these terms in an assignment to ask the students to reflect on their Jungsing experience.

We returned from Jungsing a week ago. Your experience can be symbolized in Yu Hua's novel by the narrator's dream of someone crossing a river from the left bank of ignorance to the right side of enlightenment. Put in terms of the Heroic Cycle, we can say all of us have a small self (residing in the ordinary world) who is challenged by certain experiences (in the special world) to become a Larger Self (combining the two worlds). What is the difference between these two selves that you experienced in Jungsing? Do you think that you have changed in any way since the trip? What do you need to do to become more of that Larger Self?

Student writings were excellent across the entire class; most striking was the thoughtfulness of students processing their own growth. Here are some of those responses:

Ayaan: The trip was eye-opening. I did not realize that there were people living lives like this without any control. I was not aware how bad the living conditions were at some of the orphanages. This was when I realized I displayed the traits of that smaller self. I was selfish, inconsiderate, and lazy. I was not focused on anyone but myself, but on this trip, I changed. I realized how lucky I was and stopped taking things for granted, I value little things like food a lot more. I made an effort to become more of that Larger Self, to be more awake and use the opportunities I have been given to excel.

Blythe: My old self was self-centered and selfish, I sought to help others only to gain something myself. I had been unwilling to do work that would not benefit me. However, my new self has been able to shed that egocentric skin, which helped me see a lot of new things that I could learn from instead of just scratching at the surface of suffering. Instead of seeing sick children in a bad living environment that I did not wish to interact with, I saw individuals with their own tales of suffering that needed company and comfort. To become more of my Larger Self, I need to continue to do selfless service, keeping my barriers down at all times. By continuing to learn about and experience suffering, I will be able to stay awake.

Daniel: Since the Jungsing trip, I want to help out more in some way. One example of this, when I think about film projects, I used to only think about narratives but now I really want to use film and videos to help people in HK struggling with poverty. I think that in order to become more of that Larger Self I need to actually begin helping instead of simply thinking about helping, since thinking doesn't physically do anything for anyone or benefit the situation of any of the children in poverty.

Henrietta: Since returning from Jungsing, I have noticed a change in the way I perceive my surroundings. Before Jungsing, I was unaware of all the things that I had in my life. I would envy what others had: a house bigger than mine, parents who would obey their child's every wish, people who were born naturally very talented. It wasn't until I saw people less fortunate than I that I began to notice all the privileges that I have been given. I realized that while I was too busy being jealous of what other people had, others were jealous of what I had. I have a home, I have access to a good education, I don't have to worry about my next meal; these were the types of things that I often took for granted while other people wished desperately for them. Now, to become more of that Larger Self, I need to think about all that I already have instead of focusing on what I want.

Jason: After the Jungsing trip, I've become more appreciative of the things I have in life. My privileges, my family, my friends, list goes on. Before the Jungsing trip, I would regularly think about what I didn't have in life, and the things I had in life that I disliked and felt no appreciation towards. I realized the children in the orphanage would have died to gain what I have, no matter how small or how big because they had the ability to appreciate. They didn't have anything but some worn out playground equipment, each other, and some dirty plastic balls. Now, I'm becoming more and more appreciative of what I have and remind myself every day.

Stephen: I went to Jungsing already knowing that I needed to appreciate what I have. I've heard the phrase "be thankful for what you have" a countless amount of times, but I never understood it until I went to Jungsing. I realized how different my life was from the orphans. Even the babies there were not getting enough care. I noticed many differences from the way I live to the way they live and it helped me understand how privileged I am.

Taira: In the beginning of the trip, we were selfish and inconsiderate. The biggest problem in most of our lives was the grade on the last test. We were ignorant about the fact that there was suffering in the world, some of it very close to home. Once we reached the orphanage though, we became selfless, and fully immersed in serving others. I have to say, I was surprised about how well our class worked with the orphans. After the trip, I was able to look at the two selves: selfish and selfless. Once aware of the suffering of others and able to experience it, we were able to be compassionate and selfless.

After the trip, I took a step back and just looked at myself. How lucky I am to be born into a well-off family with a mom and dad who care for me, a private school education, and the love and compassion of my friends and family. Going to the orphanage sort of opened my eyes, and let me experience the world with kids who aren't even close to as privileged as me. In order to become more of a Larger Self, I need to open my eyes to the suffering happening around me. I have to realize that I can't seek pleasure or happiness in everyday life if I want to travel from my small self to my Larger Self.

One week following the Jungsing trip students recorded a significant shift in perspective: a greater awareness of others' suffering, guilt and gratitude about their own privilege, and a desire to lead a less self-focused life. The Jungsing trip awakens students to the possibility of living a more aware existence marked by appreciation and compassion. The goal for me as a teacher is to take these moments of realization and move students towards a permanent change in consciousness. One such best-case scenario comes from Marisa, who wrote:

> Before Jungsing, I never really thought of people who have lives different than mine. I knew I liked to help other people, but I never really focused on it and I wasn't very interested in service trips. Once we were there in the "special world" I became my

Larger Self and I had so much empathy for the children. As we spent time caring for the children, I realized how much I wanted to do more for them. Now that I am back, I want to be more involved with service trips and be less selfish in my decisions.

Two years later I received this email from Marisa:

> I got into the college that I wanted to attend and I will be studying journalism there in the fall. Thank you for all that you have taught me. I really believe your class has prepared me well in not just an academic standpoint, but also in an empathetic manner. Because of you I have learned a lot about the world and problems that I would love to be able to cover in my career in journalism.

Marisa has made an explicit link between her growth in empathy during the course with her intention to bring these values into her career as a journalist.

Returning to the Humanities I in Action curricular trajectory as a whole, coming into Jungsing students had an "arms-length" understanding of "[human]kind's essential illness" (Golding, 1954, p. 89), that all of us have a natural self-focus which leads to the litany of harm that we have studied in the first four months of the year. The role of the Jungsing experience, then, is to gently bring these teachings closer: to convince them that they, too, have this "illness," that they regularly manifest selfish, ignorant, unappreciative, and callous behaviors that we call the small self. On the other hand, confronting suffering with full awareness diminishes, at least temporarily, this self-centeredness and reveals an innate compassion for others, which we call the Larger Self. One of the students described this dichotomy with clarity:

> **Jack**: The difference between the two selves offered by the Jungsing experience is that one self is self-centered and only wishes to benefit itself, whereas the other self desires to help others before itself . . . The trip did change me, I went from being closer to the first self to the second one. Since the experience, I have become more grateful for the opportunity I have been given that the orphans may never get. To continue to become my Larger Self, I will need to open up to more experiences similar to Jungsing.

By the end of November, then, Humanities I in Action students have understood that the great heroic journey of life requires not only an outward focus—combating, for instance, discrimination, violence, or genocide—but also an inward turn from selfishness to compassion.

CONCLUSION

When I tell students back at HKIS whom I have taken previously on this trip that we have just returned from Jungsing, their eyes widen as if their hearts have just jumped. There are numerous reasons for this I'm sure—memories of a travel "adventure" with classmates, of singing on the bus, or even the relatively carefree days of being a freshman. However, I suspect something else is occurring. A few years later students seem to have vestigial impressions of how they, both individually and as a community, acted with love for a few days—in the midst of beauty and tragedy—on behalf of vulnerable children. Observing suffering, while at the same time acting empathetically within one's capacity to alleviate this suffering, diminishes the self's normal preoccupations. In so doing, they enacted in their care of children the mountaintop practice of breathing in suffering and breathing out unconditional love. For many students, the Jungsing experience leaves an indelible impression; for a few days they have walked in what a whole tradition regards as the apex of the spiritual life, Kuan Yin's special world of compassion.

CHAPTER 5

THE ELIXIR PROJECT

Initiating a Path Towards Meaningful Adulthood

> By designing curriculum around social action projects . . . [teachers] have the opportunity to help their students make a difference while on this planet.
> —*Oyler (2012, p. 1)*

> The Elixir Project helped me come to terms with my own fear of not being able to make a difference, and most importantly . . . [it] gave me hope that through awareness and understanding, the necessary changes to make the world a better place can still be made.
> —*Bea, female student,*
> *reflecting on her grade 9 Elixir Project*

INTRODUCTION

When we return from Christmas break in Humanities I in Action, the course focus shifts dramatically. We move from the question "Is ignorance bliss?" in first semester to "Can I make a difference?" during the second semester. Now that the boot camp of exploring human nature and human behavior has been survived—

The Wisdom Way of Teaching: Educating for Social Conscience and Inner Awakening in the High School Classroom, pages 63–72.
Copyright © 2022 by Information Age Publishing
www.infoagepub.com
All rights of reproduction in any form reserved.

students' own heroic journey from the ordinary world to the special world of Humanities I in Action—they are now put to the test to see if they can actually navigate successfully in this new dimension and find some kind of elixir to heal their original world. This is the mindset the "in Action" teachers bring to day one of the second semester.

INTRODUCING THE ELIXIR PROJECT

We tell the students on the first day back that our overall goal of the second semester is for them to make a difference in society, introducing a long-term community-based assignment that we call the Elixir Project. In order to energize the class for the project, we read portions of Canadian child labor and education activist Craig Kielburger's book *Free the Children* (Kielburger & Major, 1998) and watch a compelling documentary about his young life called *It Takes a Child* (WE Movement, 2017). Craig's life was dramatically changed one day when at the age of 12 he read the morning newspaper in suburban Toronto about another 12-year old, Pakistani labor activist Iqbal Masih, who had been shot and killed while riding a bike near his home. Four days later Craig spoke about this tragedy to his Social Studies class. The positive response from 12 of his classmates led to the launching of "Free the Children," an NGO which has built more than 1500 schools classrooms worldwide since 1995 and continues to garner massive student involvement not only in Canada, but in "ME to WE" chapters around the world.

Our students invariably find the gifted speaking and courageous action of this 12-year-old—two years younger than our 9th graders—deeply inspiring. Even though we only use these materials for a couple of periods, we often see students referring back to Craig's example in their final worldview essays in June. If a 12-year-old could accomplish so much, what excuse do they as 14-year-old privileged students have for doing little? This content is an inspiring start to the second semester.

We then bring in a guest speaker to generate enthusiasm for youth-led projects, and to prime student interest for the upcoming Service Summit, a half-day mini-conference on the first Saturday of the second semester. During the Service Summit, students engage in workshops led by representatives of local NGOs and listen to upperclassmen present what they did for their Elixir Projects in grade 9. The following week, they choose their Elixir Project and begin the two-week process of writing their research paper on a related topic.

Not only does taking action often initiate students' journeys of social conscience, but it also becomes a litmus test of whether they have actually gained the ability to "make a difference," even if the initial action is something as simple as talking to friends or family, or publicly taking a stand on an issue. Social conscience usually comes to fruition with a growing sense of empowerment and self-efficacy.

Thus, the overall goals of the Elixir project are for students to:

1. Grow in their social conscience through action responses to present-day social realities.
2. Consider their own sense of self-efficacy with regard to making a positive impact upon society.

We encourage students to do whatever it is that they feel drawn to, and we are always impressed by the creativity of the projects. Some days after the Service Summit, we ask students to share with the class their proposed plan of action using these guidelines:

1. Statement of Purpose/Desired Outcome: Summarize in one or two sentences specifically:
   - What you are doing,
   - Whom you are doing it for, and
   - What your ultimate goal is
2. Background of Issue
   - Provide information, facts, and images that detail the cause you are addressing.
   - Why is this a cause that needs your attention? What are the reasons that this is an issue?
3. Plan of Action: Specifically, what are the steps you will take to accomplish your goal?
4. Dates/Materials/Cost
   - What is the projected timeline of your project?
   - What materials are needed for your project?
   - If you need to spend money, detail the amount and why, and how you will get those funds.
5. Necessary Permissions: If applicable, what times, dates, and venues need to be booked to host your event/outing?
6. Contact Information of Partner Clubs or Organizations

The next step following the proposal is for students to write a 4–6 page, properly cited research paper to provide academic grounding for their chosen area of action. This matching of a research paper to a project of their choice provides an ideal opportunity for self-motivated learning, one of our school's Student Learning Results. Serious attention to research also reinforces key themes of the initial unit in the course, "Worldview Matters," which warns that many well-intentioned people in history have done more harm than good due to a poor understanding of the situation they were attempting to improve.

SAMPLE ELIXIR PROJECTS

Every year older students present their grade 9 Elixir Projects to the current group of "in Action" students at the Service Summit. The following is a sampling of

Pia (l) and Emilee (r) at the Jungsing Orphanage. Photo credit: Author.

those project descriptions as written by the students. I have added a comment after each to provide additional background as well as illustrate key themes involved in the Elixir Project.

1. **Emilee and Pia—Orangutan Habitat in Borneo**

> Our project was dedicated to protecting and educating others about orangutans in Borneo. We were able to travel to Borneo, which gave us the ability to better understand the species as well the issues impacting them.
>
> **My Comment (MC):** I'm always thrilled with Elixir projects that involve hands-on learning. The fact that Emilee and Pia, best friends in grade 9, could travel together with an adult to an orangutan reserve in Malaysia over the Chinese New Year holiday would be a lifelong memory. Their week indeed left a deep and compassionate impression on them for this endangered species. They took outstanding pictures while there and held a photo exhibition of their Borneo experience in May at Pia's father's workplace, raising a significant sum of money for the protection of orangutans at this reserve.

2. **Brittany[1] and Caroline—Teaching Empowerment**

> For our senior project, Caroline and I are developing an empowerment curriculum. This is the accumulation of years of work with international charities and social enterprises (such as Craig Kielburger's organizations "Free the Children" and "ME to WE"), leadership programs in India, and inspiring people like you. The two of us will be overseeing the curriculum on three Interim trips this year—India, Boracay, and South Africa. Come find out more about how you can get involved and develop your own program!
>
> **MC:** Sometimes an Elixir Project ignites what appears to be a decade-long, if not lifetime, passion. Another pair of best friends, Brittany and

---

[1] Brittany provides further reflection on her service experiences in Chapter 18.

Caroline, both loved the Humanities I in Action course. During Brittany's freshmen year she went on an Interim trip to South India where the HKIS team created and facilitated a student-generated "Teaching for Empowerment" curriculum. Brittany was captured by this idea and, along with Caroline, devoted tremendous energy refining the "Teaching for Empowerment" curriculum not only throughout high school, bringing it to other Interim trips, but even through their college careers as well. Their social conscience growth together was the subject of a doctoral dissertation that the girls helped to co-research (Larson, 2017).

3. **Jeffrey—HKIS Talent Website**

HKIS Talent is a website I created that showcases the work and abilities of the many talented members of our student, faculty, and alumni bodies. Inspired by the potential of technology to connect, I constructed the website with the aim to build a greater sense of community and highlight another side of HKIS. As time passes, HKIS Talent will hopefully be something that links the HKIS community forever. Come to my presentation and see how you can use something you enjoy to make a change in your community!

MC: What is noteworthy here is that Jeffrey's website aimed to do something beneficial for HKIS. While projects off campus may be more exciting and dramatic, I often feel that the hardest work of service is closest to home. While the vast majority of projects are off campus, I strongly encourage Elixir Projects like Jeffrey's that aim to improve our own school community.

4. **Aidan—Save Our Soles**

On a family visit to the Philippines during Easter Break of 2014 we noticed that the local community was poor. We were especially drawn to the children. Few wore shoes and those who did had a thin pair of flip-flops to protect their feet. Upon returning to Hong Kong, I set up my own shoe charity, Save Our Soles, at HKIS. Our shoe charity has now spread to other schools around Hong Kong.

MC: Aidan's project was picked up by his siblings (one of whom is Jordan below), and ran successfully for some years—and even was extended to other international schools in Hong Kong through an annual barefooted soccer tournament. Over the years some of the most memorable and impactful projects have been successful because of the support of family members. As I noted in Chapter 2, speaking to family members is one of the most important signs of developing self-efficacy, so adopting an Elixir Project into a family dynamic certainly deepens the learning.

Jordan (l) and Parker (r) Performing Their Song "Circle the Sun" for HKIS Elementary Students." Photo credit: Author.

5. **Jordan and Parker—Girls Scholarships in China**

Our project aimed to use our passion for music to help others. We chose to support a Hong Kong-based, student-initiated NGO called EMBER, facilitated by Concordia Welfare and Education Foundation, which raises scholarship funds to help girls in rural China stay in school. We wrote an original song, recorded it with our band in a professional studio, went to Deqing, China to film the video starring the girls, edited the entire production, and released it for donation on the CWEF site.

MC: This project worked on many levels. To begin with, the two boys are talented musicians and Parker had already created a gorgeous song for the Memoir project earlier in the year about Somaly Mam's (2009) book *The Road to Lost Innocence*, so I knew what was possible. The boys were searching for an area of interest, so I told them about a girls scholarship program run by Concordia Welfare and Education Foundation (CWEF) that I was closely involved with in southern China, and this became their cause. Following their well-written research papers on the challenges that girls face globally in receiving an education, the two boys diligently wrote their song over some weeks, and then joined a scholarship trip I was leading to the school. They taught the girls the song they had written, and then filmed them lip-syncing the lyrics. Upon returning to Hong Kong, they rented out a recording studio to create a high-quality production. I show this heart-melting song every year in class as an exemplary project, which showcases not only the boys' significant musical talents, but captures our service trip to rural China on a chilly February weekend. While their hope of fundraising didn't materialize, the song is still featured on the CWEF website. The music video is of a very high quality and can be found on YouTube by searching "alter ego circle the sun."

6. **Claire and Sherry—Singing for the Elderly**

Our project was based on singing for the elderly at a nursing home called Fung Tak Lutheran Home for the Elderly in Wong Tai Sin, and the main

Sherry (l) and Claire (r) Sharing Their Project With HKIS Elementary Students. Photo credit: Author.

goal was to lighten up their day and to not forget about the past generations, but rather bring them along with us.

MC: I always highlight Claire and Sherry's experience when I introduce the Elixir project because it was so simple and effective. Claire and Sherry visited and sang for the elderly eight times throughout the semester. Both girls loved singing, and the residents of the home, which is located in a low socio-economic area of Hong Kong that is connected to our local Lutheran church, thoroughly enjoyed having them come and brighten up their day. Many of our students default to fund-raising projects, which we certainly allow, but my common line to those students who jump first to the idea of raising money is, "You have the rest of your life to give money. Consider time as your currency as a high school student. Making human connections is really what Humanities I in Action is all about." Claire and Sherry's project epitomizes the joy of service that we want to engender within students.

Finally, I would like to tell the story of one of my students, Ananya, whose project was remarkable, though her project description is not available. Ananya wanted to help special needs children in orphanages in India. She reached out by email to an Indian orphanage early in second semester with an offer to raise money, and they replied immediately accepting her proposal. To raise funds for the orphanage, she painstakingly hand-crafted 40 greeting/birthday cards that her father sold for 100 HK [US$ 12.50] at his office in Hong Kong. Through this laborious process, she was able to raise 4000 HK [US$ 516]. Then over the Chinese New Year holiday, she flew to India to visit the orphanage. As she was touring the facility, she met a boy only two years younger who was crippled with a degenerative muscle condition that prevented him from getting adopted, even though she sensed that he was very bright. She inquired about spending her entire sum on an operation for him. The orphanage said that the surgery only had about a 10% chance of success, but Ananya felt intuitively that this was the right thing to do. Some months later he had the operation and, to everyone's amazement, it was a success. Following his rehabilitation some months later, the young man was adopted by a wealthy Indian family, who then enrolled him in one of the finest schools in India. This boy went from a condition of great hardship to high hopes in just a matter of months. It appears that this boy's life has been irreversibly changed by the dedicated work and intuitive act of service undertaken by Ananya. This is the potential good that can come from Elixir Projects.

STUDENT REFLECTIONS ON THE SERVICE SUMMIT

The Service Summit is consistently well-received by students, as can be seen in these responses.

> **Taina:** The Service Summit was such an eye-opening experience for me. I had this sensation growing throughout my body through every session I went to. Mark and Joanna's [keynote] speech really inspired me to do something. Everything they said kept echoing in my ears. One of the big takeaways was when I went to a session led by Brittany. She is an inspiration. She's so humble and modest, yet she has achieved and experienced so much to do with service. Brittany represents what I hope to become.

Taina's comment about Brittany demonstrates the importance of role models for these young students, a key theme discussed in the next chapter.

> **Lilly:** My favorite workshop was Feeding Hong Kong because I thought it was really interesting to learn about a problem where I live. It made me feel very guilty because there is so much food wasted here. I know that I waste a lot of food, and when you throw out food, or leave it on your plate I personally never think about the fact I am wasting, because it has come to be such a natural instinct for me now. Hopefully now that I am a bit more educated about hungry people in Hong Kong, I will stop wasting my food, and if I don't think I can eat it all, then I will take smaller portions for myself.

Lilly's blog comment clearly illustrates the model for the short-term impact of social conscience education introduced in Chapter 3. She had previously never been aware of the issue of food wastage in Hong Kong, but as a result of the presentation she felt "very guilty" about her actions, and vowed to stop wasting food. Each of the steps is clearly present: awareness, emotional engagement, and action.

> **Will:** My favorite workshop I attended was the "running to stop the traffik" [human trafficking] presentation. This presentation stood out to me because it involved a passion. To be honest, the only way I am ever going to make a difference is through one of my passions. When you take that passion and you use it for something good, that's when you have an effective project in my opinion. That's exactly what James was able to do.

Will's comment demonstrates the indispensable role of emotional engagement in social conscience education. A final anonymous comment speaks to the crucial issue of hope:

> When learning about how bad our world is all the time in Humanities, I kind of lose hope for the future of humanity . . . But when watching presentations on how much people actually are doing to help our world, I don't see how we are still as messed up as we are. It seems that everyone is doing so much to help out and trying to get others involved. The Service Summit helped me realize that there is hope.

This comment epitomizes the struggle for hope that most students face in the course. Often the study of the dark side of contemporary issues leaves students feeling pessimistic about the global future; however, hearing presentations about people, especially peers, who have persevered and are making a difference, inspires new possibilities.

While not all Elixir Projects are a success, the vast majority are worthwhile. Students frequently draw upon their Elixir Projects in their end-of-year writing on how their worldviews have shifted as they developed their ability to take action.

ASSESSMENT

The question of how to evaluate the Elixir Project has been a topic of much consideration in our Humanities I in Action teaching team over the years. Let me share where I presently stand on this. For a number of years, I didn't assess the Elixir Project much beyond counting it as "class participation" that would potentially bump up a student's grade, if done particularly well. Some years ago I moved to a system in which I assign two grades. First, I give them a mark for public speaking, a skill we work on explicitly in their *Enlightenment Now* speeches earlier in the spring. Secondly, I assess the overall value of the project based on the following rubric, which was composed by one of the Humanities I in Action teachers. Students need to excel in at least one of these areas in order to get an A.

1. *Beneficiary Impact*—The project has made an exceptionally deep and meaningful impact for the intended cause.
2. *Adaptability*—The project reinvented itself frequently as circumstances changed, showing exceptional resilience and creativity.
3. *Time Commitment*—The project involved an exceptional commitment of time due to some regularly scheduled service work with an established organization.
4. *Innovation*—The project piloted an original idea that could be successfully shared with future classes through a presentation at next year's Service Summit or other venues.
5. *Expert Awareness*—Student research into the project produced an exceptional level of understanding of the social issue being addressed.

Based on these parameters, I give them a grade, but then tell them that if this mark pulls down their overall average, I won't factor it into their final course grade. I do this because the Elixir Project is not only difficult to assess, but is also dependent on the cooperation of community partners. For instance, I had a couple of students who loved horseback riding and hoped to assist special needs children learn how to ride, but they simply could not get responses from target organizations in the area. While I could be hard-nosed about it and penalize them for this, it seems more reasonable to make the grade for the Elixir Project optional.

CONCLUSION

We teachers of Humanities I in Action find inspiration for the Elixir Project in the words of Bill Plotkin (2003), author of *Soulcraft*: "My utter conviction [is] that what humanity most needs now is a contemporary path of initiation into soulful adulthood" (pp. 25–26). Impelled by our belief that entry into adulthood requires the ability to enact positive change, we hope to inspire students to make some tangible difference in society. The Elixir Project is our curricular path offering students the opportunity to develop their social conscience and make a positive impact on the community.

CHAPTER 6

PRINCIPLES OF SOCIAL CONSCIENCE CURRICULUM DESIGN

INTRODUCTION

Having surveyed the theory and practice of social conscience education through a close study of key aspects of the Humanities I in Action curriculum, in these final two chapters of Part I, I share what I consider to be most salient elements of the social conscience classroom: the fundamental principles of curriculum design (Chapter 6) and the four essential roles of the social conscience teacher (Chapter 7). While I have kept some of the original quotes and analysis from my dissertation (Schmidt, 2009), Chapter 6 has been fundamentally re-written in a more personal manner to include my updated reflections more than a decade later on the findings.[1] At the end of this chapter, I offer a multi-tiered pedagogical model of how this content can be delivered in such a way that the social conscience de-

---

[1] The findings were a result of individual interviews with my HKIS colleagues, documentary evidence from student writings, and focus group interviews with students to gain their perspectives on how to best educate for social conscience.

The Wisdom Way of Teaching: Educating for Social Conscience and Inner Awakening in the High School Classroom, pages 73–82.
Copyright © 2022 by Information Age Publishing
www.infoagepub.com
All rights of reproduction in any form reserved.

velopment of students is supported. In contrast to Chapter 6, I've decided to leave Chapter 7 in the more academic tone of dissertation writing to address the question of the key roles of a social conscience teacher in the context of a literature review. Given the substantial overlap between the two chapters, it is hoped that the mix of personal and academic styles provides a more comprehensive understanding of how to teach for social conscience.

To begin, the six principles that emerged from my research on how to design courses for impacting students' social consciences are:

1. Explore the big questions
2. Use contemporary events
3. Read powerful, relevant stories
4. Aim at the emotional level
5. Study role models
6. Create curricular coherence

Each principle is addressed in turn.

1. Explore the Big Questions

The most important theme that emerged was exploring the big questions of human existence. All the Humanities I in Action teachers, for example, post the ten big questions that are investigated throughout the year in their classrooms. Here is a list of those questions, according to my own estimation, in order of curricular importance:

1. Is human nature fundamentally good or evil?
2. What is humanity's relationship to nature, ruler or part?
3. Is humankind progressing or declining?
4. What's more important, the group or the individual?
5. Which value should society emphasize more, hierarchy or equality?
6. Does the pursuit of wealth do more to improve or harm society?
7. Which determines our identity to a greater extent, nature or nature?
8. Which philosophy, essentialism or existentialism, best explains where meaning comes from?[2]
9. What is more fundamental to the universe, matter or consciousness?
10. Are gender roles biologically or socially constructed?

While posed as binaries, students understand implicitly that the goal is to understand the underlying beliefs and values that determine the choices that societies make in all their complexity. Students frequently write their final exam

---

[2] Essentialism teaches that meaning is replete and accessible in the universe at large, while existentialism holds that the universe may indeed be meaningless, but humans can create meaning with their life choices.

papers about how their worldviews have become more nuanced and sophisticated through their course of study.

Since it was impossible to do the chocolate slavery activity (Chapter 3) during COVID-19 on day one in August, 2020, I decided to draw upon Rutger Bregman's (2020) *Humankind: A Hopeful History* as my opening activity this past school year. In the excerpt we read, Bregman poses his own worldview dilemma: a plane goes down and the survivors of the crash are trying to get out alive. Do we live on Planet A where passengers work together to help as many people escape as possible or do we live on Planet B in which it's every person for themselves? In our class, 15 of the 20 of the students chose planet B, while a vocal minority argued for human goodness, which provoked an unusually spirited Zoom conversation at the start of the year.

Nine months later when students wrote their final worldview essays, the Bregman excerpts were the most single most influential course material. One of my students, Olivia, wrote:

> There is no doubt in my heart that Humanities I in Action is going to change your life. As someone who had a strong pessimistic worldview coming into the class, I thought I knew everything there was to know; that "humanity was selfish and flawed." I'd believed there was no way for a school course to actually impact my life and I greatly underestimated this Humanities course. Right on the very first day, we were presented with the moral dilemma of Planet A or B. Your decision was to either place your bet on the selfishness of humanity like the majority, or to pick the optimistic choice and go against the group. Everyone thought the same thing. "Humanity has to be selfish. Or else how would you explain all the terrible things happening in the world?" To my surprise, we were wrong. As we looked through examples from Bregman, William Powers' "Future Zarahs"[3] and other worldview-challenging materials, it seemed that the good side of humanity was more apparent in society than I'd realized. The same sense of realization happened numerous times throughout the year as we encountered examples that challenged my worldview again and again . . . They were all moments I'll never forget.

The reason for the effectiveness of the Bregman materials is that they challenge students' default system with regard to the biggest worldview question of them all: is human nature fundamentally good or evil? Perhaps it's a sad commentary on the mindset of young people in my classes that the majority enter into even a service-oriented class like Humanities I in Action with a decidedly jaded view of the human condition, which certainly reflects their own struggles to be hopeful about the state of the planet. Exploring these big questions about the world, then, is really a form of self-exploration.

---

[3] One of the influential early pieces we use is a short writing by William Powers (2008) called "Future Zarahs" in which the author struggles with the issue of helping the one vs. the many in a world of overwhelming need. Powers' reference to Loren Eiseley's (1978) "The Star Thrower" short story is commonly reflected upon in students' worldview essays.

2. Use Contemporary Events

A second theme that emerged in my research was the importance of studying contemporary events. Two representative teacher comments speak clearly to this point:

> There is a "presentism" to Humanities I that's again very attractive to students and it's what gets them linked to the material.

> The urgency of it . . . It takes them to the immediate center. I think our course exists predominantly in the here and the now and the future.

Teachers of Humanities I in Action regularly integrate current events into their daily lessons, even if it requires substantial additional preparation. In the fall of 2019, for example, I knew that the Hong Kong protests would be an inflection point for the city's history, so I quickly cobbled together materials over the summer to provide students with the necessary background to understand the events of that fall as they unfolded.

This study of current issues comes home to students especially in the second semester as they choose their Elixir Project. It can be a defining moment for some, as they are asked: what's the one issue in our world that you want to address for a semester? Following an in-depth examination of their topic in their freshmen research paper, students then create a project to deal with their issue in a tangible way.

Another example of this focus on the present comes from the end of the 2020–21 school year when I changed my last summative from writing a dystopian piece of fiction—for many of my students, COVID-19 was already stranger and more depressing than they could have imagined—to a "Life During the Pandemic" final project in which they explored what meaning they were able to make from this unforgettable time in their lives. What emerged was a diverse mix of projects: Christine explored pressures put on families and friendships in a multi-episode podcast; Olivia compiled Zoom interviews asking how her elementary school friends, now scattered across various schools in Asia, dealt with the COVID-19 crisis; Harold chose to do a research paper on the effects of COVID-19 on Hong Kong's poor; and Elisa focused on researching the impact of "period poverty" on adolescent girls and women in South Asia, while also co-leading a drive to deliver feminine hygiene products to young women in Sri Lanka. These examples underscore what students frequently tell us: what many like about the Humanities I in Action curriculum is its relevance to their lives.

3. Read Powerful, Relevant Stories

A third major theme that emerged from my research is that humanities teachers consider stories conveyed in literature and films as exceptionally powerful tools for social conscience understanding because of their emotional power and relevance. In Humanities I in Action, *Lord of the Flies* (Golding, 1954), *To Live* (Yu, 1993), *Ishmael* (Quinn, 1992), and *Scythe* (Shusterman, 2018) have been the most important novels we have used. Students find the genocide memoirs[4] we use compelling as well, and films, such as *Shooting Dogs* about the Rwandan Genocide or *White Helmets*—an award-winning short film which daringly portrays rescue teams searching for bombing survivors in the Syrian civil war—often deeply impact students.

In fact, the whole concept of *story* is one that we draw upon frequently in not only understanding the course materials, but also in processing it more personally as well. I often use Joseph Campbell's Heroic Journey motif as a structure for various aspects of the course, including analyzing the books and films. Campbell (2008) claimed in his *Hero with a Thousand Faces* that stories cross-culturally follow a common mythological pattern: a hero who finds himself or herself in some mundane, unsatisfying life situation has a call to adventure to enter into a special world filled with tests and trials, but who also finds helpers and new inner resources to cope with the ordeal. In time, the hero receives new insights that are then brought back to re-enliven the original ordinary world.

While we apply this archetypal pattern to various stories we read or movies we watch, the whole "in Action" experience can be considered in these terms as well. After students have submitted their final worldview essays on the last day of class, the very last activity of the year involves students sharing their "heroic journeys" of their year in the course. I line up chairs for students to sit at the front of the room in a half-moon formation representing their starting point in the ordinary world, while positioning three stations towards the center of the classroom corresponding to the three inflection points of the heroic cycle. One by one students share their personal reflections at each station in this manner:

1. The call to adventure as the hero crosses the threshold from the ordinary world to the special world.
2. Their journey in the special world.
3. Their return with the elixir back to the ordinary world.

On the last day of school this year, Anita[5] shared her heroic journey of change in this way.

Station 1. Call to Adventure: Prior to this class, my entire life had already been planned out according to society's norms of success, to get perfect grades, into an Ivy League school then a 6 figure job. However, this class opened my eyes to a world outside of this selfish bubble of money and power.

---
[4] See Chapter 2 for a list of the memoirs we currently use.
[5] I also shared Anita's comments about the "HKIS narrative" in the introduction.

78 • THE WISDOM WAY OF TEACHING

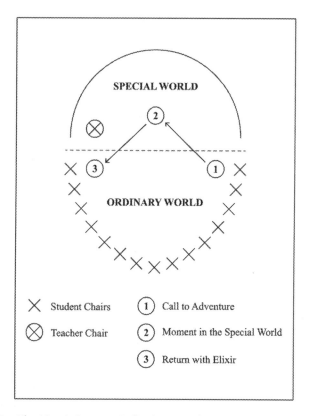

FIGURE 6.1. The Heroic Journey Reflection Ritual

Station 2. A Moment in the Special World: One guest speaker that spoke to me most was Liz Lo,[6] a graduated HKIS student. Although she grew up in an Asian household similar to mine, where grades are significantly valued, she was able to escape from the story that HKIS students are captive to and instead created her own story by pursuing her passions and raising awareness on something she cares about. Her speech made me realize that it was more than possible to stray away from the story I was captive to, and from there I was able to start thinking about a new narrative.

Station 3. Return to the Ordinary World: Because of Humanities I in Action, my worldview has changed radically, and I have walked out of this course determined to use my passion to make a difference in the world and live in my own story.

---

[6] Elizabeth Lo, graduate of HKIS in 2005, is an award-winning filmmaker who has recently completed her first feature film called "Stray," which unconventionally follows three dogs around on their daily experiences in Istanbul.

Like Anita's reflection, many stories are frequently poignant, as students share how the content and experiences of the course have impacted their lives. I have used this ritualized final debrief for two decades and have found it to be a highly effective culminating activity for classes/trips in which participants have experienced a significant amount of personal growth.

4. **Aim at the Emotional Level**

When I asked students in my research why they didn't have a social conscience—what was the essential problem we are trying to solve—there was strong agreement that overall they felt disconnected from society. These perceptions of disconnection are frequently commented on by academics and social critics about modern life in general (Maxwell, 2003; Miller, 2007; Senge et al., 2004; Shapiro, 2006; Taylor, 1991). Parker Palmer (1999) speaks of this disconnection when reflecting on his own experience with studying history in school:

> I was taught [Holocaust] history in a way . . . that made me feel as if all of those horrors happened to another species on another planet . . . They never connected with the inwardness of my life, because the inwardness of those historical events was never revealed to me. Everyone was objectified and externalized, and I ended up morally and spiritually deformed as a consequence. (p. 27)

Thus, the social conscience teacher's most fundamental task is offer students a path to reconnect to society; and the primary means to accomplish this goal is impacting students on an emotional level. Most powerfully, of course, are the out-of-the-classroom experiences that touch students' deeply, such as the Jungsing trip, the Refugee Run simulation, and the Elixir Project. But it's important to emphasize that it is possible to counteract such alienation on a daily basis as well by providing emotional connection in the classroom. Every day I seek to move my students with powerful curricular materials and in so doing re-connect them not just to the world, but to each other and to their humanity. Vicariously experiencing the plight of others elicits a range of common human emotions, which supports Bregman's (2020) claim that the "veneer theory" of human nature—that underneath our pleasant exteriors, people are seeking their own self-interest—is itself a constructed narrative open to critique.

5. **Study Role Models**

Social conscience education not only means seeing the world compassionately, but also engaging with it creatively. The status quo needs to deemed insufficient and another way sought to improve the situation. It takes notable courage, then, to undergo the journey of social conscience (as discussed in Chapter 2), which involves perspective transformation, empathy, and repeated actions to bring about change. Taking on responsibility for others may very well be perceived as a threat to one's own path to success.

80 • THE WISDOM WAY OF TEACHING

Given the energy needed for change, it's not surprising that teachers and students were in strong agreement that role models are an indispensable aspect of social conscience education, for they serve as inspiring and persuasive evidence that indeed the journey of transformation can be successfully navigated. The most prominent role model in our curriculum is Craig Kielburger (Kielburger & Major, 1998), a 12-year old Canadian boy, whose call to adventure in 1996 was the murder of Iqbal Masih, a 12-year old Pakistani carpet slave named who had himself spoken out forcefully on behalf of the issue of child labor. Craig was so moved by Iqbal's story that he recruited a group of 12 friends at his school to start a highly successful youth empowerment organization called "Free the Children." We study Craig's story as we begin the second semester in order to address the term's central question, "Can I make a difference?"

The annual "Service Summit" that we hold to kick-off the Elixir Project also works on this principle of the importance of role models. We typically have an outside speaker who visits our classes on Friday before the Summit on Saturday where a keynote speech is delivered to all the "in Action" students. The majority of breakout sessions during the Summit feature upperclassmen sharing what they did for their Elixir Project when they were in Humanities I in Action. Role models play a significant role in the "in Action" curriculum.

6.   Create Curricular Coherence

The final principle of social conscience instruction noted by teachers and students was overall coherence of the curriculum. More than a decade beyond my research, even a casual glance at the headlines suggests that the polarization of belief systems globally has only become more pronounced over time. Education in both Hong Kong and around the world seems to be increasingly a battleground of the culture wars. Beck's observation that this time in history should be called the "Age of Fragmentation" (Cohen, 2003, p. 2) seems to ring true. Writing about the Hong Kong context some years ago, Kennedy (2005) stated, "The real issue for the 21st century is how to prevent the fragmentation of the curriculum" (p. 40).

One of the best services teachers can provide for students in this era of fragmentation, then, is a coherent curriculum. Humanities I in Action teachers have constructed an academic pathway that make sense: it leads students first through a journey in which they study some of the worst experiences of modern history, and then asks them to step forward and make a difference in the ongoing issues of injustice and inadequacy in contemporary society. It's striking, then, that the image of a completed puzzle emerged a number of times in my research to describe the Humanities I in Action curriculum:

> **Teacher:** Our courses are like puzzles . . . Once they have the picture it is up to them what they want to do with it because our world is a puzzle . . . The students need to see how the puzzle works, how it all comes together.

Student: I drew a jigsaw puzzle piece because I felt like before . . . Humanities I in Action I felt like . . . I . . .had the pieces, but they didn't really fit together . . . So I drew a puzzle piece because after that course I felt like things kind of fitted together like there was a connection . . . Every piece of the puzzle has its place in the big picture and it also kind of represents how that course kind of opened my eyes to my role in the world and how I fit into the bigger social conscience picture.

While there are many benefits to coherence—learning is reinforced, engagement is higher, insights come more readily—the primary value is to offer students a sense of the whole (Selby, 2001); we all have a deep need to see "the big picture" in order to discern our place in the world. Such an orientation affords students a greater sense of purpose in their connection to society beyond their own career goals.

A SOCIAL CONSCIENCE CURRICULUM MODEL

This chapter concludes with a model for developing and teaching a social conscience curriculum, which was introduced briefly at the end of Chapter 3.

As Chapter 3 suggested, teachers and students believe that social conscience education works most powerfully when contemporary events are used to gain a perspective on the deeper questions of human existence, for they are seen as living laboratories for these philosophical deliberations. Contemplating such questions connects students to the past and provides a broader context for their understanding. The down arrow in the figure indicates the standard order of processing class materials, starting with events and ending with the big questions. The up arrow offers an alternative starting point, posing first a big question followed by linkage to a current issue.

The importance of the middle tier of psychological and sociological perspectives can be understood with a review of the definition of social conscience used

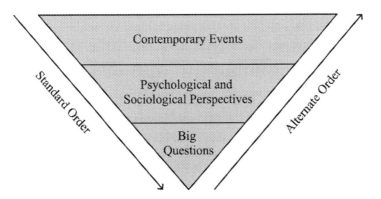

FIGURE 6.2. A Model for Teaching Social Conscience Curricula

in this book as *a personal consideration of one's role and responsibility in the context of an emotionally-engaged understanding of the world*. This statement locates social conscience at the intersection of personal identity and community engagement, which explains why powerful stories and role models are effective, for they reveal people's inner lives in relationship to decisive actions, all set against backdrops of sociopolitical challenge. A comment by a teacher of this course demonstrates the value of this middle tier to the curriculum:

> The course is built around an essential theme, again in ways that no other course I've taught, . . . looking at sociology and psychology and a sense of the potential for evil and . . . good . . . It's at the core of what's most important . . . for kids coming into 9th grade . . . The material is immediately relevant and accessible to students because the course starts with worldview questions. The readings are aimed at answering . . . those questions [with] the shift into psychology and sociology . . . It's exciting.

Teachers and students in Humanities I in Action express enthusiasm for all three levels shown in the model. As students link contemporary events in their social world to deep personal questions, they develop a critically conscious dialogue among the tiers in search of coherence. This assists students to develop a cohesive personal value system.

This model's pairing of contemporary events with observations of human behavior from within (psychology) and from without (sociology) puts Gardner's (1999) advice regarding our current educational systems today into practice. Gardner states:

> We need an education that is deeply rooted in two apparently contrasting but actually complementary considerations: what is known about the human condition . . . and what is known about the pressures, challenges, and opportunities of the contemporary (and the coming) scene. Without this double anchorage, we are doomed to an education that is dated, partial, naïve, and inadequate. (p. 20)

This curriculum model expands Gardner's "double anchorage" framework into three tiers, by explicitly inserting psychological and sociological considerations between the study of contemporary issues and the goal of developing a philosophy of life.

CONCLUSION

A decade beyond the research, these six principles—explore the big questions; use contemporary events; read powerful, relevant stories; aim at the emotional level; study role models; and create curricular coherence—remain at the heart of the Humanities I in Action course and the content we select. Now we turn our attention to the paramount role of the social conscience teacher in implementing these curricular principles in the classroom.

CHAPTER 7

THE FOUR ESSENTIAL ROLES OF SOCIAL CONSCIENCE TEACHERS

It probably comes as no surprise that the most critical aspect of educating for social conscience is the role of the teacher. In this chapter based on my research, I offer four essential roles in the form of propositions that social conscience teachers need to play in order to facilitate the growth of students' social consciences.[1]

The first three come directly from my research,[2] which are:

1. Curriculum innovator;
2. Pedagogue of critical thinking;
3. Empathetic mentor[3];

---

[1] At the risk of interrupting the personal tone of this book, I have chosen to maintain the essential dissertation format of this chapter in order to provide substantive grounding for social conscience education in the professional literature. For those less interested in this more academic approach, I pick up the narrative thread of my own teaching journey in Chapter 8.

[2] My dissertation research drew upon not only HKIS, but also a local school serving a low-income population on Hong Kong Island. The first three propositions are based on a cross-case analysis of the two schools, but I have removed most references to the local school to maintain the focus on HKIS. For more information on the findings of my research on teaching for social conscience in a Hong Kong local school, please see my dissertation (Schmidt, 2009).

[3] Being an empathetic mentor is the most important of the four roles, which explains its central position in the figure.

The Wisdom Way of Teaching: Educating for Social Conscience and Inner Awakening in the High School Classroom, pages 83–90.
Copyright © 2022 by Information Age Publishing
www.infoagepub.com
All rights of reproduction in any form reserved.   **83**

84 • THE WISDOM WAY OF TEACHING

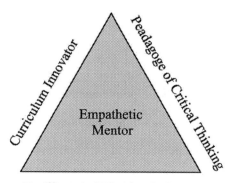

FIGURE 7.1. The Four Roles of the Social Conscience Teacher

I've also added a fourth role:

4. Facilitator of wonder and hope.

While this latter trait did not emerge specifically from my research like the other three, this fourth area seems so obvious to me in my years of teaching and has such wide support in the literature, that I include it here for the reader's consideration. Explication of the fourth role comes from the literature review of my dissertation (Schmidt, 2009).

> **Proposition 1:** One role of social conscience teachers is to be a curriculum innovator who creates units of study that confront students with local and global issues that students find engaging and worthy of study. Since students believe that the study of contemporary issues is vital to the development of social conscience, teachers should include current issues in their curricula in order to demonstrate the relevance of humanities courses to students' lives. Teachers, especially those in local school systems, should consider the possibility that their students may be far more interested in international issues than teachers presume.

Davies (2006) observes that there is almost no qualitative research that has been carried out on children's needs with regard to global citizenship education. She adds, "Had one consulted young people or listened to them one would [have] found the requirement for hard-hitting approaches and treatment of uncomfortable issues" (p. 21). Interviews with HKIS teachers and students demonstrated that both groups feel strongly that curricula need to consider pressing contemporary issues which young people deem as important. This strong preference for studying current issues is supported by many commentators (Banks, 2006; Elliott, 2007; Oxfam, 2018) and may be called "issues-based education" (Hicks, 2007, p. 5). Leung's (2006) study corroborates this finding, suggesting that one of the three conditions necessary to create active global citizens in Hong Kong schools is to teach from an issues-based perspective.

This desire for "hard-hitting approaches" was epitomized by the frequency and intensity with which students at HKIS spoke about the topic of genocide. Their high emotional engagement in this topic was due to the fact that genocide was not simply a part of history (e.g., the Holocaust), but has happened in their lifetime (e.g., Darfur), and continues unabated to this day in other parts of the world, evidence of which can be easily accessed through the Internet.

Students in the small territory of Hong Kong seem to understand intuitively that they can only understand themselves in the context of a "global gaze" (Marshall, 2005, p. 82). Thus, a local and global dynamic needs to be present in the study of contemporary issues (Hicks, 2007). It appears, then, that most students prefer what Marshall (2005) calls a "slice" model, which teaches local and global issues concurrently, rather than a more structured local-regional-global progression approach.

Teaching ever-changing contemporary issues that mesh local and global concerns is a radical departure from traditional humanities curricula rooted in the study of ancient texts. Thus, social conscience teachers need to see themselves as globally-aware curriculum innovators who select content based to a large degree on student interest in contemporary issues. While significant innovation is not possible without a substantial increase in time investment, the findings of this study suggest that the rewards are great: students become more engaged and this in turn leads them to develop greater social consciousness.

> **Proposition 2:** A second role of social conscience teachers is to be a pedagogue of critical thinking. Teachers should employ interactive, dialogical activities involving multiple perspectives to enhance students' critical thinking about their role in society. While developing critical thinking is necessary, teachers also need to bear in mind the importance of maintaining a balance between analysis requiring cognitive distance and personal integration which asks students to care for the material. Thus, the role of the critical thinking pedagogue includes helping students to make personal connections within the social conscience classroom.

Teachers and students at HKIS conceived of the primary pedagogical role of the teacher of social conscience as one that facilitated critical thinking. This research, thus, lends support to the conclusion reached in Lee's (2002) cross-cultural study that there is an "apparent universal emphasis on the need for inquiry, critical thinking, tolerance and interactive teaching in citizenship education" (p. 57).

Teachers of social conscience make many decisions every day in their teaching which are likely to affect students' critical thinking. From the selection of controversial topics, to the asking of "big questions," to the challenging of lifestyle norms, the role of the social conscience teacher is to embarrass, prod, antagonize, shock, and voice opposition to students into new ways of thinking. Teachers also need to take contrarian positions, defend minority views, or simply resist premature resolution to the ideas being discussed. Teachers who perceive themselves as provocateurs understand that social conscience growth often begins with teacher-initiated *disorienting dilemmas* (Mezirow, 2000). Yet such provocation needs to be perceived by students to be part of the larger process which contributes to their critical thinking; posturing and provoking should be integrated with authenticity and passion in order to mentor students towards growth.

Studying controversial contemporary issues, as discussed in the previous proposition, is relevant and engaging to student interest, and thus is conducive to critical thinking. However, highly engaging topics are not sufficient by themselves to reach this goal. Instructors should employ a variety of approaches to classroom questioning and discussion. For example, although students expected teachers to express opinions at times, students and teachers both agreed that the facilitative role of teachers requires that students' opportunities to engage in critical thinking should take precedence over teachers' stating their beliefs. While judicious sharing of a teacher's opinion can occur, it should be subject to challenge in class discussion like any other viewpoint. Teachers should see that their sharing is not perceived as a hint of the most acceptable and meritorious answer.

Analysis of research data also suggested that another balance needs to be struck between academic objectivity and emotional engagement. Being a pedagogue of critical thinking could be over-generalized to imply an aloof rationality towards the class materials. Thus a balance needs to be struck between academic distance for the sake of analysis, while also strengthening students' capacity for making cognitive, affective, and personal connections between themselves and the curricular materials. For example, given that the central challenge to social conscience at HKIS was disconnectedness, developing a "pedagogy of interconnectedness" (Merryfield et al., 2008, p. 8) to intentionally link students to the world's complex web of relationships seems necessary. HKIS teachers often spoke of interconnectedness as a central animating concept in their teaching.

One of the most effective ways to create connectedness to, and coherence within, the curriculum is to engage students in dialogue about the perennial questions of humankind, which revolve around issues of personal identity, life purpose, and humans' relationship to the cosmos. This use of such "big questions" is consistent with the recommendations of many educational researchers (Braskamp, 2007; Mustakova-Possardt, 2004; Nino, 2000). HKIS teachers repeatedly referred to the importance of asking and discussing these "big questions." As detailed in Chapters 2 and 6, the Humanities I in Action teachers start their course with a set of worldview questions, and students' semester and final exams ask them to write, in a critical yet personal way, about developments in their understanding of themselves in relationship to the world. Dialogue within the social conscience classroom about these questions, as Noddings (2002) states, is fundamental to students' moral development. These findings augment Haste's (2004) assertion that engaging in dialogue about issues of moral significance is highly motivating to students.

Thus, this second role of the social conscience teacher as pedagogue of critical thinking requires a set of highly complex classroom skills. Developing critical thinking, for example, implies far more than simply "critiquing" what is being studied. Critical thinking in this research involves both a differentiating and integrating dynamic that brings students into a holistic understanding of the topics being studied. This duality may be better apprehended through the use of analogy rather than definition. In Heifetz and Linsky's (2002) dance metaphor, students who have a strong orientation towards analytical thinking may need a social conscience course to get them "onto the dance floor." For students who are overly rational or excessively self-focused, it is important for them to join the "dance of life" and experience worlds beyond their own. On the other hand, naturally empathetic students, or students with intense first-hand experiences, may need to leave the dance floor and "get to the balcony." For these students withdrawing, gaining perspective, and analyzing a situation separated from their own emotional inertia may be necessary. Thus, critical thinking in the social conscience classroom is a complex dynamic requiring pedagogical finesse on the part of the teacher.

Proposition 3: A third role of the social conscience teacher is to be an empathetic mentor who facilitates the holistic growth of students. Since social conscience education involves challenging students on an emotional and personal level, not just academically, teachers need to be aware of the multi-layered needs of their students. Most importantly, teachers need to be attuned to the relational dynamics of the classroom, maintain a posture of openness and respect, and seek opportunities to mentor students towards social conscience growth.

Supporting social conscience growth is a holistic undertaking that involves challenges that are not just academic but also emotional. As students' assumptions are called into question, they often experience *disorienting dilemmas* (Mezirow, 2000). Thus, teachers of social conscience need to see their role as one of an empathetic mentor who leads students safely through this journey of disorientation to a more stable and satisfying state of mind.

Being an empathetic mentor means, first, to engage students in ways that go beyond the academic domain of the classroom. Students were in strong agreement that they wanted interactive, dialogical, and student-centered teaching methodologies, and expressed a desire for learning experiences that aimed at the emotional level. Most teachers, and especially those at HKIS, agreed that the social conscience curriculum needed to go "beyond the academic," and pay heed to the emotional and personal dimensions of learning.

Secondly, being an empathetic mentor means promoting relationships in the social conscience classroom. HKIS students emphasized that they wanted teachers who are open-minded, respectful, and who seek to develop relationships with them. Humanities I in Action teachers also were aware of the importance of developing relationships with their students and believed strongly that creating a class community was a significant part of the learning process. The abstract theme of interconnectedness, one teacher explained, could be manifested within the lived relationships of the classroom. Many teachers and students seemed to intuitively appreciate Tappan's (2006) observation that a socio-cultural approach to learning "offers a distributed, collective, shared, fundamentally *dialogical* view of moral development that stands in contrast to the individualistic, atomistic, isolated, fundamentally *psychological* view that has dominated the field for the past century" (p. 15). If social conscience aims to enhance the relationship of the self to the community, this connection should begin within the immediate context of classroom relationships (Johnston, 2006).

Mentoring students in the social conscience classroom requires that teachers be attuned to a number of areas in order to facilitate student growth. First, teachers need to be self-aware, for their own personal growth often serves to guide students about the growth process upon which students are embarking. Secondly, teachers also need to stay abreast of world events and issues beyond the classroom and be prepared to draw upon this information in their lessons. Most importantly, teachers must be attuned to the needs of their students, and should remain closely engaged in their growth process throughout a course. This process often begins in an outward direction of awareness-raising and exploration of issues and events, but the emotionally engaging nature of teaching for social conscience necessitates attention by teachers to the inward dimensions of the learning process. Teachers need to intentionally address this inner dimension, assisting students to reflect upon their learning experiences.

> **Proposition 4:** A fourth role of a social conscience teacher is to be a facilitator of wonder and hope. In studying materials that regularly make demands on learners' internal strengths, attending to the inner resources of wonder and hope are necessary to maintain forward momentum and provide the spaciousness to creatively solve problems with a compassionate consciousness. Drawing upon such positive forces of inner renewal permeates the social conscience classroom's academic endeavors and lived relationships with a communal sense of resilience.

Students seem highly attuned in the social conscience classroom to whether the teacher ultimately feels hope or despair about the issues under study and the state of the world in general. Thus, wonder and hope are vital so that the process does not overwhelm students at this impressionable stage of their development.

Parks (2005) speaks to this balance, "Consciousness and conscience are best schooled at the crossroads of suffering and wonder. Suffering and wonder pose the biggest questions" (p. 302). It is not difficult in the social conscience classroom to use shocking materials involving suffering that induce a sense of at least temporary disorientation for students. The harder task is to foster a sense of wonder and realistic hope for students to consider. Allen (1999) calls on social conscience educators to make their classrooms places of hope, in addition to places of critique and action.

In their role as facilitators of wonder and hope, instructors of social conscience can draw upon three resources in the classroom. First, as Palmer (1998) states, teachers may teach from a place of hope. Bracher (2006) makes the case that educators who have reflected deeply on the state of their own soul find not only dark motives of selfish desire and self-aggrandizement, but they also discover innate motivation to contribute to the well-being of others. The teacher can serve as a role model for students in that they have weighed the evidence of the global situation, and yet have remained committed to the task of contributing to society.

The second source of wonder and hope is in the content itself. Since engaging issues in the social conscience classroom can be stressful for students, teachers need to include stories of people, especially young people, who have confronted these issues, made sense of them, and then acted courageously to engage in positive change. As mentioned in more detail in Chapter 5, the Humanities I in Action curriculum begins the second semester studying the journey of Craig Kielburger, the 12-year old Canadian boy who created the charity "Free the Children." Humanities teachers need to include materials such as these in the curriculum to elicit hope in learners.

One intriguing research study found that reflection upon moral, aesthetic, or natural beauty in the classroom results in a measurable increase of hope (Diessner et al., 2006). Moreover, Keltner and Haidt (2003) make the case that experiences with awe, wonder, mystery, and beauty may be among the most powerful and effective means to foster personal growth. These studies suggest that in order to teach towards social conscience teachers can draw upon the power of the rich, wonder-inducing artistic resources of humanity (Edmundson, 1997; Handley, 2001); explore imaginative visions of what social life could be (Jennings & Prewitt, 1985; Parks, 2005); situate the entire human enterprise within a universe of breath-taking, awe-inspiring mystery (Purpel, 2004; Shapiro, 2006); and initiate learners into mysteries that suggest paths of transformation (Cook-Sather, 2006).

The third source of hope within the social conscience classroom is the students themselves. Ellsworth (1999) suggests that as students wrestle with hope and despair in the midst of their own existential concerns of adolescence, the very engagement with such philosophical questions can bring them relief that their concerns are being substantively addressed. Students' own intrinsic capacity to adapt to the disorientation implicit in the journey of social conscience and to seek resolution demonstrates resilience. The transformation of thoughts, feelings, and actions of teachers and students in the social conscience classroom suggests that change is possible. Inspiration can emerge from within the class itself.

Of these four roles—curriculum innovator, pedagogue of critical thinking, empathetic mentor, and facilitator of wonder and hope—it seems that the role of empathetic mentor deserves special emphasis. Social conscience teachers need first to find it deeply fulfilling to guide students through the journey of social conscience. In my interviews with HKIS teachers, it became clear that for them their main contribution to the world at large is cultivating students with a social conscience. This is the sense of vocation necessary to successfully teach for social conscience.

CONCLUSION

Here we have come to our deepest understanding of the inner life of the social conscience teacher out of which all else proceeds. Critical thinking, creativity, empathy, a mentoring spirit, hope and wonder all need to coalesce authentically with the "who" and "what" of teaching. It is a high calling to serve as a teacher of transformation. But how does one prepare teachers for such courses? The discussion so far has explored the benefits of the transformational journey for students. But this begs the question of how teachers are to be prepared for offering such an experience to students. In order to teach towards this goal, teachers must go through the same yin-yang process that is envisioned for students. The yang of social conscience suggests that, like their students, teachers need to escape their bubbles of ignorance and affluence and engage in the suffering of others in the world, while the yin of inner awakening necessitates attention to deep internal growth. This journey of inner reflect is explored in greater detail in Part II.

PART II

TEACHING FOR INNER AWAKENING

CHAPTER 8

MY JOURNEY OF TEACHING FOR INNER AWAKENING

Yesterday I was clever, so I wanted to change the world.
Today I am wise, so I am changing myself.

—*Rumi*

When asked if there is any hope for humankind, after World War II and in the midst of the Cold War, before anyone knew of climate change, the polarization of politics in the U.S, or the current threat of terrorism, Carl Jung would say, "It depends on how many people do their inner work."

—*Joyce Rockwood Hudson (2019)*

The first professor in my doctoral program gave me the gift of a name, *social conscience education*, to describe what I had been trying to accomplish through the Humanities I in Action course for some years. I immediately realized the accuracy of the phrase. I wanted students to study the world, develop an inner voice of conscience, and then take discerning actions to benefit society. This yang process of social conscience growth described in Part I occurs with amazing predictability. Every year students convey in their own unique voice how the class changes them in ways that seem, at least for some, irreversible. Years later alumni return and share how the class created an inflection point in their life's journey. I had

---

The Wisdom Way of Teaching: Educating for Social Conscience and Inner Awakening in the High School Classroom, pages 93–101.
Copyright © 2022 by Information Age Publishing
www.infoagepub.com
All rights of reproduction in any form reserved.

come to the conclusion by the time I had completed my dissertation that we were implementing a unique transformative approach that could be as beneficial to the world at large as it was for us.

As successful as the course seemed to be, however, some nagging concerns just wouldn't go away about students' service experiences. First, they often expressed that they struggled to maintain their high motivation for action once they returned to school. The initial high following a trip would eventually dissipate into cherished, but relatively impotent, memories. Second, once back on campus, students often conveyed that something was conspicuously lacking within themselves regarding their own sense of life satisfaction. These concerns came to the fore for me in a speech by an especially dedicated service-minded student at a school assembly, challenging me to reconsider the efficacy of the service path to unleash the power of education. This chapter, then, describes how these critical questions about my teaching coincided with events in my own spiritual evolution that dramatically shifted my curricular focus and provided an expanded view of what Wisdom education should look like.

FIRE AND ICE

Toward the end of any service trip students would usually ask some version of this question as we considered returning to Hong Kong, "How do we keep the fire burning?" How do we as privileged students at a highly competitive school find the internal motivation to keep making a difference on behalf of those living outside our bubble of affluence? I didn't have a clear answer beyond the default strategy of taking more service trips—in the hope that, beyond a certain tipping point, students would be propelled into a new stage of ongoing commitment. And, indeed, as a teacher passionately engaged in many service trips, this seemed to be a sensible conclusion.

It was at this time that one of our seniors, Janice, shared her experience with service at an all-school community gathering:

> For the first two years of high school, I separated life into the big and small things. The big things meant much more to me than did the small things. When I learned about the Rwandan genocide, factory farms, and other pressing global issues during Humanities in Action, I was moved to help solve these big issues. I was so busy advocating against animal abuse and the unfair treatment of refugees yet I would come home every day and act ice cold with my grandfather... Every time I think of it, I cringe in disgust and guilt.[1]

Janice's speech was a wake-up call for me, laying bare what I could no longer overlook: Humanities I in Action was not sufficient to meet certain student needs. Something more was needed beyond powerful service trips and social engagement. But I wasn't sure what was missing.

---

[1] The full text of the speech appears at the end of the chapter.

EXISTENTIAL CRISIS

Janice's comment also caused me to reflect deeply about not just my teaching but my life as well. If I were candid with myself, I had—in the wake of finishing my dissertation—entered a slow-burn, existential crisis. A part of me was experiencing Thoreau's observation that "most men lead lives of quiet desperation and go to the grave with the song still in them." Despite being involved in a teaching career that was very purposeful and rewarding, certain spiritual questions lay dormant and unresolved. While I found meaning in the visible, material world to be relatively abundant, the ability to understand the biggest questions of human existence—what is the ultimate goal of life; is support from a divine being available; what comes after death?—seemed beyond reach. I kept waiting for *Sojourners*, the inspiring Christian social justice magazine that I was particularly fond of, to write as in depth about the interior spiritual landscape as they did about social issues, but they never did.

Perhaps it was my own inner wrestling that enabled me to hear anew comments my students had expressed for years. How often they had said to me on service trips, "The people we are trying to help seem happier than we are." Much could be explored in this observation, but the mere fact that my students thought that perhaps we were *receiving* more than we were giving suggested some distress in my students' interior lives. Despite sincere acts of compassion on service trips and claims of transformation, both my students as well as myself still struggled with minds and hearts that were not at peace.

MEETING CYNTHIA

It is at this point that the oft-repeated axiom that the teacher appears when the student is ready certainly seems apropos. Six months after completing my dissertation on social conscience education in 2010, I met Cynthia Bourgeault for the first time, as she visited her daughter's family in Hong Kong and whose grandchildren attended HKIS. When I first heard her speak about her newly published book on Mary Magdalene (Bourgeault, 2010) at the Anglican Cathedral in Hong Kong, I realized I had met someone of insight unlike I had ever encountered before. Here was someone whose verbal eloquence seemed to satisfy both my intellectual questions and spiritual yearnings in equal measure. Yet strangely, even though she was manifestly highly intelligent, her teachings frequently warned of the dangerous allure of mental constructions. Her articulate explanations paradoxically advocated the letting go of one's rational faculties through spiritual practices, including her strong commendation of Centering Prayer, a form of Christian meditation I first discovered in the mid-1990s with well-known Trappist monk Father Basil Pennington.

Sensing some untapped vein of spiritual potential, I hungrily dove into Cynthia's writings.[2] And what she revealed was stunning to me in both its breath-

---

[2] Perhaps a preliminary clarification is in order for readers whose principle interest may be pedagogy rather than my own spiritual path which led there. While most of the forthcoming chapters in this book employ spiritual themes in their role as aspects of our curriculum, elements of what follows

taking profundity and daring relatability. Interpreting her own experience in light of Western spiritual masters, Cynthia made the extraordinary metaphysical claim that existential longing—such as I was experiencing—lies at the heart of the universe's *own* journey. It was just such an ache in the Godhead,[3] she claims, that brought the universe into being (Bourgeault, 2013). In her view, the endless unity of God-as-Spirit was broken by God's deep desire for self-revelation and relationship. These notions are succinctly expressed in the Islamic saying, "I was a hidden treasure and I longed to be known. And so I created the worlds visible and invisible." From Cynthia's perspective, the desire of God's Spirit to be known by something other than Itself gave birth to its ontological opposite, matter, in the creation of the universe. Over the long history of the cosmos, the Wisdom tradition asserts, the invisible Spirit of God and the physical matter of the universe have become increasingly entangled in a dynamic fusion such that matter has become spiritualized and spirit is materialized. In Christian theology the exemplar of this integration, of course, is the person of Jesus, fully human and fully divine. Drawing upon the teachings of visionary French paleontologist and Jesuit priest Teilhard de Chardin (King, 1999), Cynthia contends that this spirit-matter comingling is the evolutionary arrow of planetary civilization.

Reconsidering my own worldview, I came to see that my beliefs had divided the world into matter and some distant sense of spirit. These beliefs, I reflected, were a marked departure from Wisdom teachings across the centuries. Viewed from the Wisdom vantage point, I came to consider my modernity-influenced matter-spirit dualism as an impoverished neglect of these holistic teachings. On what grounds could I confidently hold to my "exceptional" beliefs, while the weight of esoteric spiritual traditions across time and space held an alternative perspective? This process of contemplating new perspectives began to loosen and transmute the hardpan of my listlessness into fertile new possibilities. And these changes in me would in due time nurture my sense that adapting and distilling many of the insights within this Wisdom tradition could open students to a more enlivened and profound inner life.

SICKNESS AND RECOVERY

In the middle of this metaphysical soul-searching, another fundamental crisis occurred, this time to my physical health. I had been sick on and off for much of the previous decade, which culminated with continuous flu-like symptoms from mid-January until late April, 2012. I considered that I might simply not have the con-

---

reflect my own understandings, aspects of my own individual quest. As pivotal as certain theological reflections are in how my own belief system developed, they do not in themselves represent any kind of requisite understanding in order to teach our religion curriculum.

[3] The word "Godhead" is in keeping with the original source material. It is not intended to show partiality towards any one faith tradition in describing what is perceived to be divine reality or ultimate reality by nearly all human cultures.

stitution to maintain my teaching, even fearing that some chronic disease would eventually lead to a shortened life.

With my first spiritual retreat with Cynthia approaching in early May in Assisi, Italy, my desperation grew. On something of a whim, I googled, "Strengthen immune system." And to my surprise, one of the top responses was "meditation." I could not dismiss what seemed to be the ironic message. I was going to visit my spiritual teacher in a month—who advocated Centering Prayer in all of her teaching—without a regular meditation practice. This was just the motivation I needed. I finally started meditating.

In that same fortuitous month of April another event of equal significance occurred. In my desperate search for insight into my health woes, I consulted my chiropractor who recommended a newly-opened clinic that used a Chinese medicine-based electromagnetic therapy called *bioresonance*. I went immediately, did the diagnostic exercise, and in one visit had a plausible diagnosis for my many health woes over the years in Hong Kong. I had a threadbare immune system caused by: (1) insufficient nutrition in my diet, (2) energy blockages, and

I Always Think of My First Spiritual Retreat With Cynthia in Assisi in May, 2012 as the Inflection Point in Which My Teaching Emphasis Shifted From a Primary Focus on the Yang of Social Conscience to a More Balanced Perspective Inclusive of the Yin of Inner Awakening. I'm very grateful for my fellow travelers, Richard and Suzanne Fredericks, who joined me on the retreat. Richard's personal reflections can be found at the end of Chapter 17. Photo credit: Author."

(3) heavy metal poisoning (e.g., mercury, lead, aluminum). I began to change my diet, did the electromagnetic therapy, and began cleansing my system of toxicity. To my great surprise and joy, my body started responding within a matter of days.

So, I had rather quickly entered a new stage of life in which (1) Cynthia became my spiritual teacher (2) Centering Prayer became a regular part of my life (3) better nutrition and medical treatments began my journey toward greater physical health, and (4) I began paying attention to all aspects of my body in unprecedented ways. Even then as I went off to Assisi, I had a sense that I was undergoing some major shift.

A NEW WORLDVIEW

The retreat in Assisi did more than simply confirm for me that Cynthia's Wisdom teachings were a brilliant articulation of what I was sensing in my own developing belief system. More importantly, in the weeks and months that followed, I ever so slowly began to live into new perspectives to my big questions. My chronic existential crisis slowly gave way to an engagement with and trust in a realm of subtle energies—whether they be called prayer, chi, chakras, or bioresonance—that has only grown in the intervening years. While I have had no dramatic experiential breakthroughs to such a realm, my yearning to know and be known by that dimension continues to rise like an ocean swell.

My gradual existential healing can best be understood, from within my Christian symbolic universe, by the biblical image of the valley of dry bones (Ezekiel 37). In this extended metaphor, the prophet Ezekiel testifies how God breathes his Spirit into dry, dead, and disjointed limbs that then spontaneously reconstitute themselves and come to life. Similarly, I slowly, almost imperceptibly, reconsidered at the level of a felt sense that matter and spirit were in some way intertwined. What had once been a static, bifurcated existence with only hope of some mystical breakthrough, or perhaps a vague life after death, slowly became an inner stirring of possibility in which matter and spirit interacted. I came to assume that my students had the same yearning to come into harmony with themselves and "all their relations," which included the natural world and invisible energies. Even the trees and foliage outside my classroom were not something devoid of spirit, but somehow in their physicality resonant with my own aliveness. In all, my body-mind-heart self responded with an underlying buoyancy that suggested that my own attunement to Cynthia's teachings and practices was taking effect. It was as though the underlying core of my life was supported by a new foundation. Or to draw upon a Buddhist metaphor, I sensed that above the same frenetic life spanned a perpetually brilliant blue sky. I was now situated in relationship to reality in ways that were healthier, both physically and spiritually.

This new integration of matter and spirit seemed to resolve the question of what was missing in my service learning: the role of inner work in compassionate action. My new habit of Centering Prayer allowed me to see what surely is obvious to those who approach social justice efforts from a spiritual perspective:

the necessity of a regular spiritual practice to purify one's self-referential motivations. This insight had escaped me up to this point simply because I myself had not developed my own consistent practice and was unaware of its essential value for the work of changing the world.

With the benefit of a decade's hindsight, I can definitely say that my life was fundamentally shifted by the events of spring 2012. On the physical plane, I became far healthier and more aware of the needs of my body. Knowing how to maintain my general health has brought great relief after years of anxiety about "what's wrong with me."

At a spiritual level, the process of slowly becoming conscious of integrating my body, mind, and heart has subtly transformed me as well. First, even though I generally consider myself fairly mild-mannered, I did have a tendency towards anger and self-righteousness in my social conscience teachings. Yet it seems that these reactivities have slowly evaporated as I have re-focused my energy towards the inner life. I had to let go of my naïve hope of changing the world without the simultaneous deep work of self-cultivation. In time, my teaching responsibilities, too, began to reflect these shifting priorities. While I maintained my commitment to the important work of Humanities I in Action, I began to adjust my religion curricula to reflect the principles and practices of the Wisdom tradition. Both personally and professionally I came to see that social conscience instruction needed the complement of inner awakening.

A second change occurred as I made "waking up" to the present moment a daily priority. On one of Cynthia's retreats, she commented:

> Our responsibility is simply in each moment to be, as best we can, yielded, willing, curious and present. Not to squander now a moment for the future but to be here. I love the quote made by [author and Sufi teacher] Kabir Helminski, "If you can make all cares into one care, the care for simply being present, you will be cared for by that Presence, which is the Creative Love." (Bourgeault, 2011)

This universal teaching of present moment awareness in the Wisdom tradition is something I've gladly come to accept and has become a cornerstone of my teaching and personal life. Daily mindfulness practices of conscious walking, conscious breathing, and sensing the tripartite body-mind-heart self both inside and outside of the classroom has become the means by which I attempt to regularly cultivate presence during the mental busyness of high school teaching.

Thirdly, I am increasingly drawn to the notion that a core function of mature spiritual traditions is to help overcome the tendency of the mind to perceive reality in polarizing dualities rather than higher, or seemingly paradoxical, points of agreement. Whether such black-white thinking involves matter vs. spirit, Christianity vs. "other" religions, conservatives vs. liberals, Asia vs. the West or other binaries, those committed to spiritual practices seem to embody greater inclusivity, sensitivity, and creativity. An intuitive capacity develops to see beneath easily visible labels for hidden essences.

Looking back, these major life events of facing my existential fears, starting a meditation practice, receiving energetic healing treatments, and attending Cynthia's Assisi retreat, propelled me into a new stage of development. My spiritual crisis slowly dissipated as I started to heal physically and grow spiritually. A new enthusiasm for all things manifesting this spirit-matter fusion began.

As the value of these new insights became increasingly clear in my personal life, I also considered that perhaps these ideas could be implemented in my religion classes. Just as the body-mind-heart framework offered me a new stage of growth, it seemed to suggest an avenue for students to address what was missing not only in their service learning experiences, but in their overall life satisfaction as well.

TEACHING FOR INNER AWAKENING

Meeting Cynthia nearly a decade ago was the start of a contemplative turn that has gradually worked its way into all of my religion classes, what I'm calling the yin of inner awakening. The chapters that follow provide examples of how these physical, mental, emotional and spiritual changes came to manifest themselves in a junior-senior elective course called "Service, Society, and the Sacred" (Chapter 9), a freshman religion course "World Religions" (Chapter 10), and our newly-created core courses called "Spiritual Explorations" (Chapters 11 and 12).

The response of students to spiritual practices has been much like my own. As they gradually experience greater positivity, a gathered attention, and the relief of letting go, they naturally welcome the perspectives and practices of the Wisdom tradition. In fact, every year students have encouraged me to place ever greater emphasis on such practices.

Now it seems so obvious that Humanities I in Action, for all its catalytic potential, trains its transformative sights primarily on cognitive change, even if the emotions are deeply touched and the body is involved through service responses. However, to effect primarily a cognitive change *without* conscious attention to the heart and body diminishes these essential elements of the self, and is certainly going to be less effective than an approach that groundtruths transformation in the full human panoply. What I have come to understand is that the world's spiritual traditions have a storehouse of methods to bring the mind into alignment with the Wisdom of the body and the heart. Given that I had been so enamored with social conscience instruction as my answer to the question of power in education for many years, this contemplative turn became a major shift in my thinking, which is the foundation of what I share in Part II.

I close by including Janice's speech in full. It shows a student very capable of investigating her own conscience in terms of her engagement with others. It also illustrates numerous themes of this chapter in rich detail.

> For the first two years of high school, I separated life into the big and small things. The big things meant much more to me than did the small things. When I learned

about the Rwandan genocide, factory farms, and other pressing global issues during Humanities in Action, I was moved to help solve these big issues. I was so busy advocating against animal abuse and the unfair treatment of refugees, yet I would come home every day and act ice cold with my grandfather. My grandfather used to live with me at home; he was a very skilled engineer and mathematician and that's all I saw him as. My grandfather loved solving math problems. Every day when I got home he'd ask me if I had any math homework and for a while I would show it to him so that he could double check my answers. I did this because academics was a big thing in my life as I thought it determined how successful I was or could become. But when he got sick, he started to do the problems slower and make more careless mistakes. I was a freshman during this time, and I was just so selfish and inconsiderate. When I started to notice this, I started to tell him that I didn't have any math homework because I thought that this way, I would waste less of his and my time. This was so much more than just him helping me with math, but I didn't see it until it was too late. Every time I think of it, I cringe in disgust and guilt. I deprived him of this small thing that made him happy and I really just missed out on creating a bond that could have been special.

That's when I realized that the small things are really the big things in life. Letting him help me with math homework, or even just striking a conversation with him more at home just to show that I loved him would have made a huge difference. It would have showed him that I was there for him always. During that time there were also many instances when I gave my parents the cold shoulder, I said no to hangouts with friends, and put my needs before my friends' needs. I really hope it's not too late, but two years later I am finally starting to understand the importance of the small things in life.

I sort of think of these small things as connecting the dots. Continuous small gestures mean so much more than just one grand display of love. When you begin to commit to these small acts of love, you can start to connect the dots between all this joy and ultimately end up helping to change the world for the better. My thinking now is this. If we all start caring more about others, smiling at strangers, sacrificing our needs for others, then slowly everyone will become more considerate towards each other and we'll hopefully be able to alleviate the major issues of injustice towards humans, animals, and the environment in our world. While I was figuring this out, I came across a scripture from Matthew 25 that said, "Whatever you do for one of the least of these brothers and sisters of mine, you do for me." In this way, God showed me how these small acts of love, added up, will be the reason why things change for the better on this planet.

When I learned this, it was impossible for me to not look around at everyone and not be happy or grateful for being around such a loving community. We are all one and the same. We all find happiness in sharing it with others. As Mother Teresa said, "We can do no great things, only small things with great love." I hope that we can all start doing more of these small things.

CHAPTER 9

THE ESSENTIALS OF A CURRICULUM FOR SELF-UNDERSTANDING

The Body-Mind-Heart Framework in Service, Society, and the Sacred

Knowing yourself is the beginning of all wisdom.

—*Aristotle*

Education as it is currently understood, particularly in the West, ignores the human soul, or essential Self. This essential Self is not some vague entity whose existence is a matter of speculation, but our fundamental "I," which has been covered over by social conditioning and by the superficiality of our rational mind. In North America we are in great need of a form of training that would contribute to the awakening of the essential Self. Such forms of training have existed in other eras and cultures and have been available to those with the yearning to awaken from the sleep of their limited conditioning and know the potential latent in the human being.

—*Kabir Helminski (1992, p. 7)*

The Wisdom Way of Teaching: Educating for Social Conscience and Inner Awakening in the High School Classroom, pages 103–116.
Copyright © 2022 by Information Age Publishing
www.infoagepub.com
All rights of reproduction in any form reserved.

> In Humanities in Action, I learned how to be of service to other people; in Service, Society, and Sacred I learned how to be of service to myself. The combination of these two has made me feel like a more complete person.
> —*Ana, grade 12 female student*

INTRODUCTION

As I noted in Chapter 1, my experience at Ateneo High School in Manila in 1997 was a lightbulb moment that prompted me to envision an integrated service learning course at HKIS. However, it wasn't until January, 2000 that this initial vision became a reality. It was then that my colleague George Coombs and I began teaching a religion elective called, "Service, Society, and the Sacred" (SSS), which weaved together social justice, service, and spirituality in a single course. The initial impulse of SSS was indeed the interplay that I am describing in this book; namely, that social conscience education should address not just changing the world's social structures, but pay attention to the inner dimensions of the human soul as well.

As I write this exactly twenty years since we first began teaching SSS, I see how pivotal that moment was. These two themes of social change and spiritual growth that George and I sought to encapsulate in that one-semester course eventually manifested into two pathways in our Humanities curriculum. One was the social conscience direction, which resulted in the creation of Humanities I in Action in 2003, which is the focus of Part I. The other path was inner awakening, which is described in Part II.

I have been searching my entire career for what power in education really means. Certainly in my first two decades at HKIS I believed that service learning was most the powerful and transformative pedagogy available in my school context. However, following a time of reflection that involved Janice's comment and my Assisi retreat experience in 2012, I began to investigate the inner work of transformation with new energy. Guided by Cynthia's books *The Wisdom Way of Knowing* (2003) and *Centering Prayer and Inner Awakening* (2004), I sought for efficacious ways to operationalize her profound teachings into my religion classes. I was especially drawn to her chapter "Three-Centered Awareness" in *The Wisdom Way of Knowing* in which she explicated the roles of the body, mind, and heart in the awakening process. In her view, educating for inner awakening seeks to re-balance the "one-brained" student into a triangulating, multi-sensory being. Cynthia defines these three aspects in this way:

- Body: *Sensing* is the work of the moving body center. It operates through a directly embodied or kinesthetic knowing.
- Mind: *Thinking* is the work of the intellectual center. It operates through deduction, logic and analysis, comparison, measuring and weighing.

- Heart: *Feeling* is the work of the heart center. It operates through vibrational resonance (i.e., empathy). (Bourgeault, 2014)

Inspired by these teachings, in 2015 I re-organized SSS around these three domains of the self as centers of intelligence. What emerged in the course was four main throughlines:

1. The three intelligences of the body-mind-heart;
2. The Enneagram;
3. Spiritual practices; and
4. Horizontal/physical and vertical/spiritual dimensions of life.

The evolution of the curriculum over the last twenty years has been a gradual unfolding in which student feedback and continual adjustments were essential ingredients. The end product could not have been foreseen in the early years. Thus, it is particularly gratifying that, after so many years of experimenting, I have finally found a stable curriculum framework for the course. This chapter offers an extended explanation of the course design, which laid the foundations for future courses and approaches that are described in the rest of the book.

COURSE OVERVIEW

My overarching aim in redesigning the SSS course was to meet the distinct developmental needs of our students, particularly juniors and seniors. With college looming, students face a number of intense, self-defining questions: what college should I attend, and for what overall purpose? It's the biggest question of their teenage years and maybe of their life trajectory: what is worthy of their time? And deeper still lies the question of identity: who do they want to be, as they consider the broad expanse of their lives?

Yet the frantic nature of high school makes it difficult for students to explore such important questions in a poised, reflective manner. The following is a typical example of a hard-working, conscientious, and ultimately successful (in terms of college admission) student named Jocelyn narrating her struggles throughout high school:

> Starting . . . in sophomore year, things were getting harder and I wasn't "being" but merely "living" every day with fear and dread. "I have to take hard APs[1] in sophomore, junior, and senior year so that college will see that I am competent; I have to maintain a good GPA; I have to have more extracurricular activities; I have to create this amount of artwork," I told myself. With this mentality, I started getting 4–6 hours of sleep, started consuming a lot of junk food, stopped exercising as much, doing devotions, and spending time with friends and family. For a period of time in

---

[1] APs are "Advanced Placement" courses in the American school system produced by the College Board. These exam-based courses are considered more rigorous than other courses and are seen as essential to strengthen students' bids to get accepted at highly competitive universities.

Madeline in SSS Class Beginning a Labyrinth Walk as a Spiritual Practice. Photo Credit: Author.

> junior year, I remember staying at the school's library during my frees and lunches, and my friends could not contact me at all. At home, I would . . . study and miss some of my family dinners. I would even bring my books to study at a restaurant if I really had to go. These incidents led to misunderstandings, which ultimately hurt my relationships.

I sympathize with the real angst that students like Jocelyn suffer. And in terms of answering the big questions of SSS with regard to what's worthy of their time in the coming decades, their overstressed state of mind undermines soulful inquiry into such important decisions. So, what can educators do to help foster greater wholeness? Rather than using personal interest surveys or applying a strengths finder approach, SSS opts for a more intuitive method. Drawing upon the Wisdom tradition, I employ a body-mind-heart framework which helps each center of the self to become more aware, enlivened, and integrated.

Thus, the course description lays out the core course themes as follows:

> This junior-senior religion elective aims to enable students to gain a better sense of life direction through a holistic exploration of their bodies, minds, and hearts. The starting point of this journey is the assumption that each aspect of the self—body, mind, and heart—has its own unique intelligence that it brings to bear in addressing the question of purpose in life. The class, then, consists in teaching about and training of each intelligence to bring it into greater sympathetic resonance with other aspects of the self. The training of the body asks students to find ways to improve their physical health; the training of the mind helps them to identify and understand their personality type; and training of the heart uses various spiritual practices to cultivate a more open, grateful, and empathetic disposition. It is hoped that this in-

tensive self-exploration will enable students to be more at ease with themselves and better able to understand how they can lead a life of purpose and service to society.

Students will:
- Enhance their nutritional intake and physical health.
- Discover their personality type and learn how to rebalance their type through a variety of spiritual practices and meditations.
- Observe their emotional reactions and learn how to respond more positively with acceptance and gratitude.
- Create their own personalized wellness practice.
- Apply their new sense of self and perspective to their future university, career, and life choices.

In using this body-mind-heart framework as the organizing principle of the course, I find myself in agreement with Jacob Needleman's (1999) assessment of these three centers: "[A person's] confusion, lack of unity, unnecessary suffering, immorality—in fact everything that characterizes the sorrow of the human condition—come about because these centers of perception are wrongly related, wrongly functioning, and because [people do] not see or care to know this about [themselves]." Reducing suffering, then, comes about through a re-integration of these three centers of intelligence.

THE BODY-MIND-HEART FRAMEWORK

In Chapter 3 of *The Wisdom Way of Knowing* (2003), Cynthia outlines her understanding of the life and teachings of enigmatic spiritual teacher G.I. Gurdjieff, who first explicated the role and purpose of these three fundamental intelligences within the Western esoteric stream in the early 20th century (Ouspensky, 2001). Gurdjieff stated that humans are "three-brained" beings: the body, the mind, and the heart all have ways of perceiving and orienting, as well communicating with other aspects of the self. A healthy self, then, has all three intelligences interacting as an entrained trio. By contrast, to be operating out of only one center, which in modern society is almost always the mind, means that we are functionally asleep. We need to wake up the body and the heart in order to come to greater self-understanding.

The Body Center

The focus of the opening unit is on the body center, and its role is prominent throughout the semester.[2] While modern thinking tends to marginalize the

---

[2] While I use the term "body center" quite generically in my teaching as a contrast to the mental and emotional faculties, it's important to note that Cynthia specifically refers to the body center as the "moving center." She describes this domain as consisting of "two subsets: the instinctive center, which regulates the inner operational systems of the body; and the moving center proper, which concerns our outward and voluntary interactions with the physical world through our five senses and in movement and rhythm. You might picture them as the hard drive and software, respectively, of our

body, somatic intelligence has been an essential aspect of Wisdom traditions for thousands of years. Contemporary education has begun to take a more accepting stance toward the body, in part due to the inclusion of body-kinesthetic as one of Gardner's multiple intelligences (Gardner, 2011). However, much more is possible in terms of seeing body intelligence as an essential element of spiritual development.

Seeing the body as a partner in the quest for wisdom requires a paradigm shift for most of us. Cynthia writes,

> In many spiritual traditions of the world, the body is viewed with fear and suspicion, considered to be the seat of desire and at best a dumb beast that must trained and brought into submission to the personal will. But what is missed here—and it is of crucial importance—is that the moving center also carries unique perceptive gifts, the most important of which is the capacity to understand the language of faith in sacred gesture. (Bourgeault, 2003, p. 28)

What could the body possibly have to do with self-understanding or student decisions regarding their future? The Wisdom tradition's response is that in a mind-obsessed culture, the practice of coming into centeredness through the body by sensing one's feet, breath, or other sensory experiences is the easiest way to wake ourselves up from the habitual tendency to leave body-mind-heart integrated consciousness and go into mental autopilot mode. Secondly, and even more intriguingly, is the concept of the "intelligence of the body." That is, the body has a *way of knowing* that is different than the mind and heart. Understanding oneself and one's place in the world, according to the Wisdom tradition, is intimately connected to how well we can tap into this intelligence of "embodied knowing."

Many contemporary spiritual writers speak of this intelligence of the body. Writer Philip Shepherd (Buchbinder, 2013) calls the gut "the second brain." Michael Brown's (2010) *Presence Process* teaches meditators how to follow their emotion-laden sensations deep into their bodies in order to liberate them. Similarly, Edwin McMahon and Peter Campbell (2010) contend in their book *Rediscovering the Lost Body-Connection within Christian Spirituality* that the "intellect's eye cannot easily penetrate this inner world of *felt meaning*" (p. 30) that is stored in our cells and tissues. Finally, Cynthia's teaching of the Welcoming Prayer (Bourgeault, 2008, pp. 176–180), which deals with daily emotional pain, instructs that when strong negative emotion hits, pause and experience that emotion's bodily sensation in an attempt to integrate the energy rather than repress it.

All religions use bodily movement—bowing, prostrations, symbolic hand gestures, sitting postures, conscious walking—to interlink the body, mind, and heart together to foster holistic understanding. Consider the power of adding a hand gesture moving from the chest outward to a song about opening the heart. The ac-

---

physical embodiment" (Bourgeault, 2003, p. 28). Cynthia deliberately engages this moving center on her retreats through periods of conscious work and sacred movement in order to integrate energies generated in her teaching and meditation sessions.

tivity of singing, which itself is largely mental and susceptible to autopilot mode, can become embodied in a way that the Wisdom tradition suggests works on both the conscious and subconscious levels of the individual.

It's helpful to think of the body as an interface between the inner subjective self and an objective world beyond the self. Sensitizing the body to become a medium that links self and world, a role for which it seems purpose-built, gives our physical body an integrative function far more profound than its frequent dismissal as a mere machine.

Of the three centers, certainly it is the body as a way of knowing that seems the most difficult for modern students to understand. Accordingly, Cynthia states that bodily intelligence is our weakest center. She explains,

> I have learned through years and years of spiritual work that it's from a finely developed inner sensing that you really get the information you need to make accurate discernments in your inner journey. Both the mind and the emotions are easily blindsided or manipulated by the personal will. But the sensing/moving center never lies. If I am making a decision and sense inner constriction, I know that no matter how much I try to convince myself that my preferred option is the correct one, in fact it is not. It has taken years to learn to discern from sensation. (Bourgeault, 2014, day 5)

Students' positive responses to exercising of this underutilized somatic intelligence explains their general receptivity to all kinds of embodied spiritual practices, such as conscious walking, body scans, and prostrations. Employing the body's natural capacity for meaningful movement is usually both engaging and relaxing, and allows students to be present in the moment, which gives the anxious mind much-needed rest and rejuvenation.

The Mind Center

The strengths of the mind—understanding, critical thinking, analysis, multiple perspectives, self-reflectivity, discernment—are quite evident to students. What is far less obvious, however, especially in a school setting, are the hazards of over-reliance on this particular faculty. Cynthia explains,

> The intellectual center . . . [has a] natural aptitude for reasoning, doubting, making fine discriminations. In their own right, these discriminatory skills are legitimate and profoundly necessary, built into the structure of the human mind itself. But in terms of the spiritual journey, trying to find faith with the intellectual center is something like trying to play a violin with a saw: it's simply the wrong tool for the job. This is one reason why all religious traditions have universally insisted that religious life cannot be done with the mind alone; that is the biggest single impediment to spiritual becoming. (Bourgeault, 2003, p. 31)

Is it any wonder, then, in the frenetic and mind-intensive atmosphere of high school that students find it difficult to come to any kind of abiding faith in deeply held causes, values, or beliefs? To reiterate, the mind is the wrong tool for the job. Cynthia continues,

> The other reason why the mind has been regarded with a certain amount of suspicion is its tendency to pull us into a smaller, mentally constructed sense of ourselves: to confuse being with thinking. That was Descartes' mistake in his notorious "*Cognito, ergo sum*" ["*I think, therefore, I am*"]. It's a vicious circle: the process of thinking intensifies our identification of ourselves with the thinker and makes us more and more dependent on thinking as the way of maintaining our sense of identity. In terms of Wisdom, this is like racing round and round in a squirrel cage. Nothing real can happen until we find our way out. (Bourgeault, 2003, pp. 31–32)

What is the proper role of the mind from the perspective of the Wisdom tradition? To be clear, schools should certainly continue to prepare students for intellectual rigor and academic excellence. In the Wisdom tradition, there is no ground for neglecting the mind any more than there is for overlooking other faculties. Rather, the overall goal is to bring the over-exercised muscle of the mind into sympathetic harmony with a revitalized body and heart. A mind properly attuned to the whole human self and its environment realizes its potential as an organ capable of articulating a higher wisdom, far more intuitive than its more obvious utility as a purveyor of cognition and logic alone. When informed by an alive body and heart, the mind can provide a combination of understanding and intuition that articulates "the big picture" of our role in our communities, extending even to our existential place in the universe. In a world with an ever-increasing overabundance of data but a dearth of wisdom-sensitive priorities, the value of a properly discerning mind cannot be overestimated.

The Heart Center

The third aspect of the trio is heart, which in contemporary parlance is often equated with one's emotions. However, Cynthia explains that this is an unfortunate misunderstanding with dangerous implications:

> In the psychological climate of our times, our emotions are almost always considered to be virtually identical with our personal authenticity, and the more freely they flow, the more we are seen to be honest and "in touch." A person who gravitates to a mental mode of operation is criticized for being "in [their] head;" when feeling dominates, we proclaim with approval that such a person is "in [their] heart." In the Wisdom tradition, this would be a serious misuse of the term *heart*. The real mark of personal authenticity is not how intensely we can express our feelings but how honestly we can look at where they're coming from and spot the elements of clinging, manipulation, and personal agendas that make up so much of what we experience as our emotional life today. A person with serious control issues . . . [is] more at the mercy of her emotional agendas. (Bourgeault, 2003, pp. 32–33)

So often high school students are exhorted to find their "passion" in life, which should in time, we are told, guide their career choice. In popular culture, "passion" can take on a range of associations such that the potentially positive meanings are easily conflated with overreactive or even destructive forms of passion. Even the popular adage "follow your passion" is usually understood to do whatever one loves rather than a cultivated sense of the heart in the Wisdom tradition. Cynthia offers a word of caution about our unquestioning praise of passion.

> In the teachings of the Christian Desert Fathers and Mothers, these intense feelings arousing out of personal issues were known as the "passions," and most of the Desert spiritual training had to do with learning to spot these land mines and get free of them before they did serious psychic damage . . . Passion [was seen] as a diminishment of being. It meant falling into passivity, into a state of being acted upon (which is what the Latin *passio* actually means), rather than clear and conscious engagement. Instead of enlivening the heart, according to one Desert Father, the real damage inflicted by the passions is that "they divided our heart in two." (Bourgeault, 2003, p. 33)

There is another deeper sense of heart, however, that evokes a more profound intuition. Through proper training it can develop within students a new capacity for spiritual awareness. Cynthia explains,

> The heart, in the ancient sacred traditions, has a very specific and perhaps surprising meaning. It is not the seat of our personal affective life—or even, ultimately, of our personal identity—but an organ for the perception of divine purpose and beauty. It is our antenna, so to speak, given to us to orient us toward the divine radiance and to synchronize our being with its more subtle movements. The heart is not for personal expression but for divine perception. (Bourgeault, 2003, p. 33)

If life direction is about a calling from something beyond oneself—discerning "divine purpose and beauty"—then awakening the heart gives students a new form of perception, a purified sensitivity, of what they feel they should do with their lives.

To give a better sense of the heart's gifts beyond its caricature of emotionality, Cynthia frequently quotes modern Sufi master Kabir Helminski (1992):

> We have subtle subconscious faculties we are not using. In addition to the limited analytic intellect is a vast realm of mind that includes psychic and extrasensory abilities; intuition; wisdom; a sense of unity; aesthetic, qualitative and creative capacities; and image-forming and symbolic capacities . . . This total mind we call 'heart.' (p. 157)

Expansive heart intelligence offers gifts of greater wholeness unattainable by the mind alone. However, this is a countercultural message for most students. Whereas school entails nearly 15 years of instruction of how to think before going off to university, our formal educational settings spend little time *teaching us how to feel*, a description that even sounds rather odd. By contrast, the Wisdom tradition speaks of the paramount importance of the heart. Jesus in one of his most famous teachings proclaims: "Blessed are the pure in heart, for they shall see God" (Matthew 5:3). Accordingly, the Wisdom tradition teaches that the path to meaningful contribution and ultimate contentment goes straight through the purified heart.

The Heart's Reconciling Force

What is the interrelationship between these three ways of knowing? Cynthia envisions the three centers as playing distinct, but synergistic functions. Borrowing concepts from Gurdjieff's Law of Three (Bourgeault, 2013), she sets up the Wisdom playing field in this way:

> In the ancient language of Wisdom, the moving center [or body] carries the "affirming force;" its natural aptitude is for reaching out, embracing, making contact. The intellectual center carries the "denying force," cautioning and questioning the body's desire to connect. (Bourgeault, 2003, p. 33)

The heart, then, as an organ of spiritual perception, is the reconciling force,

> a bridge between the mind and the body and also between our usual physical world and this invisible other realm. When properly attuned, the emotional center's most striking capacity, lacking in the mind alone, is the ability to comprehend the language of paradox. Logical inconsistencies that the mind must reduce into a simple "either-or" can be held by the heart in "both-and"—and even more important—felt that way—without needing to resolve, close down or protect oneself from the pain that ambiguity always brings. (Bourgeault, 2003, p. 35)

Whether it be matter vs. spirit, the yang of action vs. the yin of contemplation, or other binaries implicit in life, the heart's specialty is in resolving or living with such paradoxes.

What happens when body, mind, and heart all function properly and in harmony? When a person is poised in all three centers, balanced and alert, a shift happens in consciousness. Rather than being trapped in our usual mind, with its well-informed rut tracks of habitual thinking patterns and agendas we deal with life from a deeper, steadier, and quieter place. We are *present*, in the words of the Wisdom tradition, fully occupying the now in which we find ourselves.

> This state of presence is extraordinarily important to know and taste in oneself. For sacred tradition is emphatic in its insistence that real Wisdom can be given and received only in a state of presence, with all three centers of our being engaged and awake. Anything less is known in the tradition as "sleep" and results in an immediate loss of receptivity to higher meaning. (Bourgeault, 2003, pp. 36–37)

If all this sounds overly daunting, consider this final observation from Cynthia that comes late in the *Wisdom Way of Knowing*:

Awakening the heart may sound like one of those lofty but unattainable ideals, beyond what a human being can accomplish. But actually, it's only the words that are lofty; the task itself is quite doable. You could even say that we were born for it, because only with awakened hearts are we actually able to fulfill our purpose with the cosmos. (Bourgeault, 2003, p. 100)

THE ESSENTIALS

Given the preceding overview of the body-mind-heart framework, the following are the essential dimensions of the new course structure and the accompanying larger assignments (called "summatives") that proceed out of this pedagogical approach:

1. Starting premise: in the midst of making important and far-reaching decisions about their futures, students face great personal challenges managing their high school experience.
2. Approach: The body-mind-heart framework offers students a balanced way to reconnect to themselves and recover a sense of self.
3. Body awareness: The "Be Healthier Today" project (summative #1) focuses on the foundation of proactively making healthier eating choices, which not only strengthens students physically and connects them to their body centers, but also empowers them to develop the muscle of new habits, a skill that will be applied to their emotional and spiritual lives later in the semester.
4. Mind insights: The Enneagram helps students understand and accept their personality type with all of their strengths, quirks and contradictions.[3] In addition, it helps students gain understanding of how their type interacts with family and friends.
5. Heart integration: Following from their deep self-exploration through the Enneagram, the Spiritual Practices project (summative #2) provides students with a practical daily routine to work towards rebalancing their physical, mental and emotional centers.
6. Emotional Intelligence: Throughout the course practices and experiences are introduced to help students explore the intelligence of their hearts, such as dealing with the Inner Critic, non-reactivity, burning regrets, and engaging in meaningful rituals.

---

[3] The Enneagram has come to play an increasingly important role in many of my classes over the last five years. I frequently say that the Enneagram is the most powerful in-the-classroom material that I have ever taught. I've decided not to venture in this book into an explanation of my teaching of the Enneagram, but I will mention that I use Don Riso and Russ Hudson's *Personality Types* (1996) and *Wisdom of the Enneagram* (1999) in SSS and SPEX classes. I've also included several entries on teaching the Enneagram on my "Social Conscience and Inner Awakening" blog.

7. Application: The DIY wellness project (summative #3) asks students to develop for themselves a holistic practice that can sustain their body-mind-heart selves.
8. Culmination: A 3–6 page final paper (summative #4) summarizing their learning, which they then share in a final "Heroic Journey" ritual[4] on the last day of class.

STUDENT IMPACT

The biggest benefit for most students is that SSS gives them permission to take a sustained look at themselves. One student, Jason, explained, "Service, Society, and the Sacred has been the most unique course at HKIS I have taken because it was about me. I hate to seem self-centered, but focusing on myself for once in a classroom setting was refreshing, and to be honest, much needed." Another student, Zach, succinctly explained a few years ago, "SSS was like Humanities I in Action for the inside." The following are some recent examples of student reflections on the course.

For Hollis, the main benefit was getting in touch with her physical body amid the whirlwind of activities and classes she was involved with:

> The class has been crucial to my wellbeing as it has been a refuge during the day for me to take time to focus on myself, to stop comparing myself to others and to ultimately, listen to my body. In this sense, it has been an extremely beneficial course for me to take in several ways. The diet change project, identifying my Enneagram type and a comprehensive introduction to kinesiology have all contributed to my journey of becoming my most healthy self, physically and mentally.

Ali also expressed similar sentiments in the context of his desire to make a positive impact on the world:

> Before I focus on fixing societal issues, which I am extremely passionate about, I must concentrate on bettering myself both mentally and physically. As a result of the "Be Healthier Today" project, my Spiritual Practices project, and learning about the Enneagram, this course has given me the perfect platform to make myself healthier.

Sharon was able to counteract her extremely stressful first semester with a regular habit of meditation:

> Through SSS, I realized the importance of the balance between body, mind, and heart, and the consequences that can follow the imbalance. I will bring my learning to college and through life, of letting go, eating healthy, and meditating.

---
[4] See Chapter 6 for more details on this ritual.

After an uplifting and academically successful grade 9 year, Sandra's high school career spiraled downward. It wasn't until SSS, three years later, that she was able to put all the pieces back together again:

> From praying before meals, to learning how important gut health is (second brain), to realizing that superbrain yoga represents the importance of exercise, to finding myself as a type 2 "Helper" on the Enneagram, knowing that Loving Kindness meditation is the most effective for me, all have contributed to another year of feeling enlightened. I have never been so grateful for such an experience. The unfinished puzzle after Humanities I in Action and World Religions in freshman year has finally been completed.

Like Sandra, Ivy[5] also appreciated how SSS was a valuable complement to Humanities I in Action, leading to the beautiful phrase that she now "radiate[s] with life:"

> Humanities I in Action challenged me to step outside my bubble and instilled in me a passion for service. SSS guided me in integrating that energy in a way that is cognizant of my immediate surroundings. As I work on my gratitude project and think about how to make the best out of my remaining time here, I feel myself radiate with life. Throughout my journey, I've learned how to live.

Amar described how SSS provided a necessary counterbalance to his vision of contributing to society through environmental research that he first considered in Humanities I in Action, resulting in a sense of "profound wakefulness:"

> Service, Society, and the Sacred reminded me of the paramount importance of intimately knowing my inner self in order to purify these outward efforts . . . I believe I now have the tools to lead a life of more profound wakefulness and to constantly seek out wisdom for the betterment of my pursuits.

The following are a number of other student comments that reflect the value of a course that allows students to do self-work that has been neglected throughout much of high school:

- **Jazmin:** Through almost every activity that we did, SSS class helped me be honest with myself and recognize when I need help from others, and to not be afraid to ask for that help. It has taught me healthy ways to deal with my emotions instead of being reluctant to open up to others, which is my main takeaway from this course.
- **Kenna:** The most impactful gain [was] my development of self-love on the physical, intellectual and spiritual levels.

---

[5] Ivy's and Amar's final SSS essays are the finest sustained reflections I've seen revealing what's possible when students combine the yang of social conscience with the yin of inner awakening over a four-year career at HKIS. I have included their papers in Appendix B.

- **Khushi:** After learning about and trying out various spiritual and holistic practices, I realized how crucial it was for me to create this balance in my own life to stop the destructive cycle I had created and was going through in my life.
- **Teenie:** It has been a hectic 4 years, and taking SSS has helped me slow down, breathe and actually work on myself, my body and soul rather than just focusing on my mind . . . I finally got the time to learn more about myself and how to be a better version of myself. I've always felt lost, not knowing who I am and what I'm good at and I think this was a great class that led me to finally make some time for my heart and my body.

CONCLUSION

Many years ago I began teaching with the desire to discover power in education. Encountering Cynthia's teaching of the need to balance the body, mind, and heart was a watershed moment; I re-organized my SSS curriculum around this insight, which students have unanimously welcomed. What I have learned is that there is indeed a deep yearning to make a positive impact on the world; yet without interior practice, such an impact ultimately remains unsustainable and unsatisfying. The imperative of transformative education, then, is to balance the yang of social change with the yin of inner awakening, a harmony elegantly expressed in Gandhi's frequently-quoted directive: "Be the change you want to see in the world."

A Happy Group of Seniors in Our Service, Society, and the Sacred Class on Their Last Day of High School.

CHAPTER 10

BALANCING BODY, MIND, AND HEART

Introducing the Wisdom Tradition in a World Religions Class

Almost 80 percent of both undergraduates and faculty said that they considered themselves spiritual and that they were committed to a search for purpose and meaning. When asked how often they experienced such a search in the classroom, almost 60 percent . . . reported never.
—*Palmer et al. (2010, pp. ix–x)*

Our three-hour session at the monastery began with 10 minutes of chanting . . . The sound we created was resonant and hypnotizing. Within a minute, I had entered that state of "nothingness" and just continued chanting subconsciously. Then, we followed with twenty minutes of meditation and 324 total prostrations . . . At the end of the day, I came to realize that without even noticing, I had actually gained a state of awareness that I did not have previously. For a brief time, this state of awareness allowed me to think and reflect about what and who I truly am . . . I was confident that the state of

"nothingness" and level of awareness I have achieved through these spiritual practices was what spirituality feels like. It was almost like an inner awakening.
—*Brian, grade 9 male World Religions student*

INTRODUCTION

Service, Society, and the Sacred (Chapter 9) has always been my venue for developing new ideas, so the body-mind-heart framework first appeared in that course as the key ingredient of the yin of inner awakening. Over time, however, I gained enough confidence in this approach to share it in my grade 9 World Religions class. Given last chapter's in-depth description of Cynthia's understanding of this three-centered approach, the reader can now see how I translate her relatively complex ideas into content appropriate for my grade 9 classroom. In this chapter, I address students directly, sharing as simply as I can the relevance of the body-mind-heart teaching to personal growth in a World Religions class.[1]

COURSE INTRODUCTION

Dear World Religions Students,

Welcome to high school, and especially my World Religions class! I'd really like to teach you something valuable this semester. Of course, you'll learn a lot academically about Hinduism, Buddhism, Judaism, and Islam, but I'm hoping you will actually come away with something far more important that can be applied to your life. So far in this class I have made the point that religions envision the entire universe as being composed of two dimensions—a visible, every day existence that I'm calling "the horizontal," and an invisible dimension of reality—"the vertical"—that might be referred to as God, Ultimate Reality, the Sacred, Brahman, or the Kingdom of Heaven.[2] Religions across the world teach that deeper happiness is possible when one lives at the intersection of these two dimensions.

---

[1] I have never actually given this letter to my students, but such an artifice has served as an effective vehicle to process my own core messages that I do share through my curricular choices and personal conversations with students.

[2] We have found that the five most salient questions for students to address regarding their beliefs about this so-called "vertical dimension" are:
  1. Is there some intrinsic purpose in the universe or is reality essentially random?
  2. Is the universe (e.g., God) "on our side" or is it indifferent to our existence?
  3. What happens after we die? Do we return to the ground or is there some spiritual reality that enables us to live on after death?
  4. What is more foundational to the underlying existence of the universe, matter or consciousness?
  5. Are we connected to everyone and everything in some fundamental way?

We use a set of 40 questions to help students identify their relationship to this horizontal-vertical matrix, which is included in Appendix C: "My Worldview: Do I Believe in a Vertical Dimension?"

you hear. Try to avoid falling into thinking/imagining about anything outside of these three physical aspects of your experience.

Heart Intelligence

1. Loving Kindness Meditation: I recommend using Mark Williams' "Befriending" meditation online (Ko, 2016a), or find your own guided "Loving Kindness Meditation" on the Internet.
2. HeartMath breathing technique (HeartMath Institute, 2012): Read their description online as an introduction to this practice.
3. Emotional Journal: Write down at least three events/day in which you had a **positive or negative emotional response** to something. Note the event that caused the reaction, the reaction itself, and what you learned about yourself. The goal is to simply *observe* yourself; no need to try to change.

What's Next?

Don't worry! Take this one step at a time. In fact, growth in the spiritual life generally comes only when you are RELAXED. So, yes, class time will include a lot of academic learning, but in order for you to truly learn something useful for your life, I'm going to offer you the opportunity to let go of stress so that you can harmonize your body-mind-heart self. In my experience with students, the lowest level of impact will simply be that these practices will enable you to manage your stress better, which, given that this is the number one problem for HKIS students, is no small matter.

But understand that my ambitions for you this semester are actually far greater than simply developing mental health coping strategies, as important as they are. For most of you, this class is likely to be your most sustained study of world religions in your lifetime. All of us are trying to figure out what these different religions have spent millennia studying—how to lead a meaningful and satisfying life, both in its horizontal and vertical dimensions. My hope for you is that by the end of the semester you will have gained some insight into the big questions that religions address, such as:

- How can I become a happier human being?
- Does a spiritual world exist?
- What is the purpose of my life?
- How does one grow in the spiritual life?
- Do ancient religions have any wisdom to offer to modern people?

Of course, there are no guarantees that anything positive will happen, and your grade is never dependent on having certain kinds of "experiences" or coming to were quite balanced with the growth of your intellect, but over time your mental intelligence became highly developed, while your other intelligences atrophied. If I asked how many hours you have spent since birth training your brain, most of you would put the number well above 10,000. This qualifies you to be an expert, according to writer Malcolm Gladwell (2008), and our prestigious college acceptances confirm our efforts. But if I asked how many hours you've spent training your bodily intelligence, or how much time you've put into conditioning your heart to be in resonance with the vertical dimension, you would probably struggle to even comprehend the question!

World religions say that if you are primarily rooted in one center—your mind—then you are technically asleep! And when I look at students in my classes who are seated for six hours a day trying to develop mostly their minds, many of you indeed look rather tired and bored far more than anticipating the "joy of learning." Maybe we need a new approach!

So, the key understanding is that moving from sleep to a state of wakefulness requires a whole new way of being, one in which you pay more attention to your body and to your heart. Bringing a new awareness to your body-mind-heart will not only make you a more balanced person, but will over time, say these traditions, allow you to slowly access this Presence, and give you the opportunity to integrate the small and Large Selves. This is the path to becoming a fulfilled human being.

How Do We Start?

So what's the first step? The place to start is to interrupt your addictive preoccupation with things of the mind (think of your phone or computer!), and focus instead on the body and the heart. You reed to train your mind to pay attention to your bodily and emotional intelligences.

Your homework, then, is to choose a practice from below to begin your self-exploration.

Body Intelligence

1. Body scan: You may want to use Mark Williams' online program to guide your practice (Ko, 2016b).
2. Yoga: Find an online video to help you, such as the very gentle yoga stretches introduced by Stanford professor Kelly McGonigal (2014).
3. Food journal: Write down everything you eat and drink, and put each item into one of these three categories: healthy, passable, unhealthy.
4. Conscious Walking: Spend 10 minutes walking somewhere by yourself in which you try to focus on (1) your feet, (2) what you see, and (3) what

it is very conditional. If your persona is unmasked and your unairbrushed self revealed, your social world may reject you.

The world's religious traditions, by contrast, consider your persona or small self to be something of an imposter because it is a part that claims to be the whole. I hope you see that religion offers us a truly beautiful idea: your Larger Self, the true source of your identity, is a gift of unconditional love that lies secure in the vertical dimension. You don't try to earn it; you can only recognize, and therefore slowly receive it, as a gradually growing sense of self.

Actually, your true security comes from something that can't be won or lost. It simply *is*—and it is always available. You and I have this Presence within us, and religions across the world claim that it is our true source of identity and value. It's a gift to be accepted by anyone and everyone rather than a prize only available to a talented few. This does not mean that your small self is not precious in its own way. In everyday life you still get to fully develop all of who you are—your classes, extracurriculars and social life all still matter—but at the same time you don't get tricked into thinking that your personality is the most important part of you.

This semester as we study about four different world religions, I want to offer you the chance to explore this Larger Self. Is it actually possible that you can find some measure of true happiness inside yourself that lies outside of school and life achievements? Most of you have probably never considered this possibility because our school environment, like modern culture in general, doesn't teach you about the Larger Self.

Training Your Three Brains

How do you move from an exclusive focus on the small self to the possibility that a Larger Self exists? This is the most important question. World religions have an almost infinite variety of ways to help you let go of that small self and allow the Larger Self to be experienced. But most of us are never taught these things, so we have to start at the beginning.

Let's start with a proposal that comes from the inner Wisdom traditions in both Asia and the West about what it means to be an awakened human being. Humans are often thought to have three aspects—a body, a mind, and a heart. All three are what we might call "intelligences." You could even say that you have three brains—one in your gut, one in your heart, and of course the one in your head. In order to sense Presence, these three brains need to be sensitized and connected to each other.

The problem, of course, is that the vast majority of your time at school is focused on your mental intelligence. As a baby, your emotional life and physical body

The Two Selves

Just as there are two dimensions of the world *out there*, all world religions teach that similarly there are also two aspects of yourself *in here*. We can call the horizontal part of yourself the "small self," and the vertical part the "Larger Self." Your small self is all the parts of your personality—your strengths and weaknesses, likes and dislikes, gifts and interests. So much of school is about developing your small self—whether it's your academic subjects, your sports and clubs, or your social life. All those numbers that seem so important in high school—GPA, SAT, school rankings—are part of the small self. This is the self that you will put forward to college admissions. We at HKIS celebrate when students do really well in this system. This is obviously a very real and important aspect of who you are.

Religions say that honoring this part of yourself is well and good—as long as we realize its place in the scale of things; it's just the small self. But there is a Larger Self that offers a truer happiness that is not dependent on these horizontal achievements. Religions call this by different names: atman, the Buddha Nature, the soul, the image of God. The source of this Self is in the vertical dimension.

The Purpose of Religion

The purpose of religion, which literally means to "re-connect," is to offer each person the opportunity to combine the small self and the Larger Self into a unique personal expression of someone whose security is grounded in the unconditional Presence of God (or whatever you want to call this power) rather than simply your own personality.

The challenge is that modern society wants us to think that nothing else exists besides the small self. We are afraid that if we don't develop this small self into someone "important" or "valued" by society—in the form of making money, recognition of our talents, some respectable social status—then we will be considered a nobody or even a failure, someone who does not have value. If we fail to achieve as a student, we fear that we have amounted to nothing, a disappointment, and we'll suffer from the low opinion of others and, even worse, our own self-rejection. Students tell me that most HKIS students are quite insecure and feel threatened by low self-esteem because they just can't be "good enough" in the eyes of our culture that has such high expectations. This is what makes school so stressful for so many of us!

In addition, our culture trains us to think of ourselves as equal to our personalities. Actually, the word "personality" is linked to "persona," which in Latin refers to a theatrical mask. Your persona is the face you show to others, the role you play, which you act out in order to survive. But it usually is not who you really are. And the same conclusions as I present. Honesty and integrity are always the first priority. Skeptics welcome! So with that said, welcome to World Religions and I hope you enjoy your exploration this semester.

Student Responses

This chapter explains how I introduce the body-mind-heart framework in the context of a World Religions course. Early on, then, students understand that the main goal of the course is to give them the opportunity to become a more integrated and in touch version of themselves, primarily through body and heart-based practices. This culminates about two-thirds of the way through the course with the Spiritual Practices project, which I describe in Chapter 12. Here I present excerpts from three students whose final papers reflected on their two-week experience with a practice. These exemplars illustrate the power of spiritual practices in the context of the body-mind-heart framework.

1. Julia's mindful singing as a spiritual practice

   All my life I have been pressured to be great at singing and accomplish big things. For that little bit of time [during my spiritual practice], I let the pressure go and just sang to enjoy it. Not because I was trying to impress my family and friends. I thought about the words that I sang and nothing else, my mind was blank and the thing I could hear was my voice singing words I had never heard before. I felt like I was awakened and it was lovely . . . When I clear my mind from distractions while I sing, I connect my mind to my body. I do this by thinking of the notes and the length of time I need to hold them for then I connect that to my body by taking the right breath needed to support that note. Also, the note is projected by my vocal cords, so by thinking about that I am connected.

2. Moqiu's calligraphy practice of writing the Heart Sutra

   When I first started copying [in Chinese] the Heart Sutra, I was always nervous, and one of the challenges I had was over-reacting negatively when I thought a stroke didn't look aesthetically pleasant. Due to this, I would sometimes even hold my breath to prevent my breathing from making my hand shake. Throughout this entire project, I noticed that I used extremely shallow breaths, as my breathing correlated with the strokes I wrote, but these breaths changed from being nervous and caught to being steady and meditative once I started focusing on the concept of letting go and keeping in mind the actual message of the Heart Sutra. For my ending sessions, I found that I was able to concentrate entirely on the calligraphy and use my shallow breathing, which had once been a barrier in my path, to assist my hand movements and concentration. I went from only noticing the surface of the calligraphy I was writing to better understanding the teaching of the Heart Sutra and using the calming movements of calligraphy to move one step closer to the inner peace I hope to achieve.

3. Anton's use of photography as a spiritual practice

Calmly breathing in, while following the eagle gliding above me, holding down the trigger, snapping eight photos of the moving giant bird, looking down at the display, and seeing I got the perfect shot. A smile grew across my face, but I wanted one more photo, a better photo. This has become an addiction, going out every day for two weeks and taking photos. It all started off with a World Religions project focusing on calming my body down. This had become a great passion out of nowhere; I had become so into it . . . When I was standing on the top of the Dragon's Back taking photos, it would not matter if I were cool; nothing mattered when I was with myself. This was just what I wanted; I had been drawn into a world where there was no [interpersonal] drama.

CONCLUSION

What these experiences indicate is that the yin of inner awakening requires comprehensive, but relatively simple frameworks, as described in my explanation to students and accompanied by spiritual practices to match. When the Wisdom tradition's theory and practice come together in the context of studying the world's great religions, student growth arises as naturally as seeds emerging from soil. As Jesus puts it, "The kingdom of God is like a man who scatters seed on the ground. Night and day he sleeps and wakes, and the seed sprouts and grows, though he knows not how. All by itself the earth produces a crop" (Mark 4:26-28). "All by itself . . . he knows not how." In the Wisdom way of teaching, inspiration and energy arise often and simply. It seems we are trading in mysteries.

CHAPTER 11

WAKING UP TO THE VERTICAL DIMENSION

Student Reflections on a Practice-Based Religion Curriculum in Spiritual Explorations

The near absence of research on secular, school-based spirituality programs in youth reflects the general shortage of those types of interventions. This is an explorative time for spirituality.

—*Cobb et al.(2016, p. 253)*

Not only has World Religions provided me with insightful knowledge of the course material, it has also fueled me with the ambition to learn more about the benefits of spiritual practice in relation to religion and how it answers the basic human problem . . . I now believe it is quintessential to add spiritual practices to your life. It is a way to connect your physical body with your soul and in some ways, with the universe itself.

—*Joseph, grade 10 male student*

INTRODUCTION

At a curriculum meeting in December, 2016 a small group of my religion colleagues and I found ourselves taking steps that would in time prove decisive and impactful. In the short span of 45 minutes we dismantled our well-established and generally successful religion program and created an entirely new four-year framework.[1] The changes aimed to address students' developmental needs in a number of ways, particularly by more intentionally integrating wellness approaches into the curriculum. The new approach would make our religion classes more experiential and participatory throughout all four years of high school rather than the more academically-focused two-semester course requirement that students had previously taken. These new religion courses, we envisioned, would be part of a larger wellness block,[2] which would seek to make connections between curricula from three departments—PE (the body), counseling (the mind), and religion (the heart)—to support the whole-person development of our students.

It felt like a gamble. We had no prototypes for creating such religion courses, and—as the first epigraph attests—research in this area is nearly non-existent, yet the experiences of students like Joseph suggested that a new practice-based approach might be both efficacious and genuinely welcomed. Of perhaps greater concern, we had no idea if our group of religion instructors, each manifesting their own distinct strengths and spiritual vantage points, could pull together and implement a coherent curriculum aimed at spiritual growth. All of us were by turns excited and apprehensive about the prospect, and some of us, myself included, advocated at one point for postponing the course until after another year of preparation. Yet, in the end it seemed that the fundamental appeal of an integrated body-mind-heart wellness block would not be turned back.[3]

INTRODUCING SPIRITUAL EXPLORATIONS

Then came the hard work: how do we create a curricular structure to wake up young people to the spiritual dimension of life? We gathered for several sessions

---

[1] We chose to discard our two required semester courses, World Religions and Biblical Traditions, in favor of this new curriculum. Appendix D provides an overview of the four-year Spiritual Explorations curriculum in its current form.

[2] A new wellness block was created in student schedules for the 2017–2018 school year that combined PE, counseling, and religion courses. Specifically, grade 9 PE, a counseling course called "Seminar," and religion's "Spiritual Explorations" were integrated into a new wellness period in students' timetables. The goal of the wellness curriculum is to enable students to gain physical, mental, emotional, and spiritual well-being in their lives. By so doing we hope students will demonstrate increased self-knowledge and resilience, and greater capacity to make informed decisions about their future beyond HKIS.

[3] While wellness and well-being had been frequent discussion points at HKIS for some years, the speed with which this change was implemented from a small group discussion in early December to becoming a pivot for scheduling the following year's freshmen and teacher timetables by mid-January was striking. It seemed that once this potential curricular change was broached, it became an obvious and necessary step for student well-being. In short, the wellness block was an idea whose time had come.

Religion Teachers Meet to Construct the New Spiritual Explorations Curriculum. Jeremy Seehafer, second from the right, made the suggestion to include a spiritual practice in every class, which proved to be a turning point in our pedagogical approach.

during the spring semester as a teaching team to brainstorm and begin to assemble a curriculum for inner awakening. One of our early discussion points was what to call this series of courses. For some time we considered naming them "Spiritual Formation" courses, but eventually we decided on "Spiritual Explorations," the abbreviated form of which—SPEX —not only had a nice ring to it, but also associated openness with seeing clearly. The most important point of agreement occurred when one of our teachers, Jeremy Seehafer (whose reflections on this process are included in Chapter 17), suggested that every SPEX class should include a spiritual practice. To my surprise, everyone was in agreement—and a new paradigm of spiritual education was launched!

Would it work? Not until we received our first student papers eight weeks into the initial Grade 9 course did we know how students were responding to the new structure. What follows in this chapter is my analysis of reading those papers from my two SPEX classes over Chinese New Year holiday in February, 2018. Thus, my commentary below comes from those initial impressions of creating the SPEX 9 curriculum and the first student responses. At the end of the chapter, I reflect on the curricular process from the vantage point of having now completed teaching the four-year curriculum for the first time.

THE SPEX APPROACH

In the past year our SPEX team of five teachers has gathered regularly to construct a curriculum that invites our students to cultivate a more meaningful and balanced life. Starting from a blank slate was daunting, but enthusiasm was high. We were

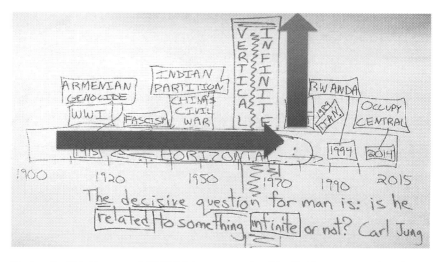

During the Third Lesson of SPEX 9 I Attempt to Graphically Demonstrate That the Spiritual Life Involves Considering Another Plane of Reality Than Our Normal Existence. Photo credit: Author

embarking on what we felt even at the onset was a bold new path that held real promise.

Through our discussions and planning, we came to envision three aspects of the SPEX curriculum that would make it a departure from conventional academic instruction. First, since SPEX meets only about once a week, the goal of each class would be focused on a dynamic experiential theme. For example, the first class introduces the overall SPEX 9 aim of Waking Up. We show a video rendition of David Foster Wallace's famed graduation speech *This is Water* (Mosley, 2014) and then ask students to put this into practice by doing a conscious walk through campus during the period. In the third class I want my students to remember one of the most important SPEX concepts, the *vertical dimension* of reality. After a brainstorming session with students on the whiteboard about important historical events of the 20th century, subconsciously priming them to think in conventional linear, or "horizontal," time, I turn the conversation with Carl Jung's claim, "The decisive question for [humans] is this: [are they] related to something infinite or not. That is the telling question of [their lives]" (Whitmont, 1979, p. 289). Then I dramatically draw a vertical bar through the horizontal timeline to visually demonstrate that religion aims to investigate a whole other plane of reality that can be called the "vertical dimension." Students then engage in dialogue involving 40 key questions about whether they believe in such an invisible dimension.[4] The

---

[4] See theme 1 and Appendix C for a fuller explanation of this activity.

goal, then, is to create something of an *event* rather than lead a series of content-based activities.

Second, each class includes a spiritual practice, which usually means some form of mindfulness. Their homework, too, is mostly practice-oriented. Students will be assigned a practice—say, the Loving Kindness Meditation—and practice it several times before the next class. We might ask students to express gratitude for unacknowledged blessings, or to smile at someone whom they usually don't engage with in this way. Fundamental here is the aim of engaging spiritual content in a way that advances overall student wellness.

A third unique feature of SPEX classes is that as a pass-fail course, grades are nearly inconsequential. Our teaching team designed four major assignments, which we call "summatives," that SPEX 9 students need to complete at a "pass" level:

1. Summative #1: Paper summarizing students' spiritual and religious background and learnings from the first unit.
2. Summative #2: Class presentation about a visit to a worship site in Hong Kong. (With COVID-19, the team changed this summative to one in which students interview a person who is deeply committed to a faith tradition or, possibly, humanism, existentialism or some other non-theistic belief system.)
3. Summative #3: Small group reflection in which students share their 10-day experience of doing a spiritual practice. (This project is the focus of Chapter 12.)
4. Summative #4: A final video in which students describe the SPEX 9 course to incoming 8th grade students and share their overall learnings from the course.

In contrast to their academically-oriented courses, these summatives were designed purposefully with their well-being in mind and are not graded on a comparison basis with other students. All three aspects—event-oriented, practice-based, and grade-neutral—are significant features of the approach.

TEACHING STUDENTS HOW TO WAKE UP

In January of 2018, we rolled out our first unit, "It's Time to Wake Up!" The key themes and activities are explained below:

1. The first step on the spiritual journey is to wake up to a different perception of lived reality. We use a video version of David Foster Wallace's commencement address *This is Water* (Mosley, 2014) in which he explains that we are like fish that don't know what water is.

2. All pre-modern cultures believed in the existence of a vertical (spiritual) aspect of life that is infinite, more powerful, and more beautiful than the horizontal (material) plane of daily life.
3. Religion uses powerful metaphors to talk about this vertical dimension and what it means to live at the intersection of the horizontal and the vertical: a burning bush, a staircase, a repaired pot (in Japanese, *kintsukuroi* pottery).
4. Our beliefs about the vertical dimension are greatly influenced by our upbringing—our family and cultural background—especially the religious practice and spiritual orientation of our grandparents and parents.
5. A major obstacle that prevents many of us from aligning with one of the universal messages of the world's religions—that each of us is of infinite value—is a self-denigrating voice called the Inner Critic that tells us that we are not good enough.
6. We break out of habitual horizontal autopilot behaviors and open to the vertical by cultivating the intelligences of the body, mind, and heart.
7. These intelligences can be trained through regular spiritual practice, such as meditation, conscious walking, Loving Kindness Meditation, body scans, and gratefulness activities.
8. All of us are on a spiritual journey navigating our way through one of three stages: constructing a faith or belief system (which may include scientism, atheism, or agnosticism); deconstructing in part or whole what we were taught/received; or reconstructing a worldview that fits our new experience of reality.

These eight themes were the essential elements of the first eight class periods.

THEMES OF STUDENT ESSAYS

To close out the first unit, we asked students to write a paper for their first summative in which they answered a series of questions related to these themes. To see if the first unit of SPEX was truly hitting the desired target, I analyzed the papers, distilling their insights into six themes. Each theme is introduced with my interpretation of student perceptions and then followed by a series of student quotes illustrating my analysis.

Theme 1: A Sense of Orientation and Spiritual Direction

The student essays make it clear that our 14- and 15-year-old students have received many conflicting messages about what to believe about religion and spirituality. While many have some religious background in their families, the majority of these students seem to have lost the positive dimensions of their tradition. Other students, perhaps equal in number to those with some religious heritage,

Elizabeth (left), Alix (middle), and Hannah (right) Engage in an Animated Conversation About Their Views of the Horizontal and Vertical Dimensions of reality. Photo credit: Author.

have been raised in an atheist or agnostic background and have had little direct exposure to religion.

The key ideas that we introduce in this unit, especially the horizontal and vertical dimensions and the emphasis on using body-mind-heart practices to help students cultivate their own spiritual beliefs, have provided a map-like orientation which enables students to directly participate in what often is called the "spiritual journey." The key activity is student conversations in small groups of 40 questions investigating their beliefs concerning the horizontal and vertical dimensions. Following these engaging conversations, students respond individually to these same 40 questions in a diagnostic questionnaire format[5] that allows them to place themselves in one (or a combination) of five categories:

1. Committed horizontalist: those who firmly believe only in a material world
2. Agnostic horizontalist: those who believe in a material world, but are open to the possibilities of a vertical dimension
3. Traditional vertical: those who find their beliefs consistent with the teachings of an established religion (e.g., Christianity, Hinduism, Buddhism)
4. Fading vertical: those raised in a traditional religion, but who now find that they are questioning their beliefs
5. Progressive vertical: those who question the traditional views of a given religion, but who have come to find the teachings "true" in some other way, usually symbolically.

This fairly simple, open-ended laying out of a "playing field" has been easily grasped by students and has invited them to engage in profound questions on not

---
[5] See Appendix C for the worksheet that we give to students.

just an intellectual level, but even more so at the level of direct experience. The following comments illustrate these points:

- **Female student (1):** Being in Humanities I in Action and Spiritual Explorations I think I now have a grasp of what I want my life to be like. I used to be very ungrateful, selfish, and full of hate. Learning from Humanities I in Action, I don't want to live in the horizontal world. In my eyes, it is filled with greed, envy, hate, materialism, and competition. I used to only be in the horizontal world. In my eyes, the vertical world is loving, accepting, and full of forgiveness. I think that learning about spirituality and the real world has helped me in rebuilding my life. I now want to do service, make others happy, and be a forgiving person.
- **Female student (2):** Soon I decided that I wasn't much of a religious person, just a spiritual one. I'm at the early stage of reconstruction right now, because my mind is evolving. Knowledge is power, and the more I learned about the world, the more I became sure of myself and my inner being. I don't quite know what I am, but I know that I'm on the journey to figuring it out. This semester, I think my biggest goal is to just absorb information like a sponge. Making decisions about my spirituality can only result from sufficient knowledge, and I definitely don't have enough.
- **Male student (3):** This spiritual unit has really made me reflect about who I am as a person, and question the spiritual practice I have been living with for many years. The practice that has been THE most useful is no doubt meditation at school, home or practically anywhere where I can do it. This makes me think about the non-materialistic things about life and how I can improve on the deeper things in life . . . The goal I am going to set is to meditate at least three times a week, as it helps me find myself at times of trouble and, ultimately, keep myself calm. I will not only use this practice, but keep in consideration all of the things I have learned in class!

Theme 2: New Insights into the Spiritual Life

The combination of laying out a field of exploration and then giving learners the opportunity to start exploring resulted in genuine spiritual insights in the papers. The comments that follow are the most incisive ones in the two classes. However, many others wrote convincingly about their intentions to learn more about the vertical dimension, or experience greater relaxation through spiritual practice. Nearly every paper showed respect for and curiosity toward this supposed invisible dimension of reality that all past cultures before our own have claimed as true and accessible. Even the students who identified themselves as "committed horizontalists" stated that they were open to spiritual growth, but simply had had no exposure or experience with something beyond the material world.

It is indeed quite surprising that in only eight class periods, which included one period for writing and peer review, that students could make such insightful remarks. Here are some of the most striking student observations:

- **Male student (4):** Everything in the world needs balance [of your body, mind, and heart], especially your life . . . Unfortunately, the society we live in today is unbalanced, which messes up the balance of your own life. School is primarily focused on strengthening the mind, sometimes the body, but practically never the heart. This is a particularly devastating issue, because the heart is arguably the most important of the three. When I'm really old and about to die, I don't want to know how to solve quadratic equations or all the comma rules, but instead be surrounded by people I love. Strengthening the mind is a great practice, but if it's not balanced with the other two it'll end up doing more harm than good.
- **Female student (5):** Talking about my past beliefs made me think about what I used to believe in, reminding me of the importance of faith. Therefore, I think that I am in the "fading vertical" phase but simultaneously "fading horizontal" phase due to the faint return of my faith. Just after a few weeks of SPEX, I already think that I have a new insight; I should focus on the vertical dimension more. To do so, I need to concentrate on my body and heart more by walking and eating consciously, and become more present to the moment. In conclusion, I should become more present and take care of my body and heart better.
- **Female student (6):** In the end, I have learned more about myself from the past few classes. I have learned that I am very much a spiritual person more than I am religious. I want to keep on learning more about this and learning about myself. I want to work on connecting more with my heart and my body instead of just using my mind. I want to continue to learn how [to] shut off autopilot and my brain when I am not in school. I want to connect to the vertical dimension more and more. I want to bring myself to living fully in both worlds at all time. I want to keep on learning about me.

It seems that the most central course concepts—horizontal vs. vertical dimensions, body-mind-heart framework—had a discernible impact upon a good number of students. Some who had adopted an atheist or agnostic worldview seemed open and explicitly curious to hear more about this invisible realm.

Theme 3: Gratitude for Time to Make Sense of Life

One unexpected theme in the papers was a sense of gratitude or perhaps relief that the school was providing time for this kind of exploration that students would like to engage in but feel they just can't find time for in their busy schedules. Even for students who have no particular interest in religion, having time to slow down, reflect, and do some kind of relaxation practice was welcome, and seemed for many to be a source of renewal during their day.

- **Female student (7):** I was extremely grateful for Spiritual Explorations and the part of the class that was scheduled JUST for meditation, meaning I wouldn't have to make an effort to plan to do it later on in my day. I especially enjoyed the Loving Kindness Meditation because it allowed me to be aware of and spread kindness toward myself, and even some people who I may not be getting along with. This part of the meditation really made me feel at peace . . . As of now, I believe my spiritual beliefs are in the process of reconstruction, as I am actively using resources such as this class to investigate the spiritual realm, as well as to fortify or create a new foundation for myself.
- **Female student (8):** Having time to think, to take a breath, it's also helped me heal. One of the reasons why I'm thankful for spirituality class is because it teaches me to have a balanced life. I never have any time to use my other brains, which is why I think my "starting over" point was so hard to cross. I only ever really used my mind, and never my heart. Because of this I didn't know how to heal when my heart was broken . . . I hope that with SPEX I'll learn more about the life I want to reconstruct for myself, I'll start to build the stairs up to the door, and I'll learn how to have balance in my life.
- **Male student (9):** Spiritual Explorations has clearly helped me to live a better life for the time being, as I have reflected more and noticed more. However, I think the most important thing for me going into the future is to ensure that I keep up with some of the things that we do in this class, whether it be the conscious walking or the short meditations. Every time we learn something in any class or even outside of school, it can feel extremely temporary. For the rest of the semester I'm really hoping that what we do in class lasts instead of just fading away over the years.

Theme 4: Positive Impact of Spiritual Practice

The most common theme of all was that students were already beginning to reap the benefits of spiritual practice in their lives. The most beneficial practice was conscious walking in which they attempted to break out of their hurried, getting-from-point-A-to-point-B routine and instead observe the natural beauty of our outdoor campus or note its award-winning architectural design. Even for me as a teacher who has implemented these practices for the last six years in World Religions, the impact upon students, especially boys, of something so simple as mindful walking[6] in such a small number of classes has exceeded any expectation I had.

- **Male student (10):** I think my favorite and most impactful practice so far this year would be the conscious walking. I had heard about this before from parents, friends etc., but I never had the urge to do it. When I was forced to do it by Mr. Schmidt, I was amazed by the results. I was asked to walk around the school (places I've been to hundreds of times) and just be aware of my surroundings. The first time I did this, I focused on other people. While I was doing my conscious walking, I came across a lady in the noodle shop just outside the cafeteria. It was January and freezing outside and all she had was an apron and a short sleeve shirt. I immediately felt a large sense of empathy when I realized how cold she was. Although I didn't do anything at the time because we had to return to the classroom, this experience showed how there are many small things you can do to make a person's day. With the conscious walking, I looked at things from a different perspective. I was able to drift away from the autopilot mindset that I am often fixated on. I believe that doing activities such as these can make an enormous impact on becoming your best future self.
- **Male student (11):** The way I perform conscious walking is using my experience of walking as the center of my attention. I am aware of what happens outside. Awareness of objects, the wind, the sun and the rain, but also the sounds of nature, people, cars. This allows me to be in a vulnerable state of mind, which unlocks the possibility of entering the divine world . . . My goal is to utilize the body, mind, and heart plus spiritual practices to attain a balance between the finite and infinite world during the remainder of the course, allowing me to progress on my spiritual journey.
- **Male student (12):** In this [mindful walking] exercise we first did some meditation and then walked outside to all of our classes in our schedule in slow motion. Doing this I noticed things I never see when going to my classes as I am either with my friends or on my phone. I was almost confused not knowing what to do or what to pay attention to. This made me realize that sometimes I need to pause and look at my surroundings and see what's around me. This helps you achieve a balanced and healthy life as you are no longer following the same routine, you get to pay attention to your body and mind. You get to push your thoughts away and think about

---

[6] I continue to be struck three years later by how many students, especially boys who seem to benefit most from the physicality of the practice, value conscious walking. Stanford neuroscientist Andrew Huberman (2021) discusses in his new podcast series how viewing nature scenes, even at a distance, destresses the body. When the act of walking is added, the process of moving forward turns on the dopamine reward system, which helps students tackle challenges they face, such as getting their homework done. Finally, he explains that any activity that creates horizontal eye moment, such as walking, also destresses the body. Many students are genuinely surprised to discover the therapeutic value of the simple activity of taking a walk.

the present time instead of the past or future. This helps you lead a very healthy life.

Other students benefited from the sitting meditation that we did in class or that they have done as homework, especially the Loving Kindness Meditation (LKM):

- **Female student (13):** A few things in SPEX that has helped me realize how much easier it is being in touch with the vertical world is the LKM and the mindfulness walk. With the LKM, I realized how much easier it is to heal when I only exude forgiveness and love. With the mindfulness walk, sometimes I would take it as a time to reflect. I think reflecting on my "past life" will help me rebuild my new one.
- **Male student (14):** I also think the 3 minute breathing exercise has really helped me and been the most beneficial to me. This breathing exercise has been used in many places for me. Sometimes when I think about something and get mad, I stop for a second and just breathe, I would do this exercise and it would calm me down. Another use of this exercise is when I'm trying to go to sleep. It only takes me three minutes of just breathing for me to fall asleep.
- **Female student (15):** I don't know why but this [LKM] practice brings me a sense of peace and happiness.
- **Female student (16):** I have found that both meditation and conscious walking have helped me become more optimistic about life in general after only doing it a few times.

Given that our fundamental commitment in the course is to provide time in every class for spiritual practice, it is indeed deeply affirming that students valued these experiences in even the initial unit of this four-year program; this portends well for the cumulative benefits that we expect lie ahead.

Theme 5: Dampening of the Inner Critic

During the fifth lesson I explain that a universal message in the world's religions is that each person is of infinite value. What pulls us out of this realization for most people in modern society is a voice in our heads that says we are not good enough to meet the "standard" in so many areas. This voice can be called the Inner Critic (explored in Chapter 16). Although this concept was taught for just one class period, a surprising number of students picked up on this theme as significant to their self-perception as they dealt with this problem by doing the LKM.

During that class period in which I introduced the concept of the Inner Critic, one female student wrote that she had no personal identity apart from her Inner Critic. Heartbreakingly, she even wrote that she wasn't worth the breath that kept her alive. So, it was a great relief to see how her tone shifted in a subsequent comment a couple of weeks later: "I have been doing the LKM. I really enjoy this practice and it has helped greatly not only to silence my Inner Critic but to relax me. I haven't really seen a lot of my Inner Critic lately and I think that could be because of this practice."

Other students benefited a great deal even from this very brief treatment of the Inner Critic.

- **Female student (17):** Since 6th grade, I have my Inner Critic to make me think that I am not good enough and that I won't ever be. I have been criticizing myself badly for the whole of middle school, and I have finally started to stop once entering SPEX class . . . [Doing the LKM] reduced my believing what it [Inner Critic] was saying.
- **Female student (18):** I also want to learn to be more familiar with my Inner Critic. I want to know how the other Clara operates and how it negatively and positively impacts me. My Inner Critic will dwell within me forever and I think it's important to learn how to deal with it when it starts talking.
- **Male student (19):** Conscious walking has improved my self-confidence and subdued the Inner Critic which pervaded my mind before I began this spiritual practice.

Theme 6: Greater Life Balance and Less Stress

The number one complaint of HKIS students, and a widely discussed issue among teachers and parents as well, is that they are always stressed out. While this has been true at our school for years, there is good reason to suspect that the 24/7 inundation by technology more recently is keeping students, as predicted by the Wisdom tradition, ever more pre-occupied by the mind center, compounding their anxieties (Twenge, 2017). As a result, it appears that students are suffering from the effects of stress far more than in the past. Encouragingly, time and again students in our practice-oriented classes have noted how even a few minutes of conscious breathing, walking, drawing, eating, or other spiritual practices on a regular basis can shift their stress levels. To a remarkable and pervasive degree, students have embraced the need to balance their bodies, minds, and hearts, which they already are reporting brings some otherwise elusive calm into their lives.

- **Male student (20):** I want to use my mind, body, and heart through everything, in everything I do. I want to be a more spiritual intact person and be calm and unstressed with every challenge . . . Before [SPEX] I [was] always stressed and wondering how I would do the next assignment and when things were due. Now I still pay attention to those things, but I just am not stressing as much over it. I'm able to be more calm when a huge summative is coming up. That's what I feel like is the point of Spiritual Explorations: to be less stressed and more calm, while also being attentive, through connecting with my three minds and using all three.

138 • THE WISDOM WAY OF TEACHING

- **Male student (21):** A great spiritual practice that we use in class is in fact meditation. This helps me reconnect to the body, mind, and the spirit. I have been intending to have a balanced approach to life.
- **Female student (22):** The more times I do the exercise of meditation, I have been told by my family that there has been a change in my mood. Usually, I am stressed and negative about the people around me. However, I believe that the Loving Kindness Meditation has made me a calmer and kinder person.
- **Male student (23):** To me, the breathing space practice is the most useful. This practice is to breathe and take deep breaths and relax oneself. During the process, my stress and worries fade away. I feel relieved and more relaxed. For example, I was stressing about the summative the following day and feel afraid of it, even though I took time studying for it. But after the breathing space, I feel like "I got this" "don't worry," etc.

We as SPEX teachers are thrilled to see such comments, and it is indeed quite surprising that grade 9 students are able to speak articulately about their spiritual identity after only eight class periods. In the student responses, we see real readiness to engage in issues of deep interiority in their freshmen year of high school. Of course, this is not to claim that students were in some way fundamentally transformed, but the findings do demonstrate that they were developmentally prepared to engage in surprisingly mature spiritual reflection.

CONCLUSION (WRITTEN IN 2018)

Several years ago HKIS religion teachers met and reimagined the religious education program. To our surprise, the school quickly embraced the concept, which re-organized student schedules for the coming year, combining periods for PE, Counseling, and SPEX into a new wellness block, a comprehensive curricular change that took effect with lightning speed. I attribute its swift acceptance to the intuitive sense among our school administration and faculty that we needed a program that intentionally integrates the body, mind, and heart of our students. Even as it happened, it felt like a once-in-a-generation opportunity to re-orient school life towards something beyond its primary academic focus.[7] At the start there was significant uncertainty about how rapidly to proceed. With such high stakes, some of us, myself included, felt it should be delayed to allow more time to develop the materials. Thus, exploring the papers has brought no small measure of relief that our curricular gamble of employing a practice-based approach is paying off, affirmed the underlying intuition that the time was ripe for change.

---

[7] This comment is in no way intended to denigrate the role of intellectual exploration in general or its role in the spiritual life in particular, but rather to reposition the life of the mind in a concerted interplay with the body and the heart. One of our next steps in curriculum development is to create additional courses outside the four-year SPEX curriculum that do strengthen the intellectual domain of the study of faith and spirituality.

Over the next three years SPEX will expand to grades 10, 11, and 12, so that in three years' time all 750+ students will have nearly 20 experientially-based classes a year focused on strengthening their spiritual lives. This only increases our resolve to return to the papers and lesson plans, confident that we are easing the burdens of our students and helping them to discover a holistic orientation to life that offers them happier, healthier, and more meaningful experiences throughout their high school careers.

REFLECTION (WRITTEN IN 2021)

Now reflecting on the creation and implementation of the SPEX program several years later, the crystalizing event in my memory is that of Jeremy making the unexpected suggestion during an early planning session that every class include a spiritual practice, which the teaching team endorsed wholeheartedly. This decision reflected a paradigm shift: we were willing to stake the success or failure of the program on whether a practice-based, body-and-heart engaged pedagogy would accomplish our aims better than the previous mind-centric paradigm. The student responses, as well as evident teacher enthusiasm, validate that we made the right call.

Given this experience with our SPEX classes, I am in full agreement with Glanzer et al.'s (2017) findings in their study *The Quest for Purpose: The Collegiate Search for a Meaningful Life*. In the book's conclusion, they remark:

> Focusing on having conversations may mean we do not ask students to engage in *practices beyond discourse that may prove transformative* in helping students discover their purpose. What we found is that students often discovered their purpose and meaning by engaging in such practices. Rarely did this kind of transformative participatory experience occur in the classroom. In fact, one of the noteworthy things we did not find, when asking students about their curricular life, were courses that encouraged students to *examine their own practices and not merely their thinking*. (p. 333, italics mine)

Our SPEX courses do exactly what the authors suggest: we ask students to focus on their practices—both in and out of class—as the most important part of the curriculum. From surveys we do at the end of each SPEX course, we know that students' favorite and most impactful aspects of the courses are the practices, be they more traditional forms such as meditation or simple action-oriented practices like cleaning one's room. Our experience with the SPEX curriculum is in striking alignment with the Wisdom tradition, which emphasizes the essential roles of the body and heart intelligences in spiritual growth, while cautioning frequently about the overreliance on the mental domain. Moving from a mind-centered teaching style to a body-mind-heart integrated pedagogy was the fundamental paradigm shift that teachers and students have come to embrace in the SPEX courses to much positive effect.

CHAPTER 12

TEACHING TOWARD INNER AWAKENING THROUGH A SPIRITUAL PRACTICES PROJECT IN SPEX

People seldom understand the power of repetition. What is repeated over and over can become enduring; what is done in a moment is seldom lasting. If farmers do not tend to their fields every day, they cannot expect a harvest. The same is true of spiritual practice. It is not the grand declaration or the colorful initiation that means anything. It is only the daily living of a spiritual life that has meaning.

—*Deng Ming-Dao (n.d.)*

The issue that I struggle with the most with my personality is self-love . . . I found this [Loving Kindness] meditation to be very effective. I did it every day—once a day for 10 minutes—for 12 days, either in the morning or at night. It helped me sleep better, and started off my day in a better mood and mindset. I found myself stopping myself whenever I would begin to have negative thoughts. For example, if I was having a bad day at school and would start feeling bad about myself, I would realize and be aware of these negative thoughts and stop myself from thinking this way. This is a result of the meditation working on my subconscious.

—*Kiki, grade 11 female student*

INTRODUCTION

When I first began teaching World Religions nearly a decade ago, I wondered if there could be a yin of inner awakening pedagogical strategy equivalent to the bubble-bursting, social conscience-creating Jungsing Orphanage experience in Humanities I in Action (Chapter 4). The first inkling that I might be onto something came in 2012 when I asked students to design and implement their own spiritual practice, and report out on what they had learned four days later. What seemed like a small, insignificant assignment yielded far more insights than I could have imagined. Since that time, I have gradually expanded this assignment to include ten practices over two weeks in all my religion classes. I have come to see that just as the trip to the orphanage is the most powerful means by which to kindle student sensitivity to the yang of social conscience, it seems—to my even greater surprise— that student engagement with spiritual practices is the most reliable path towards the yin of inner awakening. Thus, this chapter explains how teachers lead students in engaging with spiritual practices in the SPEX classes, culminating in a two-week Spiritual Practices project.

TEACHING SPIRITUAL PRACTICES

Leading up to the Spiritual Practices project, SPEX teachers introduce various spiritual practices in their lessons. One of the growth areas for SPEX teachers, then, is how to lead such practices, certainly an area which we were never trained in. Here are some practical tips we have gained through our experience about how to lead practices in a classroom setting:

1. The most important factor is that teachers themselves have developed a comfort level with a range of spiritual practices in their own personal lives, which in time makes sharing them with students far more authentic.
2. Some teachers start the period with a practice to set a more contemplative mood at the beginning, while others embed the practice later in the lesson to reinforce the theme. One teacher, Simone (whose articulate reflection on teaching SPEX can be found in chapter 17), starts every class in a greeting circle, simply asking every student to share what is on their mind or heart. I've adopted this practice recently with smaller classes, and it's been very effective.
3. SPEX teachers frequently use online audios provided by Mark Williams, the founding director of the Oxford Mindfulness Center (Williams and Penman, 2011). His 3-minute breathing space, 8-minute breath and body practice, and 15-minute body scan are all part of our repertoire. The 3-minute breathing space is my most frequently used practice in my SPEX classes.
4. While these online audios are very serviceable, part of SPEX teachers' growth has been to gain facility in leading practices themselves. One of our teachers, in fact, ended his final SPEX 12 class a few months ago by

Teaching Toward Inner Awakening • 143

leading a practice using a script he wrote, saying proudly, "Look at all of us! After four years you can easily sit through a meditation practice and I can now lead one. We've all been on a journey!"

5. Some students, especially boys, prefer not to close their eyes during a meditation period. And certainly some will use the time to make eye contact with other students or try to sneak a peek at their phones. What should a teacher do? My approach has been to join those classes—closing my eyes and participating fully—that I can trust will do the practice without much supervision, while with the other groups, I position myself at strategic points in the classroom with "one eye open" to keep the squirrely students more focused.

6. I also have meditation cushions in my room so that students can lie down on the floor during the meditation time, although COVID-19 has made students far more reticent to lay on the floor.

7. While meditation is the most practical spiritual practice to use for a SPEX class, I always keep in mind the possibility of using other more active practices, such as conscious walking (out of the classroom), simple tai chi, touching acupuncture points for stress relief, rock stacking, etc. In SPEX 12 we brought in a tai chi teacher for a class period, which was well-received by students. One of our growth areas is to develop practices that are more movement-based.

8. If we introduce a new practice that comes from a specific tradition (e.g., om chanting from Hinduism), we assure students that there is no attempt to "convert" anyone to become a member of that faith tradition. Furthermore, we say if for some reason such a practice makes a student feel uncomfortable in relationship to their own faith tradition, of course there is no pressure to participate in any way. Our experience is that as long as we are sensitive to students' preferences and give them permission to opt out of any practice, students feel comfortable with our multi-tradition approach.

9. We have also incorporated more drawing or doodling practices (sometimes called "Zentangle") recently. Near the end of the first half of SPEX 10 after having had six classes in a row on various aspects of the self (e.g., open, hidden, blind, unknown, interconnected, etc.), we put on some calming music and give students half an hour to draw/doodle on an A3 piece of paper with the course themes about the self scattered across the sheet. Following this relaxed and creative extended quiet time, we then ask students to conclude the class by writing a reflection in their journal about their takeaways about themselves.

10. Our team is currently debating whether we should teach a progression of mindfulness skills along with a set of "standard" practices. At this point we have not put in place any kind of "developmental" path of spiritual practices; teachers choose practices that they are comfortable with as they see fit.

INTRODUCING THE PROJECT

I introduce the Spiritual Practices project, summative #3 in the SPEX 9 course, in the context of teaching a one-period lesson on the four spiritual paths of Hinduism. To set a Hindu temple-like atmosphere in my classroom, students take off their shoes at the door and enter into a room with a candle-lit shrine on ceremonial cloths surrounded by meditation cushions. After I explain that the goal is in no way to make students Hindu, but rather to appreciate the strengths of this faith tradition (as we will do in succeeding weeks for Buddhism, Judaism, Christianity, and Islam), we discuss the four paths of Hinduism in terms of the body-mind-heart framework. I explain that the great insight of Hinduism is that different personality types seek to integrate the horizontal and vertical dimensions into their lives in different ways. Students learn that there are distinct forms of yoga to develop each element in the framework.

1. BODY—Karma Yoga: For active, body-oriented types who like to accomplish physical tasks or do service.
2. MIND—Jnana Yoga: For reflective, mind-centered types for whom ideas are powerful and alive.
3. HEART—Bhakti Yoga: For emotional, heart-attuned types who are drawn to love, relationships, and devotion.
4. MEDITATION—Raja Yoga: For spiritual, holistic types who want to find the Larger Self through various spiritual practices.

In light of these teachings which attempt to match personality types with certain practices, I explain that each student will pick and implement a specific practice over the next two weeks with the aim of benefiting their spiritual life. I also mention that for most students this project is the highlight of the course. Then I distribute the following assignment sheet.

SUMMATIVE #3: SPIRITUAL PRACTICES PROJECT

You should find this experiential project both interesting and personally beneficial! You are to individually explore and implement a spiritual practice of your choice. Just as athletes or musicians need practice to develop their skills, so we also need to practice integrating our body-mind-heart selves in order to experience various benefits in our lives. While up until this point in the course we have been using specific spiritual practices in each class to help you understand yourself better, now we want you to choose a practice to help better balance yourself and open yourself up to the vertical dimension. This may be a practice we have already tried in class, another practice listed below, or one you create yourself in consultation with your teacher.

Follow These Steps:

1. Personality Reflection: Consider whether you are a body, mind, or heart type, and think about if you would like to strengthen one of these areas, or address an aspect of your body-mind-heart self that has been underdeveloped.
   - As you think about your body-mind-heart self, what are the core problems/issues that you are hoping that your spiritual practice can address, such as a positive behavior that you want to develop more fully (e.g., compassion, openness, peace, hope, living in the present, exploration of a potential vertical dimension) or an area of concern (e.g., anxiety, moodiness, self-focus, superficiality, an overactive Inner Critic, emotion-driven behavior)?
   - What practice would you like to choose and why? What is your intention?
2. Spiritual Practice Background: Research your particular practice. If it comes from a religious tradition, research how it moves practitioners from the horizontal to the vertical dimension, or seeks to integrate both dimensions? How does it bring about personal peace or inner aliveness? (If you create your own practice, then you don't need to do this step.)

Given these considerations, you are to propose a spiritual practice which:

- Can be done alone a minimum of 10 times over the next two weeks.
- Involves creativity on your part in designing the activity.

Best place to start: What kind of spiritual practice would you like to do?

TABLE 12.1. List of Spiritual Practices for the Spiritual Practices Project

Brewing and Drinking Tea	Gratitude Journal / Letters	Phone Deprivation
Calligraphy	Guided Meditations	Playing an Instrument
Chanting	Hiking/Walking in Nature	Poetry Writing
Coloring	Intentional Acts of Kindness	Pre-meal Prayers
Daily Prayer Recitation	Intentional Isolation/Silence	Social Media Detox
Daily Scripture Reading	Making/Giving a Gift	Stretching
Doing a Chore (e.g., washing dishes)	Mindful Eating / Drinking	Tai Chi
Drawing/Painting/Artistic Creation	Mindful Listening to Music	Walking / Caring for a Pet
Gardening/Planting	Mindful Walking/Movement	Yoga
Giving Compliments	Mindfulness Training via an App	Zentangle
Giving Someone a Hug	Nightly Journal ("3 Good Things")	Others?

SPIRITUAL PRACTICE LOG

Complete the "Spiritual Practice Log" (Figure 12.1) after each practice. Include documentary evidence, such as pictures, video, lyrics, etc., to demonstrate your engagement in a practice.

In preparation for your summative #3 small group discussion, consider these questions:

1. What practice did you do and why did you choose this practice? What aspect of yourself were you hoping to develop?
2. How did it go? Share high and low points of your practice. How effective was it? If your spiritual practice comes from a specific tradition, did you feel that your experience verified what the tradition claims about this practice or not?

SAMPLE STUDENT SPIRITUAL PRACTICES PROJECTS

Here is an array of spiritual practices projects from previous classes.

1. **Christian Prayer**: A student named James wrote a prayer that he recited twice a day and then allowed himself the opportunity during this prayer to add in his own thoughts and requests. While he questioned whether he even believed in God at the beginning of the project, by the end he felt that some kind of Higher Power had helped to modify his behavior and attitudes. (See excerpts of James' detailed log under "Student Project Reflection.")

Name	
What practice have you chosen?	
WHY have you chosen this practice? In what ways do you (your body, mind, and heart) hope to benefit from this practice?	

Date	Length of Time (in minutes)	Reflection	Documentary Evidence

FIGURE 12.1 Spiritual Practice Log

2. **Creating and Destroying a Mandala**: Adrienne did a mix of meditation (about 10 minutes) and drawing of mandalas (15 minutes or more), completing several of them through the 10 sessions. She felt calmer about life and very satisfied with her mandalas, even though she found it difficult to burn one of them in the end. However, she decided that she also wanted to ceremoniously burn a personal journal that she had written. She realized that there was a lot of emotional baggage in her writing and it felt like a relief to let it go. (See excerpts of Adrienne's detailed log under "Student Project Reflection.")

3. **Death Meditation:** Following the class visit of a Buddhist monk who meditated daily for 45 minutes on his own death, Zach attempted to do such a practice for 15–20 minutes/day. Although initially it was a struggle, by the third session Zach was able to escape his own initial uncertainty around how to do the practice and venture into areas he had never experienced. Through this practice, Zach, who saw himself as a "math-science" type, felt that for the first time he began to develop his own spiritual identity beyond the day-to-day horizontal dimension. The second outcome for Zach was that contemplating death helped him relax about his tests and homework and place his academic concerns into a larger life context.

4. **Gratitude Letters:** As a second semester senior, Jocelyn wanted to bring a sense of completion to her high school career by writing letters of gratitude. She began each note with a 3-minute meditation to center herself, and then hand-wrote letters to people whom she wanted to thank. This allowed her to think deeply about those who had made a big difference in her life. Another student, Celine, wrote letters to important people in her life and then cut the letters into extraordinarily elegant paper lace.

5. **Journaling:** Both Jade and Natasha had written their own journals in the past, but in this project they applied this technique as a spiritual practice. To prepare, Jade listened to the insights of Buddhist teacher Adyashanti (2012), and Natasha meditated (paradoxically) on the benefits of failure and the detriments of success. These practices reframed their journaling, enabling them to write with a previously unexperienced spaciousness. Both girls felt that this kind of writing provided them with a newfound ability to allow for the healthy flow of emotions.

6. **Painting**: A high-achieving student throughout high school, Claudia had struggled for years with stress-induced headaches. She chose painting as her spiritual practice so that she could rekindle a love for creating art that she had neglected throughout her high school career. While she initially approached painting as a way to distract her mind from stress, she came to understand that this practice required her to engage consciously with the physicality of painting through the processes of executing the strokes, listening to the sound of the brush on the canvas, and deciding on color.

Using painting as a therapy, she realized, was actually the opposite of distraction. Rather, she needed to fully engage her mind in the activity. Not only did she produce a stunning piece of art, but more importantly she came to see the therapeutic value of her latent talent for painting.

7. **Calligraphy with Loving Kindness Meditation:** Soobin started with a few minutes of Loving Kindness Meditation to calm herself, and then began writing Chinese characters that she found meaningful for 10–20 minutes. She felt that this practice helped her get a sense of the true purpose of calligraphy, which she understood to be imprinting herself with spiritual values.

8. **Drawing Global Problems:** Denise started with places that she likes to visit (e.g., a beach) and then imagined how climate change might affect these places. Through this practice she brought good intentions to global problems, such as hunger, war, religious conflict, and homelessness. The outcome of this project was that she felt very grateful for the peace and stability of her life that she usually takes for granted. In addition, she came to feel that she should do some kind of service work in the community.

9. **Eating Mindfully:** A female student of Indian heritage named Samiya performed a Hindu prayer before she ate her meals in order to eat more slowly and mindfully. She used a prayer from her tradition before her meals:

O lord Hari, you are the giver of food.
You are the enjoyer of food,
and you are the creator of food.
Therefore, I offer all that I consume at your lotus feet.

The highlight of the project was when Samiya went to a Christian student's home for Thanksgiving and felt an immense sense of gratitude for the food and friendship.

10. **Hindu Chanting:** A male student of Indian heritage named Sid chanted a 25-minute religious song called the Amritvani.[1] While initially he didn't feel any difference, by the third time and throughout the rest of

---

[1] While the majority of students try practices outside of their religious heritage, we strongly encourage students of all faiths to choose a practice from within their tradition to help them connect to their family, religious, and cultural traditions. One of our concerns at the onset about the SPEX course at a Christian school was that perhaps Christian students would feel threatened by this multi-tradition approach. My experience is that most, if not all, Christian students enjoy the SPEX classes and appreciate that they are encouraged to practice their faith during the spiritual practice project, some version of which occurs every year in SPEX. As a Christian teacher, I'm very happy to brainstorm creative practices to affirm students' Christian heritage. Given my experience with Cynthia's practice-based approach, I enthusiastically introduce Christian students to practices within their tradition, such as Centering Prayer or Lectio Divina, which most students have never heard of.

the sessions, he felt that the practice helped him become calmer, more focused, and in a better mood.
11. **Bathing gods:** Riana performed a variety of rituals in which she washed the gods at her family's Hindu shrine in her flat. She had always done these before with her mom, but for the first time she began to do the rituals for herself. What started as a required project without much meaning became an experience in which she felt more connected to her tradition and closer to God.
12. **Transcendental Meditation:** As an artist, Samantha came to this project with a desire to overcome the sense of being "stuck" in her creativity that she was experiencing in her senior year. Inspired by filmmaker David Lynch's enthusiastic endorsement of meditation, she did a daily 20-minute Transcendental Meditation practice. By the end of the project, Samantha felt that her art had begun to flow in ways that she hadn't experienced for some time, transforming her paintings from harsh and depressing images to flowing, flowery images of rebirth.

LOVING KINDNESS MEDITATION

This discussion would be incomplete without giving some attention to the Loving Kindness Meditation (LKM), which has proven to be among the most valued of the practices that we do. Emerging from the Buddhist tradition, the LKM focuses first on generating self-compassion, asking practitioners to say, for example, "May I be healthy and happy," "May I be filled with loving compassion," and "May I live in peace." Next this wish of loving compassion is applied to others, "May [a person] be healthy and happy," etc. One academic claims that there are 18 research-supported reasons to practice the LKM (Seppälä, 2014).

The following two comments come from students who used the LKM to help themselves with various life challenges. A female student named Nana, for example, describes how the LKM revived the most endearing aspects of her character:

> In any emotional situation, most people come to me for help because I give off a very caring and compassionate energy, or so I am told . . . In recent years, however, I have become less compassionate due to stress. I used to have a very sweet and bubbly character, especially to my parents, but in recent years I have lashed out at them and at other people that I normally would not have. I remember being very focused during the LKM. After the first meditation, I felt a change in my energy and my soul. I felt my old character revived; it was amazing. I got so many comments about my changed character from my peers. It was crazy to me that people around me could sense a change in my character that was motivated by a simple meditation. I made people happier around me because I was more compassionate due to meditating every day for 20 minutes. I became aware of how powerful the LKM is. I had a talk with Dr. Schmidt after class one day about loving kindness and it really hit me how life-changing this meditation can be.

Another powerful example comes from Natalia, a student who was deeply moved and distraught by her weekend experience at the Jungsing orphanage. To deal with this emotional disturbance, she used the LKM in combination with piano improvisation to help her through this "grieving process," which she describes as follows:

> On the first day I did an impromptu one-minute piano piece to express my feelings about the trip, which came out in a cold minor key. Then in the next eight sessions I did a LKM where I tried to imagine a utopia in the world where the orphans each had caring families to support them. The meditation really helped alleviate some of the guilt and shame that had accumulated by the end of the trip, and allowed me to gradually understand the perspectives of the parents who had abandoned the children. I told myself that I was going to love my family like the orphans would have if they had been given the chance, and was therefore able to have a positive takeaway from the experience. Then, for my last spiritual practice I wanted to see if there was a change in my emotions, as reflected in a second improvised musical composition. The second time was in a heart-warming major key.

STUDENT PROJECT REFLECTION

In the student project reflection, each student records their ten or more spiritual practices in their log and provides a brief reflection on each experience. Here I highlight the first two projects in the foregoing list to show through selective reflections how these students grew through the process.

1. **Christian Prayer (#1 above):** James comes from a Christian family, but he had a lot of doubts about whether he actually believed in God or not. To investigate this question, he wrote a prayer that he recited twice a day for total of ten minutes for 15 days. The following is a selection of his log entries:
   - **Day 1:** Since this was the first time doing my practice, I didn't really expect much. I just read the notecard and didn't think much of it.
   - **Day 2:** Tried again today, but didn't feel anything. I'm not really expecting much.
   - **Day 4:** Getting a little bit skeptical about this whole praying thing. It's still only the fourth time but still. Also, I think if the rest of the sessions continue to be like this, I might really reconsider my belief in Christianity or religion altogether.
   - **Day 6:** I'm not sure if this is just a placebo effect of prayer, but I think I'm thinking more optimistically.
   - **Day 7:** Today was a really tiring day because I had three tests. However, during my night prayer, I felt more energetic and peaceful. I slept well.
   - **Day 8:** I'm starting to feel the real power of prayer and belief in a higher power. I'm still not certain, but I feel that it may have not only been an emotional effect but a physical one as well.

- **Day 9:** Today I got into a discussion with my mom over my grades and I noticed something different about the way I behaved. Instead of going straight to yelling, I caught myself and decided to resolve it calmly. I'd never actually thought about arguing with my mom without shouting in the past, so it was actually a surprise to me as well. I think this whole prayer thing might be working.
- **Day 11:** After my night prayer today, I felt a weird calmness that hasn't ever happened. My body just lost all energy and I felt extremely relaxed. It was as if my whole body and consciousness was letting out a sigh of satisfaction. I'd like to think it was God, but it could've just been the thought of sleep getting to me.
- **Day 12:** I'm starting to see a real difference in my behavior at home and at school. I feel like I'm politer and more cheerful.
- **Day 13:** My friend commented on my cheerfulness. He told me I look happier than usual when I didn't really have anything to be particularly happy about. I think this actually proves that now, it's not just me noticing changes but people around me as well.
- **Day 14:** I am positive now that by doing this spiritual practice, my behavior and outlook on life has been changed. I feel significantly more happy throughout the day compared to when I started.
- **Day 15:** This was the last time I did my spiritual practice and honestly, I was quite surprised with my results. Although at the beginning it was either this would have no effect on me or I would become the Buddha, I realized that I ended up somewhere in between these two expectations. I'm still not sure if God is real, but it confirmed to me that there is in fact a higher power. It also proved to me that there is an effect related to praying and behavior. It's been a very interesting experience.

2. **Drawing a Mandala** (#2 above): Adrienne chose to do a meditation and mandala spiritual project because she thoroughly enjoys doing art.
   - **Day 2:** Today I tried not meditating first and just going straight into drawing my mandalas and I got bored really quickly, so I think I might try meditating again next time and see if there's a difference.
   - **Day 6:** I meditated for ten minutes this time because it worked for me very well last time when I meditated for ten minutes only. I'm finding it helps me concentrate much better on my mandalas and I don't get bored as easily. Today I continued with my mandala drawing and I'm really happy with the end result.
   - **Day 8:** I'm starting to enjoy spending effort and time on this much more than when I started. Since I'm working with oil paint, the whole process is taking much more effort and work to finish, but I'm enjoying it.

- **Day 9:** I didn't get bored of doing it at all. In fact, I found it put me in a better mood and calmed me down a lot more than before since I was stressed out today.
- **Day 10:** After meditating, I finished off some details of my mandala and I'm extremely happy with the results. I feel really comforted and in a great mood because I finished something well and I focused and put a lot of effort in it.
- **Day 11:** Today is the final day and it's also the day that I have to destroy what I have made since it's an important part of the process. Although I couldn't get the strength to burn my last mandala, I did burn my first two pieces and also my journal which I keep and write in almost every day. I think that at first it hurt to burn my journal since it kept so many of my memories and emotions, but it also weirdly felt good to burn it because there were bad memories in there too and now that I've burned it, it's like nothing ever happened and now I can make new and better memories.

Both examples reveal the struggles many students have in starting a new spiritual practice. Most students have never been taught how to take up a practice to help them deepen their spiritual lives. However, as illustrated by these two projects, many students feel that in the middle of the process—often around the fourth or fifth day—they begin to benefit personally from their chosen practice. Overall, the vast majority of SPEX students found this activity to be the most valuable of the four summatives in helping them to relax, develop more positivity in their lives, and grow in their spiritual identity.

CONCLUSION

While most students don't come into our religion classes with burning questions, from the first time when I introduce the extraordinary claim that religion enables followers to combine the material and spiritual dimensions of life into a meaningful, energizing whole, many students are intrigued and are willing to experiment with our suggested practices. SPEX 9 teachers have found that having students generate their own spiritual practice regimen does indeed bring some sense of calm, balance, and purpose to many of them, initiating them on a path to explore the possibility of life beyond the visible. Such practices, I've come to believe, are the best way for young people to begin the great Wisdom work of inner awakening.

CHAPTER 13

THE WISDOM WAY OF KNOWING AND TEACHING

The Epistemological Foundations of SPEX Teachers

The way we interact with the world in knowing it becomes the way we interact with the world as we live in it . . . Our epistemology is quietly transformed into our ethic.
—*Parker Palmer (1983, p. 21)*

This new approach revolutionized my teaching. I came back daily and shared with Marty the incredible reflections students were writing in their daily "homeplay" assignments and in-class spiritual practices. Words of encouragement, mindful walks, daily meditations, gratitude journals and others positive psychology avenues to happiness were explored. Student responses blew me away . . . I will never teach the course the same way again.
—*Jeremy Seehafer,[1] current HKIS Humanities teacher*

---

[1] Jeremy's full reflections on teaching SPEX classes can be found in Chapter 17.

The Wisdom Way of Teaching: Educating for Social Conscience and Inner Awakening in the High School Classroom, pages 153–158.
Copyright © 2022 by Information Age Publishing
www.infoagepub.com
All rights of reproduction in any form reserved.

INTRODUCTION

At the end of Part I, I proposed that the deepest understanding of social conscience teachers' inner lives could be understand through four role descriptions—curricular innovator, pedagogue of critical thinking, empathetic mentor, and facilitator of wonder and hope. As I conclude part II, I would like to consider similarly the interior life of SPEX instructors, with a particular emphasis on their belief formation. What internal disposition does it take to teach a spiritually-oriented curriculum aimed at the inner awakening of high school students? I offer the following from our experience as a starting point to contemplate this important question about the inner life of a Wisdom teacher seeking to inspire spiritual growth in students. The focus of this chapter, then, is to go "under the waterline" and explore the deeper epistemological foundations of SPEX teachers to knowing itself. This does not mean epistemological foundations in the headiest sense of systematic philosophizing, but rather the more commonplace sense of reflection on lived experience that goes into belief formation.

SPEX PEDAGOGY

Religion teachers at HKIS began teaching the Spiritual Explorations (SPEX) program, starting with grade 9, in 2018. Chapter 11 describes the first unit of SPEX 9 on "waking up" to a spiritual life and students' positive responses, while Chapter 12 shares the most impactful aspect of the course, the 10-day Spiritual Practices project. The SPEX pedagogy, I proposed, involves three defining characteristics, which I review again.

Over the last several years religion teachers at HKIS have gradually implemented the SPEX concepts and practices throughout the four years of high school. The overall goal of the four-course sequence is to prioritize body-mind-heart coherence over mind-centric critical analysis. Thus, a first defining characteristic of the SPEX pedagogy is the role of spiritual practices in the curriculum in bringing about such integration. Every class includes a spiritual practice and most assignments ask students to cultivate these practices in their daily lives.

A second distinctive characteristic of SPEX is that it is event-oriented. Because the class meets only once a week, day-to-day continuity that would otherwise build content knowledge retention can't be counted on; instead, instructors create individual stand-alone classes that are complete unto themselves and employ activities that aim to have a singular, memorable experience (e.g., burning regrets in a fire, waking up to our school campus through conscious walking, learning the five love languages).

Thirdly, all major assessments are based on a credit-or-no-credit format; there are no letter grades. Students need to receive credit on all four of the major (summative) assignments in order to pass the course. Since students are already subject to a great deal of grading pressure in their other classes, our message is that we can offer a high quality educational experience without holding the carrot and stick of academic grades above their heads.

All three aspects of the new SPEX approach—practice-based, event-oriented, and grade-neutral—are reflective of the Wisdom path itself, which offers an experiential, non-judgmental invitation to live life at a higher vibrational energy leading to greater self-knowledge and a deeper sense of connectedness to the world. By placing student wholeness at its heart, the SPEX curriculum holds a non-coercive curricular space for overly stressed students to relax, rebalance and restore their generally overstretched lives.

SPEX EPISTEMOLOGY

The key themes of the SPEX curriculum—waking from sleep; horizontal and vertical dimensions; body, mind, and heart as "three-centered awareness;" and the emphasis on the direct experience of spiritual practices—reflect Cynthia's understanding of the Wisdom tradition. Perhaps, then, it is not surprising that the SPEX epistemology has striking similarities to the contemporary American contemplative tradition. Paula Pryce (2018) in her book *The Monk's Cell*—a phenomenological study of this tradition, including substantial focus on Cynthia's teachings—describes in detail the characteristics of this community:

> Cosmopolitan and well-educated, this is a specialized community of Euro-American professionals from the upper middle class . . . a subsector of America's intelligentsia . . . well-traveled and globally aware . . . The Christianities they practiced in childhood could not bear the weight of the world's breadth as they knew it—neither the goodness and wonder of its expansiveness nor the burdens of its violence and contradiction . . . Yet rather than becoming secular in response to churches which they felt were at odds with worldly complexity, this group responded by taking up a seemingly paradoxical commitment to deepen knowledge while simultaneously allowing for doubt, ambiguity, and mystery in their understandings of the divine (p. 14).

Pryce's characterization aptly describes SPEX teachers as well, who indeed are experienced and well-traveled Euro-American international school educators who find teaching in a place like Hong Kong highly engaging. These teachers are also in agreement that the religious traditions of their youth failed to grapple with the world's complexity in all of its beauty and distress. These inadequacies drove the instructors to explore all forms of knowledge—secular and religious, Christian and non-Christian—to get at the root of humankind's existential dilemmas. Thus, the "doubt, ambiguity, and mystery" they experienced in their adult years caused them to winnow, and then expand, their childhood faith rather than jettison it.

What then is the epistemological method our SPEX teachers at HKIS employ in order to come to a personal determination of what elements of religion and spirituality are most intrinsically engaging and important? Pryce's explanation provides insight into this discernment process:

156 • THE WISDOM WAY OF TEACHING

> For this community, the largesse of a chaotic world did not prompt clinging to dogmatic tenets, but instead inspired a creative bridging of knowing and "unknowing." This dynamic tension between **scholarly knowledge, lived experience, and religious ambiguity** suggests an epistemological embrace of a complex world that allows for no easy answers (p. 14, bold mine).

I would like to suggest that Pryce's insights accurately characterize the SPEX approach to understanding the world in all its mesmerizing and disturbing complexity.

1. **Scholarly knowledge:** While most of the teachers were raised in parochial communities that inculcated beliefs through worship liturgies, creeds, and catechisms, SPEX teachers have distanced themselves from these frequently uncritical pathways, viewing those explanations as oversimplified. This gap creates ambiguity that risks, or perhaps guarantees, living without ready-made answers to many crucial questions. This drives SPEX teachers to search further afield, drawing upon scientific and secular forms of knowing as well as the world's wide array of religious traditions as guides for the formation of their worldviews. An open, trusting, and discerning attitude towards a rich diversity of knowledge sources is needed to teach the wide-ranging SPEX curriculum.
2. **Lived experience:** Breaking away from the centripetal force of parochial upbringings has resulted in educators who trust their own subjective experiences more than that of received, tradition-transmitted explanations. The centrality of personal meaning-making helps explain the prominent role of spiritual practices in SPEX courses.
3. **Religious ambiguity:** While most of the SPEX teachers come from Christian backgrounds, genuine respect for all religions—and an inclination to perceive similarities among traditions rather than differences—characterize this approach. The first year's theme of "waking up," for example, is certainly a shared interreligious concept. So, teachers ask themselves as they prepare a lesson on this topic: what aspects of Hinduism, Buddhism, Judaism, etc., enable their respective followers to awaken to divine reality? Spiritual resources from the world's major religious traditions are marshalled in support of the overall goal of awakening rather than privileging one faith tradition above others.

The preceding three characteristics suggest a reformulation of the epistemological foundations of teachers' upbringings. These are summarized in Table 13.1.

It is not surprising, then, that SPEX teachers feel that in creating the SPEX curriculum they are breaking new ground. Whether in their daily lessons or their deeper philosophical commitments, teaching SPEX involves a significant departure from how religion was inculcated in these instructors' formative years. It is understandable, then, that these educators approach their teaching with a mix of

TABLE 13.1. Comparison of the Epistemological Foundations of SPEX Teachers' Parochial Upbringing to Their Current Worldview

Epistemological Aspect	Parochial Upbringing	Contemplative/SPEX Innovation
Scholarly Knowledge	Sacred revelation privileged above secular understanding.	All knowledge is welcome with no clear-cut distinction between sacred and secular.
Lived Experience	Lived experience is understood, interpreted, and articulated within a tradition's epistemological constructs.	Lived experience is an important source of insight in and of itself.
Religious Ambiguity	One's sacred tradition is considered true and all others are to some degree incomplete, empty, or wrong.	Openness to all traditions in search of specific interreligious themes that are compelling by virtue of their near unanimity across the world's religious traditions and affirmed by lived experience.

boldness and trepidation: the former because student feedback strongly indicates that they are indeed meeting students' spiritual needs more effectively than in the past, validating the SPEX method; the latter as they hear the real or imagined voices of disapproval from those who faithfully raised them in religious communities in their youth. This is presumably the ambiguity of religious innovation across time.

CONCLUSION

SPEX teachers seem aware of the pioneering and experimental nature of their new curricula. Thus, it comes as some comfort to find that their approach to spiritual learning shows parallels to the epistemological traits of contemporary American contemplatives, as understood in Pryce's study. Perhaps one of Cynthia's lineage bearers, 20th century French paleontologist and Jesuit priest Pierre Teilhard de Chardin, foresaw instruction like SPEX emerging in the future when he named a new human-initiated biospherical entity coming into being across the planet called the *noosphere*, a global thought form united by a shared planetary wisdom (King, 1996). The prolific scholar, who was exiled to China in the 1920s during his most productive years for his daring theological writings, sought holistic understanding and spiritual insight through scientific exploration *and* spiritual contemplation in equal measure. SPEX teachers living in Hong Kong share some of these traits, happily ensconced in some form of self-imposed exile from distant systems and impractical theologies, enjoying the noosphere-sensitive freedom to create courses that draw upon both secular and spiritual knowledge sources to support students' psychospiritual well-being.

SPEX teachers realize that they are fortunate to belong to a community of like-minded educators who agree that the creation of the SPEX curriculum has been among their most rewarding collaborative experiences of their careers. And perhaps the reason why is that at a deeper philosophical level these teachers found co-innovators who subconsciously understood that new wine couldn't simply be poured into old wineskins. At some point new containers of truth—new epistemological frameworks—were needed.

PART III

SPECIAL TOPICS IN INNER AWAKENING

The next three chapters focus on specific themes—body consciousness, non-reactivity, and the Inner Critic—that we consider essential elements of inner awakening and frequently teach about across various religion classes. Chapters 14 and 16 are co-authored with Dr. Sangeeta Bansal, a mindfulness instructor who lived in Hong Kong for four years and who has come to the school as a visiting teacher for several years. Sangeeta and I have team-taught classes and led spiritual retreats for students, parents, and teachers during her visits.

Sangeeta and the Author Co-Leading a Faculty Spiritual Retreat at Tao Fung Shan in Hong Kong. Photo credit: Mekala Weerakoon.

Discussing the Chinese spiritual classic the Tao Te Ching at a faculty retreat. Photo credit: Sangeeta Bansal.

Author leading parents in a meditation at a spiritual retreat at HKIS. Photo credit: Sangeeta Bansal.

CHAPTER 14

TEACHING CONSCIOUSNESS OF THE BODY

Two Practitioners in Dialogue

Sangeeta Bansal and Martin E. Schmidt

The meaning of life is not something to be discerned and known intellectually by the mind, but to be felt in the depths of our flesh.
— *Jorge Ferrer (2008, p. 4)*

I experienced a powerful example of bodily intelligence in making one of the biggest decisions of my life to this point. When [film producer] Paul Saltzman visited our class, he advised that in deciding on a university one should meditate, envisioning oneself living life on each campus, and observe which university felt "right." So, in my college decision, I underwent Saltzman's meditation and surrendered the expanse of information I had gathered on each university to raw, simple feeling. When I completed the meditation, I could feel which school was right for me, and assuredly made my decision. The level of intuition I employed in this anecdote couldn't have arisen from the logic-driven mind—it was a tangible testament to the body-mind-heart framework of wisdom. I will continue to utilize this wisdom in the future to guide my most consequential moments.
—*Amar, grade 12 male student*

This chapter explores understandings about the role of the body in inner awakening in the form of a conversation between myself and Sangeeta Bansal, a mindfulness instructor based in New York, concerning how and why we teach about the body in our respective classes. Our underlying assumption is that the body is an intelligence on par with the brain, a belief that challenges the preconceptions of our students.

Marty (M): Several years ago I re-organized my Service, Society, and the Sacred (SSS) course around the theme of wisdom. I went for a practical, low-bar, senior-friendly definition: wisdom is figuring out what you want to devote your professional time and energy to in the coming decades. I've had conversations with lots of alumni over the last year, and most struggle big time with this issue, so the idea is to bring this question to my high school students at an earlier stage to help them be proactive in their thinking. And what I came up with, following my teacher Cynthia, is that wisdom in all spheres of life is a natural outcome of developing what she calls *three-centered awareness*, which integrates the intelligences of the body, mind, and heart. The context, then, of this dialogue is how to teach towards an integration of these three in search of wisdom.

To kick this off, I'll tell you about my starting point with three-centered awareness. If the ideal state of being awakened is employing this body-mind-heart sensitivity, then our essential problem is that most of the time we are living predominantly out of one center, which for my students is undoubtedly the mind. The body and heart have little currency in the educational sweepstakes that dominate their lives. As students progress through high school and become more "mindy" in their pursuit of competitive university acceptances, their own sense of body and heart energy is visibly drained. Living out of one center only is the Wisdom tradition's definition of sleep, which sadly is not just a spiritual metaphor for some students in my classes!

This is the fifth year that I have structured my entire SSS curriculum around the body-mind-heart concept, and I'm pleased to say that it's working! It's comprehensive in scope, yet still flexible enough to easily incorporate new materials in the curriculum. So, tell me about your work, Sangeeta. How do you teach towards the body-mind-heart connection?

Sangeeta (S): When I teach mindfulness, whether to 6th graders or MBA students, I always start with the body. Our bodies are an integral part of our mindfulness practice—and it sets the platform on which we rest our efforts. In the Satipatthana Sutta, the foundational Buddhist text from which all modern versions of mindfulness spring, the body is one of the four pillars that we bring our awareness to. The Buddha instructed his followers to "stay in your appropriate *gocharas* ("cow pastures"), otherwise the mind is easily seduced by Mara;" mindfulness of the body is the simplest and most direct way to overcome the onslaughts of the demon Mara, which personifies our desires and temptations.

It comes as a surprise to many of my students that mindfulness practice views the body as much more the solution to our temptations rather than their instigator! The body is the first of the four pillars, so the Buddha's unambiguous advice: *stay in the body*. This means becoming aware of bodily sensations, posture, gait, all five senses and, of course, the breath. These become the objects of one's concentration and contemplation, helping to anchor the mind so that Wisdom can manifest itself.

M: Cynthia—and the Wisdom tradition out of which she teaches—certainly agrees with the Buddha that the body is the starting point on the spiritual path. Cynthia explains that, contrary to common stereotypes, the father of Christian contemplation, St. Anthony, considered the body as a natural ally of the spiritual life rather than an impediment in need of harsh discipline.

So, on day 1 of SSS this year I started with the body. After introducing the theme of wisdom, I gathered the class in a circle, turned the lights off, and said, "Let's do a little thought experiment." I then slowly read five words or phrases—SATs, GPA, final exams, college acceptances, and leaving home—and asked them to pause for 30 seconds after each word and note any bodily reactions. Students had a variety of responses: some felt a tightening in their gut, throat, or arms; others felt pain in the head or around the eyes; and one felt a compulsion to spit out a laugh or maybe it was a cry. In our debrief, they all realized that there was a body-mind-heart connection that they had never paid attention to. We came around to the point that all of us have accumulated unresolved tensions that reside in the body. At the end of last semester numerous students reported that this simple exercise was a big wake-up call. While they took this little experiment as a scary realization, I turned it around and explained that this illustrates the body's finely tuned intelligence. Then we discussed what their bodies were trying to say to them. Finally, we watched the first half of a video, "What piece of advice would you give the 16-year old you?" (Merlin's Diary Podcast, 2015). Quite a few of the speakers referred to the importance of the body in gaining life wisdom.

S: Yes, the body-mind-heart connection is certainly an overlooked area in the culture that we live in. We kind of get it, but then forget. For example, we know our knees feel weak when we are scared to look down from a tall building, or our palms get sweaty before a public performance, or we feel our heart beat faster when we are excited. These are bodily reactions to mental events.

Further, we also know that to excel in anything, for example, an Olympic gold medal, physical fitness of the body is not enough. Nor is simply the mental desire or ambition to get that medal sufficient. It is a combination of mental and physical processes working in synchronicity and alignment towards a common goal, overseen by a resonant, feelingful heart. Buddhist monk Ajahn Brahmamuni (2012) remarks that it is not enough to follow the heart; one has to *train* the heart. When the messages from the body-mind-heart get garbled in the "noise" that exists in our internal and external environments, then we are unable to align these three intelligences to get to our best outcomes. We need to pay attention to the body, for it serves as the doorway to higher spiritual experiences.

If we pay attention, the body can tell us many things. When we feel constriction in the chest, or the breath becomes shallow and fast, or when we get a tightening of muscles or a clenching of the jaw, it is usually indicative of the mind being uncomfortable with a "trigger." So, the body is an early warning system for a mind-state that is arising. Only if we become aware of the alarm, however, can we choose to work with the feeling and resolve it in some way. If we are unaware of it, we may lose that window of opportunity to change our course of action, and perhaps our life's trajectory. A quote attributed to Holocaust survivor Viktor Frankl says it well, "Between stimulus and response there is a space. In that space is our power to choose our response. In our response lies our growth and our freedom."

M: The Frankl observation reminds me of an incident a couple of years ago when I entered into an unexpectedly intense discussion with my boss about an issue I cared deeply about and was quite emotionally-laden for both of us. As the conversation and tension ratcheted up, somehow my body acted, as you said, as an early warning system; but most oddly, it seemed to then act of its own accord. I felt myself breathe deeply from the belly, and it seemed to give me that split-second of awareness to think clearly and with less emotion. The conversation remained tense and frank, but not the kind of falling out that can be disastrous between colleagues. But what struck me about the whole event was the sense that my gut *breathed* me back into a state of awareness rather than the mind as "command center" saying, "Breathe, breathe! You are in a state of stress." What do you make of that?

S: I think you picked up the signal from your body and acted on it, thereby mitigating an impending disaster. But sometimes we miss these signals, and it can have devastating consequences—just as if you were driving on a precipitously high mountain road, and you missed the sign that said "Steep Curve Ahead." In mindfulness training courses, we use a variety of breathing techniques to bring us out of mental ruts. I think the expression that "whatever you can breathe through, you can live through" is very true.

I'll summarize three ways in which mindfulness training helps bring awareness to the body, and allows us to use the body to enhance mental and spiritual experience. My students love these practices and benefit enormously.

1. **Using the breath to stay present:** One of the most beautiful characteristics of our breath is that it is always in the present moment. We can never take a future breath and store it, nor can we hold on to a breath in the past. By nature's design the breath is always anchored in our moment-by-moment existence. When we allow our awareness to harness itself to the breath, we are essentially severing the mind's tendency to dwell in the past or the future. Regrets of the past and worries about the future usually cloud our moments and keep us from living life fully. This way our breath can be a powerful ally in our efforts to shut down excessive rumination and mental chatter.

2. **Using our senses to savor life:** The now famous raisin-eating activity (Williams & Penman, 2011, p. 73) is a multifaceted exercise that helps to take something small and usually inconspicuous, and elevate our experience of it. We bring our complete attention to the raisin, and using the sensory mechanisms in the body, we savor it like never before. We see it, smell it, hear it, touch it, and taste it for ten minutes and think of nothing else. This serves as a reminder of how mindlessly we usually eat, distracted by conversation or technological gadgets. We lose the ability to enjoy and give gratitude for one of the most essential aspects of our existence—bodily sustenance and nourishment. This experiment also shows us a practical way to escape the thinking mind by letting ourselves dwell on sensory experience rather than discursive thought.

3. **Using the body to relax the mind:** While much has been made of the body's tendency to react to environmental stress (the fight, flight or freeze stress response), it is less commonly known that the body also has a relaxation response. Putting the body in relaxation mode helps bring down the stress hormones cortisol and adrenaline, and activates the secretion of the feel-good hormones like oxytocin, dopamine, and endorphins. These are essential for the body's self-repair and self-healing processes to kick in, which are held at bay when the body is in a stress response. In order to switch from a stress response to the relaxation response, we practice abdominal breathing. This activates the vagus nerve, which helps start the process of relaxation in the para-

sympathetic nervous system, and switches off the sympathetic nervous system related to stress in the body.

With new information emerging from neuroscience, we are coming to better understand how the body and its functions optimize our living experience, especially its impact on our emotions and even our spiritual experiences. It's all a concert of body, mind, and heart—with no one aspect being the star. The beauty of the symphony lies in how well they are aligned and coordinated.

M: What could be more important than to bring about this kind of concerted wholeness in the lives of students who by all measures are being increasingly stressed and depressed? Most of the day they are sitting in chairs, listening and talking—all aimed at engaging their brains.

One of the most effective activities I did this semester was a conscious walking activity. I explained to the class that the whole Wisdom tradition is unanimous in exhorting us to stop living on autopilot and become aware of the present. So, I asked them during our class period, when the hallways were empty, to practice walking through the rest of their day's classes mindfully. To practice conscious walking, I asked them to either walk sensing their feet, or by tuning into what they saw or heard. The goal of both strategies was to help them temporarily pause their interior monologues and be in the present moment. To begin, I had them lie on the floor as I played a 14-minute body scan exercise (Ko, 2016b). Then I came around, tapped students one-by-one on the shoulder or leg, and allowed them to exit the room to begin their walking meditation. They returned about 15 minutes later, and I was quite surprised how something so simple could help them view their normal existence in such new ways.

Their homework was to continue this kind of conscious walking in their daily lives. Here's how Zach responded:

> Almost every day after school I walk up the hill to my house, which is surrounded by beautiful green scenery and an array of different animals, but because I normally just have my earphones on and don't pay attention to my surroundings, I never realized how truly beautiful this was. When I started walking consciously up the hill, I began to see how amazing the birds, trees and squirrels are, and it shocked me how I have completely taken this all for granted for the two and a half years I have lived there.

There's the beauty of a concerted awareness that you were referring to, Sangeeta. It's not difficult for students to get an enticing taste of three-centered awareness.

S: That's a lovely comment from Zach! Living a life where we can just "be" without always "doing" helps us to tap into that inner wisdom.

It is often counter-intuitive to think that "sitting still" and being in the present moment without having an agenda can actually make us more productive, but that's one of the key lessons in mindfulness. It reminds me of what the French poet Jules Renard said, "If I had to live my life over again, I would ask that not a thing be changed but that my eyes be opened wider."

M: I've come to the same place! The 17th century French mathematician and philosopher Blaise Pascal wrote, "All of humanity's problems stem from man's inability to sit quietly in a room alone." So much of our agitation towards others and life in general comes from an existential fear of being with ourselves and facing our discontent. The 4th century Christian desert fathers described the restlessness and emptiness of life as the "noonday demon" that visits us when our busy lives slow down. Addressing this condition, one of the desert fathers, Evagrius, advised, "Sit in your cell and it will teach you everything." Wait out the fear until a deeper, hidden wholeness emerges from within. Traditions across the world are in agreement that this is what meditation does. Is it really possible that something so seemingly simple as "sitting still" could in time bring forth a sense of calm and satisfaction? What a wonder!

Sangeeta, as we bring this to a close and you think about your work, what is the growth edge in your teaching?

S: I'm really fascinated by the whole neuroplasticity thing, which suggests that the content and nature of our thoughts change the structure and function of the brain—and these in turn change our experience of the world around us. My students find this a challenging concept to believe, despite so much scientific evidence. They can see how the work they do with their hands can carve a block of wood into a beautiful statue, or turn a blank canvas into a brilliant piece of art; but they cannot see how repetitive thoughts carve out new grooves in the brain, changing their abilities and capabilities as human beings. This fact, known by sages and monks in all Wisdom traditions, and explained in meticulous detail by the Buddha, serves as the bedrock of modern day contemplative neuroscience and secular mindfulness teachings that I bring to my classes. I'll end with this quote from the ancient Buddhist text the Dhammapada, "You are what you think. All that you are arises from your thoughts. With your thoughts you make your world."

Let me throw it back to you, Marty. What's captivated your thinking recently?

M: For me it's the whole idea that coming into the body is the way to Wisdom. I just don't think I ever considered this possibility until a few years ago. I think that at some level I had really bought into the "spirit is good" and "flesh is bad" dualism. In fact, I remember the moment a few years ago when I had visceral recognition of bodily intelligence.

Reading a brilliant interview with Philip Shepherd entitled, "Out of Our Heads" (Buchbinder, 2013), I had a very strong sense of surging body energy. Something in the article struck me as deeply true.

In the same vein, what both excites and challenges me is the bold claim made by Jorge Ferrer (2008) that "the body is the human dimension that can reveal the ultimate meaning of incarnated life. Being physical itself, the body stores within its depths the answer to the mystery of material existence . . . The meaning of life is not something to be discerned and known intellectually by the mind, but to be felt in the depths of our flesh" (p. 4). Underneath the quest for guidance about their careers, my students want to have some sense of life purpose. Could understanding something so seemingly abstract as our life purpose come from the humble, concrete task of sensing our bodies? Or more provocatively, could the body actually contain specific wisdom we need about ourselves and our lives, an idea that I'm exploring now in Classical Chinese Medicine (Shea, 2015, p. 24)? Is it possible, as Helminski (1992) suggests metaphorically, that we are unknowingly "knee deep in a river, searching for water?" (9). Like the wonder of meditation, the intelligence of the body almost seems too good to be true. In the end, then, I keep asking: how much meaning can high school students experience? And on an experiential level, for my students and myself, what does it mean for me and my students to perceive "the meaning of life . . . in the depths of our flesh?"

I think for both of us, Sangeeta, this journey of teaching our students has been full of unexpected joys and enlivening challenges. Along with the ups and down, we seem to sense that the growth we have experienced will continue in its own time. Thanks, I really enjoyed the dialogue, Sangeeta. Wishing you peace in your teaching in New York!

S: Agreed! It's been a pleasure. Wishing you happiness in your continued service at HKIS.

ABOUT THE CO-AUTHOR

Sangeeta Bansal, Ph.D., is a certified mindfulness teacher based in New York, dedicated to bringing self-awareness to the community. She has taught mindfulness at several universities and schools in the New York area, including Princeton University, NYU Stern School of Business, and Rye Country Day School.

CHAPTER 15

NON-REACTIVITY

The Supreme Practice of Everyday Life

This being human is a guest house.
Every morning a new arrival.
A joy, a depression, a meanness
Some momentary awareness comes as an unexpected visitor.
Welcome and entertain them all!
Even if they're a crowd of sorrows
Who violently sweep your house empty of its furniture.
Still, treat each guest honorably.
He may be clearing you out for some new delight.

—*Rumi*

Learning the non-reactivity meditation has not only helped me deal with my temper but in a greater sense has redeveloped my experience of letting go, letting the stimuli pass by rather than influencing my mind and body.

—*Sharon, grade 12 female student*

INTRODUCTION

Despite the love and care of many people in my formative years in the Lutheran Church, the underlying implicit directive seemed to prioritize right belief in church doctrines over inner transformation. The hope was that assent to doctrinal truth would facilitate and accompany right action in the world. So it has come as quite a surprise to me that the Wisdom tradition really asks very little of its adherents, if they can be named as such, in terms of what to believe. Although the Wisdom tradition has important concepts to convey, such as the body-mind-heart framework or the horizontal and vertical dimensions, they primarily serve as ways to explain practices to be explored experientially, with no emphasis on faith declarations or mandatory beliefs. One of the fundamental foci of our program, then, is not on beliefs, but rather on our most common experiences of dealing with emotional reactivity on a daily basis. Here in this chapter I take Cynthia's teachings—distilled from the Gurdjieff Work[1] and the writings of her mentor, Father Thomas Keating—and combine them with Stephen Batchelor's (2015) insights in his book *After Buddhism* to explain to my religion students how to deal with the trigger moments that we all struggle with routinely—and to see them as fecund sources of inner awakening. Students find that they can easily relate to this topic and are surprised that this most commonplace of experiences is at the core of the spiritual life. Much of what I teach in SSS and Spiritual Explorations is paying attention to these daily frustrations, for they are indispensable grist for the Wisdom mill.

INTRODUCING NON-REACTIVITY

Dear Students,[2]

We've been talking about the common message contained within the cross-cultural Wisdom tradition, which states that the goal of life is to marry the horizontal material existence in time with the vertical dimension of the invisible and eternal. Or more personally, we have said that the aim of life is to integrate the small self of daily life with the Larger Self that lives forever. All of these lofty and abstract ideals may be appealing, but what does it mean in real life and how do we get

---

[1] Armenian spiritual teacher G.I. Gurdjieff (1872–1949) has had a pervasive influence on Cynthia's work. She often credits Gurdjieff as the first person in the Western tradition to bring mindfulness practices to a larger audience. However, gaining some kind of overview of Gurdjieff's ideas can be a challenge for the uninitiated. I recommend Nottingham's (2018) easily accessible book The Work: Esotericism and Christian Psychology as an introduction to Gurdjieff's core teachings. For a more thorough treatment, read Ouspensky's (2001) classic text In Search of the Miraculous.

[2] Like other chapters in this text which also take the form of a letter, I usually don't share this piece with my classes when I teach about non-reactivity, preferring short presentations instead. However, this format helps me to distill the essential message I want to share with students. On the other hand, I have posted this piece on my "Social Conscience and Inner Awakening" blog and I will occasionally share it with individual students who want to investigate the ideas I present in more depth.

there? And, in keeping with body-mind-heart emphasis of the tradition, how do we make sure the spiritual journey isn't just some kind of head trip? The surprising and eminently practical answer to these questions is something that Buddhist writer Steve Batchelor (2015) calls *non-reactivity*.

The Reactive Self

Before getting into how it all works, let's start with your daily life. When you come to school, you unavoidably encounter events that make you feel nervous or downright disheartened—a low grade on a test, a close friendship that seems to be unraveling, competition between you and someone else for a coved leadership position, the moral dilemma of a friend cheating on an exam, etc. Because we are hard-wired biologically for survival—drawn to the things we like and avoiding life circumstances that threaten us—we cannot help but have emotional responses to such events in our lives.

However, the Wisdom tradition points out that responding mechanically to these "I like"/"I don't like" habits means that we live our lives on autopilot, trapped in small self reactivity. These habits affect everything: our thinking—I like high grades more than low grades; our emotions—I like to feel happy rather than feel sad; and our actions—I do things that give me a sense of reward rather than doing things that are likely to put me at risk.

When we are confronted by all the "I don't like" things in our environment, we employ one of three survival strategies: fight, flight, or freeze. The first two approaches cause us to confront or avoid the problem, while freezing means that we endure the unpleasantness, but numb out the feelings associated with the discomfort.

Regardless of the strategy, when confronted by circumstances that threaten us, the full force of our egoic habits energize our self-righteousness, which manifests itself in endless internal monologues: "I studied so hard, but then we weren't tested on the material, " or, "Cheer up—find your favorite comfort food and indulge yourself—you deserve it," or, "I'd try harder, but I know it's pointless."

What can be done?

How Reactivity and Non-Reactivity Work

Cynthia teaches that understanding how reactivity works, and then strengthening some non-reactive strategies, can help you escape your egoic habits and act from a place of independence from the small self's survival programs. Cynthia employs the following diagram to understand the habitual patterns of reactivity in her book *Centering Prayer and Inner Awakening* (2004, p. 136):

Beginning at the triangle (1), Cynthia borrows from Father Thomas Keating's (1992) starting point that all of us have unconscious emotional programs for hap-

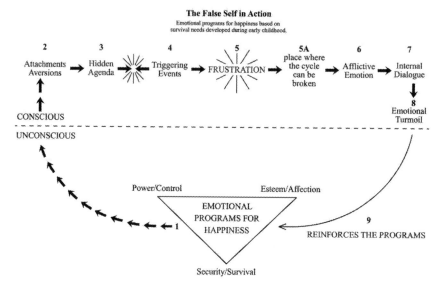

FIGURE 15.1. The False Self in Action

piness that run our conscious attention and behavior. This survival self believes that it must acquire at least one of these three essentials: a) Power/Control b) Esteem/Affection c) Security/Survival. While these needs or impulses are understandable, our automatic reaction to them can undermine our sense of well-being or our relationships with others. These are the unconscious drivers of our more conscious attachments/likes or aversions/dislikes (2), which create the hidden agendas (3) that enter into our real life situations.

Inevitably at some point a triggering event occurs (4)—something that threatens an emotional program—and frustration (5) sets in. This is followed by the habitual mind's emotional reactions (6–8) with accompanying internal dialogue that reinforce our unconscious programs for happiness. Such mindless programmed responses keep us trapped in the survival self's needy grasping, leaving the Larger Self's equanimity in tatters. According to the Wisdom tradition, it is right after the initial moment of frustration (5A) that we have the opportunity to disrupt the spinning egoic self's automatic responses. Rather than immediately going into fight, flight, or freeze mode to strengthen the small self's emotional ruts, we are able precisely at this point to implement a three-fold strategy of non-reactivity.

The Path of Non-Reactivity

The way of escape, then, is to train yourself to put into place a non-reactive strategy that follows right on the heels of a triggering event, which means you attempt to:

1. Respond with non-reactive awareness: consider yourself a third-person observer who watches your own emotional responses arise and then dissipate. Don't judge, don't try to change yourself; just observe! In time this practice will begin to cultivate a third-person perspective within yourself that sometimes is called the Inner Witness.
2. Experience the triggered emotions in your body as sensations: our most ancient and basic emotions—fear, rage, seeking, and panic (Panksepp, 2004)—correlate with neuroemotional pathways through the body and are often felt energies. Rather than fighting (acting out mindlessly on the basis of discomfort), fleeing (avoiding, repressing or denying the agitation), or freezing (numbing physical and emotional responses), this counter-intuitive strategy opens bodily sensations to the experience, again sensing-observing with non-reactive awareness.
3. Breathe and let go: attempt to breathe into these challenges, which keeps the body-mind-heart open to the moment—and to the vertical dimension—rather than shutting the full self down in fear and falling back into habitual coping behaviors. If possible, attempt to let go of all the ways that you want to energize ego-driven thoughts and emotions (e.g., justifying, defending, indulging, recruiting allies, demonizing). Try to let them go!

Cynthia emphasizes that steps 1 and 2 usually need to be repeated over and over again; and if you never get to the feeling that you can "let go," don't worry! Most of the work is already done in observing and participating mindfully in your reactivity. Put most succinctly, Cynthia often advises her students to "go down into sensation" rather than "up into story."

Once these strategies become an intuitive response, they can be used on a daily basis to deal with issues and concerns that arise, leading to a more relaxed and grounded life in the present moment.

Non-Reactivity as a Path to the Ultimate

Non-reactivity, Stephen Batchelor (2015) asserts in his book *After Buddhism*, lies at the heart of the Buddha story. When Siddhartha sat beneath the Bodhi tree and was attacked by the demon Mara, he came face to face not with an eternal metaphysical foe, but his own greed, hatred, and anger. When viewing these internal vices non-reactively, they "are seen for what they are: impermanent emotions that, when left to their own devices, will fizzle out" (p. 308). In the movie *Little Buddha* (Bertolucci, 1993), Mara's flaming arrows are turned into flower buds as they enter Siddhartha's unperturbed sphere of concentration. At the end of the dialogue between the former prince and Mara, Siddhartha states, "I know you." Siddhartha has befriended his darker inner impulses, a prominent theme in Buddhist teachings and the Wisdom tradition in general.

Batchelor claims, then, that letting go of—rather than eliminating—reactivity is the Buddha's key teaching for attaining nirvana. "Nirvanic freedom is the result of understanding how reactivity works. It is not the result of uprooting reactivity" (p. 308). When "a person's direct experience [manifests] the suspension or absence of these impulses [of greed, hatred, and confusion] . . . [this] is the definition of 'nirvana.' The experience of nirvana marks a turning point in an individual's life" (p. 41). According to Batchelor, this kind of non-reactivity is the path to nirvana.

Likewise in a Christian framework, breaking the habit of reactivity can be considered a path into the Kingdom of God, Jesus' master metaphor for the ideal divine-human relationship. While traditionally repentance of sin is seen as the way to enter the Kingdom of God, Cynthia explains that the Greek word for "repentance" is *metanoia,* which literally means to go "beyond the mind" or "into the larger mind" (Bourgeault, 2008, p. 37). Non-reactive strategies are precisely *metanoia,* opening the body to those roiling emotional felt-senses rather than mindful assertions of self-righteousness. Such *metanoia* goes hand in hand with *metamorphosis,* the power of transformation characteristic of the Kingdom of God.

Sharon's Experience

My most incisive student response to this teaching of non-reactivity comes from Sharon in my SSS class. Writing in her final paper—and in the context of our study of the Enneagram—she explains how she implemented these teachings in her life and the benefits that she received:

> Another meditation that I was introduced to as the course developed was a non-reactivity meditation. Impatience and temper have always been my weaknesses since I was young, and my family and friends have been noticing the worsening of these traits recently, due to stress and sleep deprivation. As an Enneagram type seven, the enthusiast, my basic desire is to be satisfied and content, which I achieve by keeping myself busy and occupied. In the process of reaching for the most I can handle, I tend to face situations where I become impulsive and reckless. In addition to being a seven, I am a seven-wing-eight, characterized by aggressiveness and a big temper. Small and particular things easily irritate me, and I am usually quick to judge and express my annoyance in a shouting manner. In order to channel my energy into positivity, Mr. Schmidt suggested that I observe and let the impulses pass without judging. Putting this into practice was difficult, as the impulses sustained for extended periods of time when I tried to breathe and let go. Yet again, I found repeating the practice multiple times helpful. By the fifth meditation of the week, I was able to detach myself from the triggering events and let the noise or situation continue without reacting. The basis of surrender meditation created the smallest gap needed between my surroundings and myself, which allowed my steady breathing to cue relaxation and objectivity. Learning the non-reactivity meditation has not only helped me deal with my temper but in a greater sense has redeveloped my experience of letting go, letting the stimuli pass by rather than influence my mind and body.

Sharon Studying at a U.S. University. Photo credit: Sharon Kim.

I am confident that I have regained my sense of letting go through the meditations, because I felt the same emptiness a few days ago as I was moving away from a relationship. I was holding onto the relationship for security, identity, and the memories that I have invested in and defined myself with. I was scared to let it go because I tied myself with the relationship and losing that connection would mean losing my identity that I had thought would last. In the moment, however, I was surprisingly calm and logical, and the following morning I felt the emptiness in my chest, the hole that lets just enough air through. The emptiness comes from the realization that my identity and value should and will be connected to the vertical dimension, where I will be able to anchor myself on a more profound depth. Breathing deeply now naturally calms me down without having to try hard to focus on clearing my mind. I feel in control of my emotions and mental state, and I no longer feel anxious when I am stressed.

CONCLUSION

The paradigm shift that has occurred in me from my youth to whom I am today has been dramatic. In my formative years, the emphasis was on being a kind, service-oriented, and forgiving person, but at the same time this implicitly came with a set of non-negotiable beliefs. The Wisdom tradition approaches this differently. Rather than starting with the *a priori* assumption that spiritual growth first necessitates believing certain doctrines, the Wisdom tradition begins squarely with life experience. To consider non-reactivity as the supreme practice of the spiritual life moves the fundamental task from the arena of abstract metaphysics to the nitty-gritty of everyday life. The yin of inner awakening, thus, starts with the most commonplace interactions that all students can relate to. That which appears to be most basic, in fact, has profound implications for the spiritual life. For Batchelor, letting go of reactivity is the very definition of nirvana; for Cynthia, *metanoia* beyond the small self's preoccupations lies at the heart of Jesus' message about the Kingdom of God.

CHAPTER 16

DEALING WITH THE ACCUSER

Befriending Your Inner Critic

Sangeeta Bansal and Martin E. Schmidt

> Self-compassion is not a way to judge ourselves positively, but a way to relate to ourselves compassionately, flaws and all, embracing ourselves as we are.
> —*Kristin Neff (TEDx Talks, 2013)*

> I always had trouble seeing the good in me even when I was younger. All I thought about was the bad things I did and the mistakes I made and it made me feel like I don't deserve the love I'm given by this almighty God that is perfect in all ways.
> —*Grade 9 male student*

INTRODUCTION

In this final special topic, Sangeeta and I discuss the concept of the Inner Critic, the third essential concept in teaching for inner awakening. I'm grateful to Sangeeta for first bringing this term to my attention, for I found it to be one of those rare ideas that, even from first mention, cuts through the mundane routine of a class period and speaks directly to the hearts of students. When I introduce the topic, I often tell the story related by mindfulness teacher Sharon Salzberg who asked the Dalai Lama about self-hatred (Salzberg, 2015). The spiritual teacher did not recognize the word and asked for it to be repeated. Still puzzled, he then asked for a translation of the concept into Tibetan, but none was provided. Finally, he turned back to Sharon and said, "Self-hatred? What's that?" Salzberg comments, "When I explained to him what I meant by the term—talking about the cycle of self-judgment, guilt, unproductive thought patterns—he asked me, *"How could you think of yourself that way?,"* for we all have the 'Buddha Nature.'" Students can easily see the clear contrast between the Wisdom tradition's high regard for the human person and the underlying sense of modern culture that we are never "good enough," a refrain seized upon and repeated by an invisible internal voice called the Inner Critic.

The first half of this chapter is written as a class presentation to our students. In the second half of the chapter, Sangeeta and I engage in dialogue about how we teach this concept in our classes as well as our personal reflections on the topic.

THE VOICE IN OUR HEADS

Dear Students,

If we could go back in time and tell our adolescent selves one message, it would be this: make peace with your self-critical voices. Both of us remember having strong consciences in our youth, but this gift of sensitivity oftentimes became an autoimmune attack directing its most unvarnished commentary inward. A voice inside our heads was constantly questioning, critiquing, and scolding much of our lives—our motives, actions, abilities, and potential. Its collective chronic message was, "You are not good enough." Often its tone was mean and derogatory, and its language could be quite colorful! Yet no one knew; by most outward measures we were successful academically, socially, and in our extracurricular activities. But worst of all, *we* didn't know either. The voice was an inaudible background soundtrack of our lives.

Yet even then we were aware that something was amiss: why would we be so relentlessly critical of ourselves and so unfailingly generous to our friends who might be in the exact same situation? We were aware of the contradiction, but we had no instruction about what it was, its proper role, or how to deal with it. We would like to spare you this pain and confusion by sharing with you that this voice has been discovered, understood, and named—the Inner Critic—and that it can be harnessed for good.

Our sense is that most HKIS students have highly attuned Inner Critics. Nearly every voice—from parents, siblings, peers, Hong Kong's achievement culture, and social media—speaks of the importance of attaining a competitive resume from early on in your education to survive in the high-stakes educational ecosystem in which you find yourselves. You think it's a necessary inner guide to motivate yourself to lead a successful life. We hope that you will reconsider the role that this invisible companion plays in your life.

Protector Turns Predator

By all accounts, this voice inside our heads is not a friendly one. It is unrelentingly negative, putting us down, minimizing our achievements, and reminding us of our failures. So how did we allow this destructive voice to take up permanent residence in our heads?

A psychologist would explain it this way. When we were very young—newborn to 7—our parents guided our behavior to ensure our safety and survival in the world. Once we separated from our parents—going to school or interacting with those beyond our family—those internalized voices kept us safe, whispering "don't talk to strangers," "don't go alone," "don't eat that," or "study harder." In this benign version, the inner voice plays a valuable role protecting us from engaging in reckless and potentially life-threatening actions. Our young and impressionable minds got the message that there are certain rules we must follow in order to play the game of life. Not only do we avert harmful situations, but by acquiescing to these self-imposed restrictions, we keep everyone around us happy, greatly improving our chances of survival.

But here's where it gets complicated. In our attempt to appease others, we end up short-changing ourselves. Over time our self-understanding fragments into "acceptable" and "not acceptable" areas, subjecting those rejected aspects to punitive and judgmental self-talk. The once well-meaning Protector has now turned Predator, and given that it is inside our own heads, we really have nowhere to run and hide.

As Earley and Weiss (2013) explain in their detailed work on the topic, these voices can wear many different hats. Some take on the voice of the Perfectionist, setting extremely high standards for performance or appearance. There's the Inner Controller that tries to restrict and shame you for impulsive and/or indulgent behavior, the Taskmaster that tries to motivate you by being tough, the Underminer that tries to hold you back from taking risks, the Destroyer that attacks your very existence, the Conformist that tries to get you to fit into a certain mold based on family and cultural norms, and the Guilt Tripper that attacks you for possibly harming someone else.

From the perspective of the Inner Critic, every painful experience in life becomes evidence that we did something wrong or stupid, and that we need to fix ourselves by beating ourselves up. For example, you get a bad grade in Biology and your Underminer comments, "Don't try to be good in science; you will fail and it will hurt." You didn't get invited to a party, and the voice snidely remarks, "Nobody really likes you, so you'd better not put yourself out there for further humiliation." The memory of this pain gets trapped in the innermost recesses of the body-mind complex with the warning sign: "That Hurt—Do Not Repeat!" When faced with a potential for a similar hurtful situation, alarm bells go off in the brain: "Don't go there—Danger Ahead."

Very soon the Inner Critic starts to exert its negative influence on all domains of our life that are important to us. *Because* a certain activity is meaningful and important to us, it becomes even more important to build up the defenses. The Inner Critic is most satisfied with us for NOT trying, for NOT taking on any challenge or any risk; on the other hand, it is merciless with perceived failure. The Perfectionist may pounce on writer's block to make it hard to finish a book project, the Taskmaster will make us procrastinate, and the Destroyer might turn manic and try to convince us that we don't deserve to live. Withdrawing from friends, activities and any kind of challenge, the Inner Critic eventually shrinks our world to a tiny island safely ensconced behind barricades where no one can threaten our security. We might then feel safe, but at the cost of sacrificing the best things in life—our potential for growth, creativity and joy—all of which require that we step out from our self-imposed exile.

Furthermore, the impact of this constant negative feedback and the tough stance taken by the Inner Critic has a detrimental impact on our nervous system, activating the fight-flight-freeze reactions in the brain. As neuroscience research has shown us, the brain cannot distinguish between real and perceived danger. It reacts in the same way whether a tiger is chasing you in the jungle, you feel left out from a social group, or if you subject yourself to internal bullying. Fear activates the stress response, resulting in hormones cascading through our bodies, creating havoc in our body-mind system.

The collective impact of this negative feedback from ourselves and those whom we respect and admire results in us questioning our self-worth. This self-imposed inquisition becomes present not only in our thoughts, but is also embedded in our emotions and perhaps even in the body's cellular structure.

So what does the Inner Critic sound like? Here are a few examples from HKIS students:

Grade 9 female student: *I was bullied a lot when I was a kid and I always let what people say to me get to me. If someone said I was dumb, I guess I am dumb then. I never stood up for myself either. My mom used to tell me I was a doormat and that I am weak for letting people get to me. I don't create my Inner Critic; other people do and it gets so strong that it now has a mind of its own. I am not mentally strong, I know that . . . My mind has the better control over me. I am not myself; I am my Inner Critic.*

Grade 9 male student: *Only this year did I find out that my parents weren't the ones who were putting all that pressure on me to get to good grades. It was my Inner Critic telling me that I wasn't good enough and no matter what I do, it will be bad or not up to standard.*

Grade 9 female student: *As soon as I entered high school, I found writing becoming increasingly hard until I physically couldn't write because I was scared of doing so. I would tell myself it wasn't good enough and it didn't make sense and that I would fail. That was why I constantly dreaded humanities assignments.*

Since we don't talk about this self-critical voice, many students suffer alone. It comes as a big relief to many students, then, when they realize that they aren't the only ones struggling with this negative soundtrack playing in the background. So, what can we do once we realize that this is an issue in our lives?

Strategies to Deal with the Inner Critic

We have six tips to help you manage the negative forces that have taken up residence in your subconscious mind and body, and to channel that energy into more positive outcomes.

- **Accept**: Start by accepting that the birth of the Inner Critic is a natural human phenomenon, a part of being a fully functional person. You can try to accept the idea of a common humanity, where everyone goes through a similar experience of suffering, so no one is alone in this. *"This is not just me. It happens to everyone. This is just the way the brain functions."*
- **Catch the Inner Critic in the Act**: Every time you spot it, say "hello" to it. Recognizing its subtle, but distinctive voice already begins to lessen its authority. *"Oh, there you are again."* Try rolling your eyes with that acknowledgment! When seen, the Inner Critic has the tendency to scurry away into the dark mental alleys from which it emerged. Pay attention when the Inner Critic noticeably asserts its strength. Be particularly watchful when you look in the mirror. It usually cringes or says things like *"Ouch!"* Watch out when you are about to speak in public. Your Inner Critic may warn you of how much your audience will dislike your talk. When you have to do something you've always wanted to do but never actually accomplished, it will oftentimes throw distractions in your way to keep you from your goal. When you find yourself procrastinating on a project, it may be a sign that your Inner Critic is covertly undermining your work. It's urging you to "not try," to dissuade yourself from taking on something new, saying, *"It's not a good day today."*
- **Spiritual Practice**: A mindfulness practice sensitizes the mind to the Inner Critic's more subtle movements, which will allow you to spot it before it starts sabotaging your well-laid plans. A simple practice of breath aware-

ness settles the mind enough that you can see the critic when it rears its head. *"I see you, Mr. Critic."* Try saying that while wagging your finger accusingly. With belly breathing and meditation techniques one can activate the parasympathetic nervous system that will enable you to get out of survival-based reactivity mode induced by the Inner Critic and into relaxation mode. Mindfulness practices of open awareness also allow us to get curious with the Inner Critic, to engage with it in friendly conversation and to extend compassion to it.

- **Acknowledge the Underlying Good Intentions**: Don't fight the powerful energy of the Critic, but rather acknowledge and befriend it. *"I see how you are trying to protect me, but I really want this to work. You may now leave— I got this."* When you give the Inner Critic some recognition that you understand its goals of trying to protect you, it may recede peacefully into the background. At times, you may even take on a bolder tone and say something like, *"Who asked for your opinion? Leave me alone!"*
- **Activate Your Inner Coach:** Speak to your younger/unsure self with the voice of a compassionate, cheering and loving coach. *"You can do this."* If your younger sibling or a mentee who looks up to you was bullied by someone, what kind of advice would you give him or her? Direct compassionate words of encouragement towards yourself, as you would, of course, do for a friend.
- **Develop Unconditional Positive Regard:** This can be something as simple as looking in the mirror, putting both fists in the air, and saying loudly, *"I'm just fantastic!"* This takes frequent practice and it may seem contrived or unconvincing in the beginning, but if we applaud ourselves, we go against the warnings posted by the Inner Critic, thereby reducing its vice-like grip.

We believe that these tips could have a profound impact on your whole approach to life. Give it a try and see what happens!

Loving Kindness Meditation

We want to especially emphasize that spiritual practices can help tame the Inner Critic. By helping you become more aware of what's going on in your mind, meditation enables you to catch yourself when you are engaging in unhelpful self-critiques. Then ask yourself: is that running commentary in my head useful or not? If not, attempt to let that voice go.

Sometimes letting go, however, is a lot harder than it sounds. Gaining the power to allow self-critique to enter and then pass through your mind involves building up an inner voice of self-compassion. Many students find the Loving Kindness Meditation (LKM) to be an effective practice to enable you to treat yourself with the same kind of compassion that you would provide a friend, which slowly shifts your subconscious thought patterns.

Recently Camilla, a high-achieving and ever-pleasant student, came up to me after class, "Can I talk to you, Mr. Schmidt?," as she fought back tears. She explained that she was feeling extremely anxious in not only this class, but others as well. It didn't seem to make sense, given her effervescent demeanor and high grades. After it became clear that she herself was unsure of the root issue, I recommended that she do the LKM for the next several days. A week later she wrote me an email explaining, "Thank you so much for the help, Mr. Schmidt. Truly, I feel like this week I've had a lot of improvement in regards to my anxiety . . . The meditation overall helped my security for all my classes. Thank you!" So, our advice is to try the LKM on a daily basis for a week, and see if your self-talk becomes gentler.[1]

Finally, it's not only about being kinder to yourself, but in time as you cultivate and direct generosity inward, you will also find a desire to treat everyone with this same love. This is a very different approach than when you are critiquing yourself, which leads to either judging others harshly who are "below" or envying those who are "above." The LKM meditation has a leveling effect, connecting you to the rest of humanity.

CONCLUSION

Our greatest hope is that you can recognize the inner contradiction that many young people have between harsh self-critique and open-hearted support towards friends with similar challenges. If your natural impulse is to comfort others, why are you loathe to comfort yourself? The first step in dealing with the Inner Critic is recognizing its existence and how it oftentimes sabotages what you are trying to accomplish in life. The next step is to develop a regular meditation practice to anchor that inner voice of self-compassion in your body-mind-heart self. Putting these two steps into practice will enable you to develop this life skill, and in so doing enhance the gift of yourself to the world.

REFLECTING ON AND TEACHING ABOUT THE INNER CRITIC

Marty (M): Hello Sangeeta, I want to first say thank you for bringing this issue of the Inner Critic to my attention. Prompted by your reading and teaching in this area, earlier this year I asked my 9th graders how many of them felt that they were a stronger critic of themselves than anyone else in their lives, and I was pretty shocked when 17 of the 20 students raised their hands. I thought, "Whoa, I need to investigate this more!" My sense now is that this issue is pervasive in our school community. Is that what you are gathering in your teaching of high school students in New York?

---

[1] We particularly like a 10-minute LKM called "Befriending" by Mark Williams that can be found on YouTube (Ko, 2016a). More student testimonies about the LKM can be found in Chapters 11 and 12.

Sangeeta (S): Yes, same here. Most kids raise their hands when I ask them if they have heard this critical voice inside their heads, and some even admit that they have names for them. However, they are rather taken aback when I tell them about the potential havoc that can be wreaked by the Inner Critic.

M: It rings true for me personally, too. I think that for most of my life I've suffered with an overly active Inner Critic. I remember as an adolescent being struck by the contradiction that I was far tougher on myself than I would be on a friend who had the same problem. It didn't make sense to me, but at the same time I couldn't release myself from this internal conundrum. I have a very distinct memory from college that I would like to share, put into the Christian worldview terms of my upbringing. I was standing outside the student center at my university in North Carolina, and that Inner Critic muttered to myself, "What a sinner!" I have no idea what the thought or issue was, but what made it memorable was that in the next instant some other voice responded, "But you're a forgiven sinner!" Some other more hidden part of me, it seemed, had to make the obvious point that the Christian message was all about forgiveness, so why was I beating myself up about my imperfections? Something inside me was trying to dampen that self-critical voice, but I didn't know how to grow that impulse.

S: How do you make sense, if I can ask quite candidly, of your inability as a young Christian to carry out a most basic teaching in Christianity: to love yourself?

M: Great question, and I think it's quite relevant here. Franciscan priest Richard Rohr (2016) recently commented, "Most people naturally feel that God must be pleased and placated. The isolated ego cannot imagine infinite and gratuitous love. Until we receive the Gospel on a cellular level, the little mind processes reality in some form of 'tit for tat.'" I take this to mean that our default system can only understand and accept *conditional* love, which leads to great insecurity. With all the negative voices that we have internalized from our childhood, we can't truly believe that God or anyone else values us unconditionally, a message which appears in religious traditions across the globe. So, even though we may have been taught that "God loves you" in our religious communities, the ego can't accept it as true. What a tragedy!

S: And we can go one step further. Most religious traditions teach that the goal is to become one with God, so if we cannot believe the teaching that we are deserving of unconditional love, just think how impossible it would be to absorb this even more radical non-dualistic teaching about our *oneness* with God where we become active co-creators of the world. As I became familiar with the self-critical mindset, I came to wonder if this is what holds us back from experiencing our innate divinity. This is why I see this Inner Critic concept as a gateway teaching to the most profound religious truths about unconditional love, unity with God, and creating a better universe.

M: So, Sangeeta, let's go from these profound considerations to Rohr's statement that we have to receive how deeply we are loved "on a cellular level." I'm still trying to understand this counterintuitive teaching that such sublime truths need to be discovered in bodily flesh!

S: That's why the Loving Kindness Meditation aims to impact not just the mind, but the body and heart level as well. Just as we once internalized all those negative messages about our unworthiness as children, we now need to replace that message with one that speaks of infinite and gratuitous love towards our deep physical selves—down to our energetic cellular level— where matter and energy, body and spirit are indistinguishable.

M: That's why I think we both feel that this Inner Critic issue is so important. If loving our neighbor is perhaps the fundamental religious command, but we can't even love ourselves, how authentic and consistent can our actual care be for others?

Let's turn to you, Sangeeta. Can you share your experience with the Inner Critic?

S: Well, like you, Marty, the Inner Critic has been a companion on my educational journey. As an undergrad in college I was a history major, which I loved and did very well in academically. However, when I decided to pursue a master's degree in business, there were several voices around me—friends, teachers and other well-wishers—who warned me that this was a difficult choice for someone who did not have advanced college level mathematics. Eventually I internalized those voices and whenever a difficult math problem came up, I would say to myself, "Oh, this is impossible for someone like me because I'm no good at math—I'm just a history major. These people are much smarter." I stayed away from any work opportunities that involved doing math.

Years later, when I migrated from business to teaching topics in psychology, world religions, and then eventually Buddhist and Indian philosophy, my Inner Critic once again reacted rather predictably. "Who do you think you are? There are so many experts out there. You're not anywhere as good as them. You should not be in this area. You don't know enough. You're a business major, for God's sake!" By this time, I had some understanding of how this voice was trying to keep me from making a fool of myself. It had my "best" intentions at heart. It urged me to not put myself out there for ridicule. It encouraged me to stay small and invisible.

M: So, what did you do to deal with the Inner Critic?

S: Interestingly, what worked against this "safe player" mental state, intent on shrinking my world into a safe haven where I would never get hurt, was another strong inner voice that said, "Doing this feels so good." When I chose to act out of my highest intentions for myself, not *just* the intention to play safe, I was energized by a force that can only be described as "purpose." I felt aligned with my true purpose. I noticed my body and mind going into stress mode before a big talk, and then I noticed a rush of excitement that overcame this stress. I chose to pay attention to this rush of excitement rather than the voice of the Inner Critic.

M: Both of us have this sense of distinctly different voices inside of our heads, battling it out for our attention and ultimately for our decisions to act. And I have to say that over the last five years that I've been meditating, the Inner Critic in its adversarial role has pretty much disappeared. The generosity that I can extend to other people I now extend to myself.

But here's the question I've been asked in class: has the dismissal of that "slave driver" that always tells you to do more meant that you have become less productive? In all honesty, it's possible that I do achieve less in terms of actual output. But what has happened is that as I learn about ways to heal myself through meditation and all the body-mind-heart connections, I am changing what and how I teach. I have discovered, it seems, what really matters for myself and my students. In that sense, I am more "efficient," even if the actual volume of work may be reduced. That's my take at this point on this important question. How would you address this, Sangeeta?

S: There is nothing wrong about noticing our flaws—for example, a tendency to procrastinate—and try to motivate ourselves to push harder. Very often, my students fear that if they don't have this self-critical voice, they will let themselves off the hook too easily and not get any work done. I like to emphasize that there is no problem with trying to boost self-motivation and avert slacking off. It's the delivery method and the tone of the message that we are trying to change. Over the long-term the Inner Critic does not accomplish its goal to boost motivation; in fact, over time it damages morale. A voice that is compassionate will do the opposite—it will encourage you to try again, and not beat yourself up for what happened in the past. The Inner Critic judges and condemns based on one misstep whereas the inner coach gives you several opportunities to grow.

M: That's a helpful way to reframe the question. Accepting myself has been a life-long journey, so I don't want to pretend that doing a Loving Kindness Meditation is a cure-all, but I would say that there has been a growing acceptance of who I am and who I am not. Over the years

	I have come to see that following my intuition, even when it wasn't recognized by others at the time, is a reliable guide to what I need to do with my life choices. What meditation has done for me is allow a lot of baggage that I was carrying from childhood thought patterns to recede into the background.
S:	Yes, I agree that meditation is really about changing habitual patterns of thinking and behavior, most of which we acquired before we became conscious of the damage they could do. This awareness shines new light on areas of our lives that hold us back in so many ways, keeping us from experiencing life in a joyful way.
M:	Yes, living a more abundant life seems to come from letting go of the Inner Critic, which subtly shift one's identity from this visible, tangible world—the horizontal dimension—to a more secure invisible domain. Success or failure on the horizontal is not so important now because there is a rootedness beyond it that allows a person to accept life as it comes, to somehow relax into reality. Of course, these things are not easy to describe, but my sense is that letting go of the Inner Critic in the end is a surrendering of the ego to something greater. There is a comfort in not taking oneself so seriously, and resting in something else.
S:	I love that . . . This is why I just keep reading about these new insights from professors and researchers. We are discovering new ways to apply ancient truths to our lives. It's an exciting time to be alive and I'm so grateful to have these teachings available to us!
M:	I feel the same. Can you recommend an author for us to get started with to learn more about the Inner Critic?
S:	Kristin Neff of the University of Texas has become the leading voice in the field. The insights she has gathered over the last 20 years are shared clearly in her TEDx talk (TEDx talks, 2013). Her book *Self-Compassion: The Proven Power of Being Kind to Yourself* (Neff, 2011) provides more detail about the key concepts that she speaks about.
M:	Thanks for your years of dedicated and passionate study, Sangeeta; look forward to more insights to follow.
S:	And I want to hear how you integrate these ideas into your SSS class and your exciting new Spiritual Explorations course.
M:	Will do, and let me know how this all plays out in your important work in New York.

PART IV

REFLECTIONS ON THE WISDOM WAY OF TEACHING

In this final section of the book, I have asked former and current colleagues (Chapter 17) as well as students who have been in our classes (Chapter 18) to speak to readers directly about their perspectives on education for social conscience and inner awakening. In earlier parts of the book, student testimonies were offered to demonstrate how instruction catalyzed certain aspects of social conscience and inner awakening, respectively. In Part IV, which focuses holistically on overall experiences, I attempt to offer greater personal insight into the multilayered ways in which this instruction can be impactful and the heart-felt significance that this can hold for both teachers and students, oftentimes years later.

I am deeply grateful to my colleagues and students, who have shared with me their opinions, testimonies, and epiphanies regarding their personal journeys that we have experienced together, all of whom have taken a keen interest in the wonder and mystery of these powerful educational approaches. In fact, it's not an exaggeration to say that such reflections have guided the entire Wisdom way of teaching process over the years and have compelled me to write this book. These comments, and others like them, have served as the most important benchmark for determining the efficacy of our various curricular innovations that have developed over time. Such participant feedback shows the remarkable potential of a carefully designed Wisdom education for engendering transformative experiences. I hope that their reflections will help the reader not only better understand the Wisdom way of teaching, but inspire resonant courses and programs in your own context.

Lastly, in Chapter 19, I pull together the yang of social conscience and the yin of inner awakening in a final personal reflection about my own pedagogical journey.

CHAPTER 17

TEACHER PERSPECTIVES

Every profound innovation is based on an inward bound journey.
—*Brian C. Arthur in Senge et al. (2004), p. 13*

The service learning course Humanities I in Action at HKIS was the favorite teaching experience of my 30-some-year career. The course was constructed around the goal of personal growth—for students and teachers alike.
—*Alan James, former HKIS Humanities teacher*

Including spiritual practices in the mix . . . revolutionized my teaching.
—*Jeremy Seehafer, current HKIS Humanities teacher*

What has actually inspired me to teach literature is not the bildungsroman narrative conventions of Huckleberry Finn or iambic pentameter of Hamlet, but rather the existential crisis both characters face, and the transformative grace that, at the climax of both stories, feels so powerfully and palpably close at hand.
—*Leo Zen, current HKIS Humanities teacher*

This chapter is a collection of personal testimonies written by former and current colleagues who have had direct connections with the courses and experiences shared in this book. It is hoped that these first-hand reports from those closest to the work will provide insights for teachers and practitioners who would like to apply these pedagogies in their own settings. What is particularly noteworthy in these reflections is the "inward bound" journey expressed in each piece. This illustrates perhaps the most important Wisdom principle for instructors: teaching for transformation requires going on one's own journey of deep personal change.

In keeping with the book as a whole, this chapter first offers teacher reflections—in alphabetical order by first name—on the Humanities I in Action course and social conscience education, and then moves to comments on Spiritual Explorations and teaching for inner awakening.

REFLECTIONS ON TEACHING FOR SOCIAL CONSCIENCE

Alan James on Teaching Humanities I in Action

The service learning course Humanities I in Action at HKIS was the favorite teaching experience of my 30-some year career. The course was constructed around the goal of personal growth—for students and teachers alike. I once called the course "teacher proof," not as a put down to future colleagues, but as a compliment to say that the foundational principles of the curriculum were designed foremost for the 14-year-old inquisitive mind and heart foremost. Students came into the course hungry to discover their own place in the cosmos, although it was the rare kid who knew this at the time. With 80 minutes of class time every day of the year, the interpersonal relationships were guaranteed to develop, especially when the course content revolved around issues of fairness and justice, locally and globally.

Early in the course we would travel as a class to Jungsing, China, where students were thrust into the responsibility of caring for young, often disabled, orphaned or institutionalized children. Since most of my students couldn't rely on speaking Chinese, they had to use their other senses to attend to the needs of the children. It took less than a day for my students to shift from talking about "those kids" to "my kid" as they developed a remarkably close bond with someone else. The Humanities I in Action students returned from Jungsing with a fundamentally different outlook on their classmates and their own potential in the world.

And with months more to go in the course, it was possible to build on this shared experience through readings, films, class discussions, and additional shared service experiences; this not a "one-off" trip, but a sustained eight-Saturday collective effort. Through those additional service experiences, students discovered the hard work of commitment to an outside institution, such as a center for disabled adults, children, or even in an English language support role for local Cantonese children. I loved how students studied an unvarnished version of the depravity of the human experience through such topics as genocide, child labor, and environmental degradation, but also were empowered to fight back, to make a local contribution rather than wringing their hands or abandoning their ideals. The course also expected rigor—course materials were texts from current affairs, and the literature studied contributed to their knowledge and ways of seeing the world as they were living in it.

Perhaps my favorite memory of the Humanities I in Action course came from a *Lord of the Flies* simulation we conducted on a local beach. We never told the students they were competing; we simply gave two groups a similar set of goals and a time frame. Within minutes the exercise had descended into attempts to undermine the "opposing team," a team made up of students who the day before were working in groups with them and months before had held babies together in Jungsing. When the short exercise ended, much like how the novel ends, the students ashamedly recognized that all the tasks assigned could have been far more easily attained by working together. The lesson that the "world as competition" is self-constructed carried their thinking forward and underpinned much of our worldview reflections as the year continued. Putting students and service at the center of the learning experience worked beautifully to challenge the hearts and minds of everyone in the course.

Amy Vlastelica on Applying Social Conscience Education to Museums

Social conscience education impacted my trajectory both as a student and teacher at HKIS and beyond. Unfortunately, the Humanities I in Action course did not exist when I was a student (1994–2002), but the seed for inner awakening was planted through Interim and service trips, such as those to the Jungsing orphanage. These were the most influential in developing a global mindset, and are what set me and my third culture peers apart from many of our classmates in university. The desire to further reflect on my own place in the world is in large part what drove me back to HKIS as a drama teacher from 2007 to 2009.

During my time as a teacher, collaborations with Marty and Crossroads Foundation inspired me to use my skills in theatre and design to produce "live action simulations," which employ theatrical elements of role-play, immersive sets, and narrative to encourage participants to walk in the shoes of others. Their goal is to provide a shared experience—such as the plight of a refugee—from which participants can relate, reflect, and ultimately gain empathy. In many ways, I was striving to create my own version of transformative experiences, like those I had participated in on HKIS Interims and service trips, by bringing difficult realities to students who most likely will never have the opportunity to witness these things firsthand. The resulting research formed my MFA thesis entitled *Social Action Simulations: Developing Social Conscience Through Role-Play and Choice-Making*. I studied how simulations could be hosted in informal educational venues beyond the classroom, such as museums, in hopes to reach greater audiences. Now as a creator of and consultant for museums in the US, I hope to instill these same values of social conscience into my work.

LeAnn Stanhope on Teaching Humanities I in Action

Not only is Humanities I in Action the reason why I wanted to join HKIS, but it also embodies why I wanted to change professions in my late 30s, ending a successful 14-year career in health and fitness to become a teacher.

Eight years ago I was invited to work with 150 grade 10 students in their unit on Health & Wellness. Those 8 weeks showed me that education was going through a major shift in what students were being taught and how they were navigating through that content. I enrolled in teacher training a month later and within a year I was at a teacher conference watching Marty present his research findings on a course he was running—Humanities in Action. It blew my mind. I saw a curriculum that used provocative, real world issues and inspired students to research, formulate opinions, and meet with experts in authentic learning experiences. It was a course that empowered them to take meaningful action. Listening to his presentation I was excited, then inspired, then intimidated, and then paralyzed with fear. I felt ridiculously under qualified to teach this course, which is why it took another 7 years for me to apply to the school.

Being able to teach Humanities I in Action this year has been all that I imagined it to be. We explore controversial topics and perspectives—from evangelical hate groups, to eugenics, to the Rwandan genocide—with the intent to expand our worldview, and finally to understand. We add in novels that tell stories from around the world and not just support the Western "single story" that Nigerian author Chimamanda Ngozi Adichie (TED, 2009) warns us about.

We then add in trips that humanize orphanages in China, or simulations that help us to better understand the refugee crisis, which are incredibly powerful experiences. They foster hands-on-learning that creates foundations in understanding and compassion, to help students see how they can make true systemic change in the world. In this course they do not just mindlessly do "service hours" to pass the course. Spending time with the recipients of the aid that NGOs are assisting, instead of just throwing fundraising money at the issue, helps students see people and not just poverty, real humans and not abstract problems.

Making a mid-career move was a big gamble for me, but in retrospect I see that I've really taken health and fitness to a new level. Humanities I in Action is the epitome of this new level, allowing me to bring health to my students in a whole new way—healing our misunderstandings so we can heal the world.

Zella Talbot on Teaching Humanities I in Action

The birth of Humanities I in Action came about after I had been teaching the 9th grade humanities course for almost 20 years. Rather than having students develop a bank of knowledge for its own sake, Marty and I wanted something more purposeful in their lives. We had been experimenting with community service through the 90s and knew that it could be very powerful, but the impact always seemed to be short-lived because it was outside the curriculum. It was always an "extra" rather than at the core of what we study at school. Our curricular task, then, was to integrate memorable content and experiential learning, all aimed at the high purpose of making the world a better place. We knew we were charting a new direction and therefore, like a puzzle, we had to select the content deliberately, steering the learning according to student need and interest. We sought constant feedback from the students, slowly departing from the traditional 9th grade course. The only requirement we had was to mix three core components to make Humanities I in Action authentic and purposeful: awareness of social issues, emotional impact, and inspiring students to act to change their society. While it has taken years to bring these ideas to fruition, we could sense from early on that we were creating a new vision of education. What we felt all those years ago is still true today: while the global challenges of our world are incredibly daunting, thinking alone cannot solve our problems. We need the humanities to teach our students to act with heart to foster genuine care for planet earth and its inhabitants.

REFLECTIONS ON TEACHING FOR INNER AWAKENING

Jeremy Seehafer on Teaching Peace Studies

When I created a Peace Studies course for our Humanities Department nearly a decade ago, the curricular focus was on Social Studies content such as conflict resolution, the military-industrial complex, and nonviolent civil disobedience. However, as time evolved, I felt that the course was somehow lacking in the core of what it meant to be both personally peaceful and how to help bring peace to a chaotic world. Thus, I started to tinker every year trying to find the right combination of what might work to make it more engaging, thoughtful and reflective.

Units on "peace and human nature," "restorative justice," "forgiveness," and "religious inspiration" were added and students found these topics to be engaging both intellectually, but more importantly, spiritually.[1] A significant amount of time was given for reflection, some of which was incredibly personal in nature and deeply insightful. Soon thereafter, the decision was made to offer the course as both a Social Studies *or* Religion credit. I was pleased with this shift in focus and optimistic that students might be encouraged to take the course to help them fulfill a Religion credit.

Assignments were created that focused more on the heart and offered students opportunities to explore their own spirituality. Some of these assessments included seminar discussions on peace and human nature, a simulation on restorative justice where students developed empathy, burning of regrets, visits to various

---

[1] With Jeremy's guidance, these topics eventually became the core of the SPEX 11 curriculum, which can be found in Appendix D.

places of worship in Hong Kong with personal reflections, and letters of forgiveness.

It was then that I spoke with Marty who encouraged me to consider including spiritual practices in the mix. After his sharing of successes with these in his courses, I decided to experiment and try them myself. Needless to say, I'm so glad I did! This new approach revolutionized my teaching.

I came back daily and shared with Marty the incredible reflections students were writing in their daily "homeplay" assignments and in-class spiritual practices. Words of encouragement, mindful walks, daily meditations, gratitude journals and others positive psychology avenues to happiness were explored. Student responses blew me away. They found these spiritual practices to be personally beneficial and were more than willing to try new experiences. Ultimately, this made the course more personal for them and helped them understand the essence of peace. It started with them, on their personal journey, and allowed them to take the next step in wanting to make the world a more peaceful place. I will never teach the course the same way again.

Leo Zen on Teaching Spiritual Explorations: "The Reluctant Wisdom Teacher"

Being asked to teach a course on "Spiritual Explorations" was both an exciting opportunity and one that presented, for me, a series of dilemmas. Nothing in my teacher training prepared me to teach explicitly for the development of wisdom in students. The profession of teaching has revolved largely around content knowledge, differentiating instructional practices, providing "guaranteed and viable" curricula, and assessments based on prescribed academic standards. To paraphrase a quotation often attributed to Mark Twain, my teacher training, though by turns inspiring, challenging, and ennobling, also made sure I was equipped with all the ways in which "schooling" could interfere with my students' education. It was not until the end of my teaching practicum did a professor (of literature, not education) suggest to me that perhaps schools expend a great deal of energy on developing and assessing students' intellects, but very little on their capacity for wisdom.

And yet wisdom is so often what we say we want students to seek. In all the settings I have taught—from public schools in Hawaii that served a large population of low-income indigenous and immigrant families, to a competitive and heavily exam-oriented government school in Hong Kong with average class sizes of 40 students, to an international school in Hong Kong populated by students who are as affluent as they are diverse—the students have had a common need; a need that, no matter how comprehensive the syllabus or inventive the lesson plan, was continually frustrated. Some students need to improve their spelling and grammar. Some need to comprehend texts more efficiently for multiple choice tests. Some need to construct better thesis statements. But all students—the teen mother, the Ivy League-driven violin virtuoso, the child of expatriates who spent spring break in the Seychelles—need a sense of authentic *purpose*; liberation, really, from the narrow social pressures, expectations, and definitions of success placed on their lives. And because of that, they also *all* need compassion, forgiveness, gratitude, and love.

That's a tall order, and the next dilemma that might arise when you are asked to guide students through a course on Wisdom traditions or Spiritual Explorations is that your own feelings of inadequacy will quickly surface. I had no background or "content knowledge" for teaching religion, let alone much direct experience in the mystical or esoteric contemplation of purpose and the meaning of life. The closest formal understanding I had was in the use of biblical allusions in the literature I taught, and perhaps the weekends I spent as a child mowing the lawn of our neighborhood Buddhist temple in Hawaii while my parents chanted with the monks inside. In fact, I was half-convinced that I was chosen to teach the course because of my name (though the "Zen" has less to do with my Buddhist upbringing and more to do with a mis-anglicization of my family's surname when my parents immigrated to the U.S. from Taiwan). Suffice it to say, any teacher who seeks to teach the Wisdom way will be confronted with the progress they have or have not made in their own spiritual journey. This *self*-doubt in how such a course could be realized and whether one is fit to teach it would, I imagine, give pause to even the seasoned teacher of World Religions who may be more comfortable with teaching the material as academic content and not as a transformative journey for the student.

But teachers know that despite their lack of prep and sleep, despite their anxieties and consternations, the bell for the start of the lesson will ring anyway ("ask not for whom the bell tolls"), and sometimes you just have to show up and settle in. It was in teaching the course that the Latin idiom *docendo discimus* ("by teaching, we learn") became, once again, generously apparent. There are, of course, many more books to read and teachers and guides in the Wisdom traditions to follow and retreats to attend and yoga postures to master. But there is also the resounding stillness of students breathing in unison. There is the gentle tapping of rain on the classroom window one is able to discern in that stillness. And there is a sacredness to the space of the classroom that is remembered when we are all allowed to just *be*.

Once, when I was mowing the lawn at the Buddhist temple, I asked a monk if I could go into the temple to chant with my parents. His reply? "You already are."

What I realized from the first year of teaching Spiritual Explorations is that I have been preparing (and have been prepared) to teach this course all my life—and what a gift it was. Marty has gone into marvelous detail about what such a course or way of teaching might entail. I'll only share that the teaching of wisdom was reassuringly less about *doing* for the students (or the students doing something for me) and more about *being* with the students. A relationship that is a refreshing contrast to the usual transaction of grades and judgment, and one that is far from proselytizing—more, as stated by Cynthia Bourgeault, "energetic" than "moralistic." The journey is as much yours as it is theirs.

Now, there are still moments when I think all this is better left implicit and up to interpretation. *Show, don't tell.* But then I remember my work is in service to very young and impressionable beings who are inundated with exploitive and explicit messages about what they should find unattractive about themselves, fear about the world, and aspire to possess. It is no wonder that movements like service learning, positive education, character strengths, social-emotional learning, and mindfulness in schools feel so resonant and progressive. We are all teachers of spirituality if the wellbeing, transformation, and self-transcendence of our students (and ourselves) is the goal.

I'm also willing to make the concession proposed by not a small number of my students that there may well be nothing beyond the "veil" (or no veil at all). But if there is. . . then, as Marty has suggested, what a wasted opportunity it would be to not have ever conversed, contemplated, and communed with our students and with each other about the possibilities of that invisible, infinite, and ultimate reality.

So it is with a little less reluctance that I call myself a teacher of the Wisdom tradition and spirituality. I'm not ready to surrender the moniker of "English Teacher" as my first and foremost professional identity; it is what Marty might call the outer *yang* to the inner *yin*. Marty has shown the power of social consciousness and service in facilitating our awareness of the unseen, and art—literature, films, music, comic books—can be a means to that awareness as well. After all, and all along, what has actually inspired me to teach literature is not the bildungsroman narrative conventions of *Huckleberry Finn* or iambic pentameter of *Hamlet*, but rather the existential crisis both characters face, and the transformative grace that, at the climax of both stories, feels so powerfully and palpably close at hand. Yes, I want my students to effectively analyze those texts and know how to get an "A" on the assessment, but I'd trade in a dozen "A" essays for my students to value equally why one might be moved—in body, mind, and heart—by the texts as well, and for them to have the wisdom to know the difference.

Richard Friedericks on Teaching Spiritual Practices

> The real revolution to come is the spiritual awakening of humankind, and out of that awakening will be born a civilization of love, a universal society with an engaged heart.
>
> —*Wayne Teasdale (2002, p. xxxiii)*

All my life, I've longed for this kind of revolution! As a teacher I saw it as my opportunity and responsibility to lead students and colleagues toward their own awakening. To support this, I took an online course on Contemplative Teaching in 2005. Through the course I was introduced to Buddhist meditation practices, the Integral Theory of Ken Wilber and re-acquainted with the writings of several spiritual teachers. I applied what I was learning as best I could to my own teaching at HKIS and with my media classes with various degrees of success.

I began to imagine teaching a class about the practice and purpose of meditation. In 2009 I proposed and began teaching a religion course called "Spiritual Practices of the East."[2] This was a survey of contemplative practices of the world's religions. I was pleasantly surprised when students signed up for a course that had them sit in meditation for 20 minutes at the beginning of each class session.

Over the five years I taught the course, we focused on understanding what happens when we meditate and why sitting-to-just-be might benefit each student and our community. We looked at meditation through the eyes of current scientific studies as well as the ancient teachings of the world's various spiritual traditions. We discussed human cultural and spiritual evolution through the lens of Integral Theory. I wanted to spark curiosity. I hoped they would start asking: "Where do these thoughts and feelings come from?" or "Who am I?" or "What am I part of?" I hoped they would leave the course aware of big questions: "Where are we headed as a civilization, as a planet?" and "What can I do to help make this a good place for all of us to live?"

Student responses to meditation were initially hesitant to resistant. Gradually, however, students began to see the benefits of sitting in meditation. They began meditating at home, and in class made observations about their practice. A Loving Kindness Meditation was a favorite choice. We discussed how meditation was a tool for integrating the mind with the heart. Students reported more positive interactions with others and brighter moods. We discussed what kind of society it would be if everyone practiced meditation and lived in a centered sense of joy. Teaching responsive students helped me to see that the idea of "a civilization of love," an enlightened society with "an engaged heart," is not an impossible dream.

Simon Thauvette on Teaching Spiritual Explorations

As an educator of mathematics with a spiritual bent, when I arrive at the limitations of my knowledge and understanding, I start asking theological questions and seek help from "above" in hopes for clarity and to push through a cognitive plateau. Rather than focus on keeping axioms, definitions, and the facts of mathematics separate from the explanations and interpretations of a vertical dimension, I have become completely convinced that spiritual exploration acts as an anchor and catalyst to push through physical limitations, extend my knowledge, and reach new levels of insight in all domains of my life. This personal intuition has been confirmed in my teaching of "Spiritual Explorations" this year: there is no doubt that the explicit, regular participation of addressing life's most complex and meaningful questions in my SPEX classes has not only created a glowing ef-

---

[2] Richard's course became the first one at HKIS to bring spiritual practices into the curriculum; I credit his initiative for beginning our institutional journey to what became the SPEX program nine years later.

fect within my students' bodies, minds, and hearts—as we consider life's infinite possibilities—but it has also molded a vision and belief that the more we explore the interconnectedness of all things, the more we learn, period. Now more than ever it is time for educational institutions to embrace spiritual exploration as a necessity in helping our future leaders discover and push their potential from within and place it at the very core of everything we do in academia.

Each of the SPEX classes that I led started with a "check-in" followed by a meditation lesson and practice, then continued into the core of the lesson with time for students at the end to reflect and write in their journals. The buy-in and success of each of our lessons was based on the premise that good decisions start with good listening. At the beginning of class I asked every student to respond to the question, "How are you at this moment in time?," which not only gave each student an opportunity to share, but also allowed the entire class to listen in a judgment-free and empathetic manner. Once everyone was given an opportunity to share—as much or as little as they wanted to—the progression into a meditation practice and the lesson was smooth and well-received by all individuals. This format created an avenue for the body, mind, and heart to be connected and set the tone for everyone to listen and feel their existing beliefs as well as ponder new possibilities.

As an educator who has facilitated countless math lessons, my meter of success in the past was purely based on my students' abilities to build problem-solving capacity, improve numerical fluency, and develop strong reasoning skills. After teaching SPEX, however, I have been able to reflect on my own teaching practice and realize that when we set goals, learning targets, or lesson objectives, we may get our students to explicitly converge their thinking and meet such goals, but that such learning routines set limitations and rarely get students to explore or go beyond the assessed curriculum. By contrast, the learning routines that go with a SPEX class create infinite avenues of learning based on the individual's own experience and driven by genuine curiosity and endless possibilities.

If schools truly have students at the center of their educational models, then they need to dive deeper and unpack the center of their models—the learner, the individual—and start exploring the possibilities that lie within each person and what dimension they can reach *above*. Until now, I had always sought for answers to the question, "How do we get students to care, be compassionate, and take ownership for their own learning and succeed," and had come away without clarity. Now I have been enlightened that through spiritual exploration, students themselves have the answers within as they explore their bodies, minds, and hearts in light of the vertical dimension.

* * *

In bringing these comments to a close, I want to honor my colleagues and friends who have chosen teaching as a life pathway to make a difference in the world. For it is not easy to maintain one's energy for innovation when, akin to other forms of modern life, standardization, technocratic strictures, performance pay, and the ever-present possibility of cost-cutting measures threaten to smother teachers' love of knitting together an animate curriculum within the minds and hearts of their students. I am happy to report that teaching these courses oriented towards social conscience and inner awakening has been a deeply gratifying, life-giving personal and professional experience for all of us, and will be among the most meaningful of our life experiences. I am deeply grateful for their co-creation of these and other like-minded courses, and for their continued steadfastness in converting these curricula into living, breathing experiences day-in and day-out on behalf of our students.

CHAPTER 18

STUDENT VOICES

Too much environmental and global education has been outer-directed (looking out on the world) and has denied interiority (inner journeying)... Spirituality is a recognizing of deeper levels of connection within ourselves and between ourselves and our environment.
—*Selby (2001, p. 13)*

My experience in Humanities I in Action awakened me to the world around me and guided me to my ambition of having a positive impact on this world through environmental sustainability. Service, Society, and the Sacred reminded me of the paramount importance of intimately knowing my inner self in order to purify these outward efforts... I now have the tools to lead a life of more profound wakefulness and to constantly seek out wisdom for the betterment of my pursuits. The wisdom of Humanities I in Action and SSS for "living deeply" has transformed me for the better, and its lessons will continue to influence all aspects of my life indefinitely.
—*Amar, grade 12 male student*[1]

The value of student testimony in evaluating the impact of one's teaching craft is difficult to overstate. In this chapter I ask students who have studied in our social

---
[1] Amar's full essay reflections on Humanities I in Action and SSS can be found in Appendix B.

The Wisdom Way of Teaching: Educating for Social Conscience and Inner Awakening in the High School Classroom, pages 203–218.
Copyright © 2022 by Information Age Publishing
www.infoagepub.com
All rights of reproduction in any form reserved.

conscience and inner awakening classes to speak directly to readers about their experiences. The following collection of personal reflections illustrate why I have felt compelled to share *The Wisdom Way of Teaching*. Much like the previous chapter on teacher perspectives, what seems most striking in these pieces is the degree of interior exploration—the "inward bound journey" (Senge et al., 2004, p. 13) that Selby (2001) points to as the blind spot in environmental and global education.

For the sake of organization, I have listed student contributions in alphabetical order by their first names; I have not arranged them according to social conscience or inner awakening, however, for some of the comments don't fall easily into one category or the other. I have also listed the year that they graduated from high school. Most graduated from HKIS, while a few transferred to other schools. All of the writings were solicited recently for this book.

ALYSSA FAN (2021)

Spiritual Exploration (SPEX) is a course that let me evolve, both as a student and a person. Through various, sometimes even unconventional, mindfulness practices like burning paper on which we wrote our regrets, I learned to let go of identities and beliefs that no longer served me. As a high school student, this was a skill that felt very important and empowering. I realized that beliefs such as "I need to get good grades" or "I need to be a good student" constantly gave me stress, which ultimately impeded my learning. But SPEX taught me tools that I can use to regain control of my own life, in and out of school. SPEX, in my view, is a special course that offers valuable life lessons to the next generation of change leaders. Thank you SPEX and SPEX teachers for empowering me and teaching me how to live the life I wish to live.

ARIANE DESROSIERS (2019)

I was fortunate enough to partake in two of Mr. Schmidt's classes in my freshmen year, Humanities I in Action and World Religions. I'll admit that before starting the school year, I was rather cynical of what could be learnt in an average 9th grade humanities class. I had just departed from my old school in the midst of an administrative conflict, so I came to Humanities I in Action disheartened and world-weary. I was aware of global issues and was passionate about them; my yang of social conscience was developing as we studied more about the urgent issues of our modern time, but I often felt during that first month that there was nothing I could do to change the world; it seemed too futile to even try. And then we went to Jungsing. Experiencing that euphoria of making a baby smile and holding several disabled kids by the hand for a stroll in the park is something I'll never forget. It made me realize that service learning is just as important as the standard academic way of learning, and perhaps even more, because when you experience a moment

Ariane (r) with Classmate Liberty (l) in Grade 9. Photo credit: Author.

of inner awakening, you truly start to learn about yourself and how you, personally, can change the world.

It was inspiring. By the end of the semester I was ready to go forth and "spread the light," but I also kept in mind that darkness is innate; extinguishing darkness in its entirety and adding too much light can make you blind. I think it's important to realize that (as somber as it may sound) you need to appreciate the darkness because it lets you be grateful for your experiences in the light. This concept is something I'll take with me whenever I try to enact change in the world.

Then, during second semester I began taking religion class with Mr. Schmidt as well. Again, I was skeptical of World Religions—I had never taken a religion class before and I was actually worried it would try to coerce me into being religious. I grew up agnostic and my dad would always tell me how he hated the indoctrination of the church. However, it was completely the opposite. That semester I learnt about how I had a lack of training, if you will, in the "heart" sector of the body-mind-heart system. I've always believed that spirituality has to come from within (the "know thyself" concept), and so for the entire second semester I embarked on a personal journey to discover more about myself and to develop my spirituality. I studied dreams in our religion class with the aim of gaining a deeper understanding of my outer ego/personality (the one which aims to create big change in a global context—aka, the yang), then trying to marry it with my still-developing "inner self" (the one which aims to create change that evokes personal emotion—aka, the yin). I realized that when it comes to my spirituality, I consider all things natural to be sacred, and was thus labelled by Mr. Schmidt a "mystical ecologist," which, so far, rings true. I consequently further developed my yin and as a result am more self-aware and try to envelop the cynicism that naturally occurs within me with love, hope, gratefulness and optimism. In conclusion, I believe that learning with the yin-yang process is integral to inspiring students to enact global change and create a much-needed inner balance when we are constantly pressed in an ever-changing modern world.

BEA CARANDANG (2018)

At first, Humanities in Action made me uncomfortable. On the first day of class in my freshman year of high school, Mr. Schmidt introduced the chocolate activity [Chapter 3] and led with the question "Is ignorance bliss?" This puzzled me as I didn't really know what to make of the question. As the class progressed, we began to learn the reality of how cocoa beans are sourced and how most major chocolate companies source their cocoa unethically. This was the beginning of the uncomfortable feeling that began to reside at the pit of my stomach. The feeling didn't go away as the next few classes progressed, because immediately after the first class, we dove into more and more real world issues. The feeling of unease became more and more present, and soon I realized that the feeling wasn't discomfort, but guilt. I felt guilty for choosing ignorance over reality. I felt guilty for choosing to stay safe and happy in my own expatriate bubble, and for downplaying the urgency and magnitude of the rest of the world's issues. It was then that I realized why Mr. Schmidt asked us on the very first day, "Is ignorance bliss?" I realized that my whole life I had been living in a bubble and had subconsciously put into practice an us and them mentality. I had separated myself from individuals whom I saw on the news, believing that I was immune to experiencing any of "their" problems. For this reason, I realized that it was my fear of suddenly feeling guilt that caused me to leave the room if my dad put CNN or BBC on. Although I did feel uneasy at the beginning of the class, it was necessary in order for me to realize that issues such as poverty, unethical labor, or the refugee crisis were real and happening at that very moment. It made me realize that ignorance was not bliss, and that I could no longer escape the reality that the world has issues that urgently call for change.

The Elixir Project in the second half of the year was what allowed me to come to terms with the reality that the world wasn't how I made it out to be. For my Elixir Project I focused on education in the Philippines, a topic very close to my heart, as being Filipina has always been something that I took pride in. The goal of my project wasn't necessarily to raise a certain amount of money or donations, but rather to create a video to raise awareness on the importance of education. I worked with the Virlanie Foundation, an NGO which helps impoverished and abused street children in the Philippines. I spoke to many of the children in their programs, looked at their facilities and programs, and talked to those who have successfully come out of the program. I wanted my Elixir Project to emulate my own experience in Humanities in Action in which by watching my video others could also experience what I call the "light switch" moment. By flicking on the light switch, the rest of the room suddenly becomes more clear, and in the same way, being aware of the world and its issues makes it more visible and much more tangible. The Elixir Project helped me come to terms with my own fear of not being able to make a difference, and most importantly through the Virlanie Foundation, gave me hope that through awareness and understanding, the necessary changes to make the world a better place can still be made.

Bea (l) with Miyona (r) Participating in a Flag Day Community Fundraising Event Early in Humanities I in Action. Photo credit: Author.

Looking back now four years later, I can say that Humanities in Action quite literally changed my life. This class completely broadened my worldview by encouraging me to accept the reality that the world is not perfect. It is because of this class that I have come to realize my passion for learning and talking about world affairs and my deep interest for understanding why our society is the way it is today. Today I am studying at the University of Toronto and am working at obtaining a double major in International Relations and Sociology.[2]

BRITTANY FRIED (2015)

You never expect a grade 9 course to shape your decisions throughout high school, let alone in university and beyond. Yet as a soon-to-be graduate of Georgetown University's School of Foreign Service, I can say that has exactly been the case. Humanities in Action was my first true taste of holistic education: learning that focuses on the mind, heart, and soul. It taught me that compassion, community development, and social consciousness not only can, but should be integrated into an academic setting. This knowledge has been core to my learning both in and outside the classroom since.

Humanities in Action provided a space for reflection on personal views of the world and our individual place in it. This reflection, paired with exposure to global challenges, prompted me to identify issues that spoke to me personally, and shift to long-term engagement with them. My personal topic of choice became transformative education, due to my exposure to it in Humanities in Action, and the positive impact I saw it could have on the greater global community.

As a result of this shift, my best friend Caroline and I developed a leadership and empowerment program implemented annually in India. The program

---

[2] Bea's three-minute video is the finest visual I have to introduce the Humanities I in Action course to students and teachers. Put her name and "Humanities 1 in Action" into a search engine to watch the video. She also made a second touching five-minute video detailing her Elixir Project in the Philippines. This can be found by putting her name and "Education in the Philippines" into a search engine.

was started my freshman year of high school. While Caroline and I had initiated service programs together before, taking Humanities in Action provided essential critical thinking skills that enabled us to engage the local community on a deeper level. As a result, we attempted to minimize the harm that came about from our presence—for instance through voluntourism, a concept we were exposed to in Humanities in Action—and instead aspired to provide benefit for all involved.

Our commitment to transformative education that we developed through Humanities in Action did not stop after freshman year. For the next three years Caroline and I remained engaged in the India program, and with the help of Dr. Schmidt, led the trip twice more, expanded the program to other countries, and developed an official curriculum. Beyond this, I spent a summer with the organization Me to We running "Take Action Camps," and as the school's Senator of Service worked with the school administration to incorporate a greater long-term vision into our high school service clubs.

By the time I arrived at university, it was clear that transformative education was central to my core interests and being. Continued engagement with the topic manifested itself in my major and minor, which focus on peace education and genocide studies, respectively; a semester studying peace education in Rwanda; four spring breaks conducting Holocaust study in Eastern Europe; work with a Jesuit community development organization in Zambia; and internships and service opportunities in DC. Now, my undergraduate experience is culminating in an Honors Thesis on the intersection of peace education and Ignatian pedagogy in post-conflict Timor-Leste. It is unknown what next year will bring, but one thing is clear: the pursuit of transformative education will be a part of it.

When I look back, it's very clear where this 8-year journey began: in a grade 9 classroom, when I was asked what I cared about, and how I was going to engage with it academically, physically, and spiritually. Addressing these critical questions at such an influential time in personal identity formation, and being provided the tools to engage with them through the course, allowed me to discern a topic that has and will continue to shape my life. I will forever be grateful to Dr. Schmidt and the Humanities in Action team for not only asking these critical questions of my classmates and me, but for believing we had the ability to do something about them, and for challenging us to do exactly that.

GIORGIA FRANCHI (2000)

I don't think it is an exaggeration to say that the experiences I had at HKIS in relation to social awareness and service led me to becoming a human rights lawyer and thereafter work for a humanitarian aid agency.

Looking back, I believe it was around 9th grade when I first became aware of the impact that charity work could have, both on myself and others. I had been selected to travel to Vietnam on the Christina Noble Foundation Interim. Prior to leaving for Ho Chi Minh City, we were asked to read *Bridge Across My Sorrows* by Christina Noble (1994), the founder of the organization, and this provided an amazing introduction into what we would experience once in Vietnam. It provided a whole other layer to my experience—how the will of one woman changed the lives of so many children, and how this in turn helped her grow as an individual.

In the following years I became involved in other types of community work, volunteering for Mother's Choice, World Vision, and Habitat for Humanity through another Interim. These experiences were eye-opening—not only because they put some perspective on my life, which had always been privileged, but because they also gave me an understanding of cultures, languages, and history. It was also not lost on me that as expats we could choose to "pop in and out" of these experiences—how could we really serve these communities? These were the kinds of questions that began forming in my mind.

In 10th grade I enrolled in an interdisciplinary class [a forerunner to Humanities I in Action] with Mr. Schmidt and Mr. Coombs which provided a blend of literature, history, and service work. This was the first course I had ever taken which expressly incorporated service into the curriculum. I saw that all the students—whether academically-minded or not—engaged in the service aspect of our class with enthusiasm. A highlight was a class trip to an orphanage in Jungsing which we visited for a few days. I cannot say how much we did in fact help the nurses, but it was a distinct moment in our studies where our social conscience was galvanized, where we were encouraged to step outside of our physical and emotional safety zones; to reflect; to be conscious of not only our actions but our spirituality as well. I was overwhelmed with emotions: guilt, empathy, gratitude. And I kept going back to the same questions as before—was this meaningful? What could service *really* mean for me, in a way that would not be tokenistic, selfish, imposing? Was there really a way of being of service as part of daily life?

I returned to the orphanage in Jungsing with Mr. Schmidt as an adult, ten years after my first trip there. In retrospect it was easy for me to see how that explicit marrying of service and education pushed me onto a specific career path of service—in a way that felt genuine, where I could contribute purposefulness with my own specific skillsets. It wasn't that single visit to Jungsing that did this, but it *was* that class where the seed was planted and which shaped the decisions I made as a high school student and beyond.

After university I practiced as an immigration/human rights lawyer before shifting slightly to working for a humanitarian aid agency. For the last few years I have managed research projects that look at preventing and responding to violence against women and girls in conflict settings. The charity sector is not a perfect system, and I often ask myself the same questions I had asked in Jungsing. But that's how I know I am still being conscious of my actions, of my service; still thinking about my privileges and place in the world; still learning. And I am grateful for my high school teachers who took us beyond the classroom into a world of compassion, awareness, and mindfulness.

ISABELLE NG (2013)

I was very much in my own little privileged bubble prior to Humanities in Action. I was born and raised in Hong Kong—a bustling city comprised of fancy skyscrapers, flashy neon lights, and some of the world's wealthiest people'. At the time, I was 13 years old and had little to no understanding of the cruelties of our world. Hong Kong to me was finance, advancement, and technology. I was unaware of the massive wealth gap and housing crisis that crippled countless lives. From a more general standpoint, I simply had limited knowledge of how our world history has caused systemic injustices that still hurt many populations today. I was quite literally young and naive.

In Action opened my eyes and exposed me to a brand-new worldview. This drastic shift in mindset led me to rethink my entire life and what exactly I wanted to do with it. I continuously questioned, what could I do about what I was learning and how could I apply it in my life? How could I dedicate my life to better comprehending injustices and contribute my time for the greater good?

One memory from class that sticks to me was when Mr. Schmidt showed us visually what the ratio of the wealthiest to the rest of the world looked like—the 1%. He then had us recognize that we students of HKIS were all in that 1%. I was stunned by my privilege. For my whole life, I didn't have to think about whether I had a roof over my head each night or food on my plate when I got home. I didn't have to think about affording health care or university. I lived an extremely extremely comfortable life. While in Action changed my worldview, it also made me aware of my privilege—what could I do to show that I recognize this and what could I do to take advantage of this?

Retracing back to my In Action days, I now know I have made life decisions that in part are due to having taken that course. I attended a university where I pursued biology and environmental studies. I chose courses to purposefully enrich myself on subjects such as environmental racism and water rights, all the while learning the science behind life itself. My multidisciplinary learning has widened my worldview past what I learned in high school. Humanities in Action threw more fuel to my fire—the fire being the passion I had for wildlife conservation since childhood. I know I will dedicate my life to environmental conservation, and I'm grateful for Humanities in Action for giving me the push and belief in myself to pursue this for life.

JASMINE LAU (2008)

It's difficult to pinpoint when one becomes aware of one's own self-efficacy, the moment when empowerment happens. For me, looking back, I became aware sometime in high school due to Humanities in Action and SSS. So much of my current worldview has been developed by those classes, including my purpose and my understanding of self and society. The choices that I have made in my current career—deviating from the traditional career paths like finance or consulting

Student Voices • 211

No Experience Was More Rewarding in All My Years of Doing Service Than the Decade-Long Cooperation Between Concordia Welfare and Education Foundation with HKIS students and Myself in Supporting a Girls Scholarship Program in Guangdong Province, China. I worked closely in these years with Jasmine (second from the left) and Jenn (fourth from the right), who both contributed reflections to this chapter. Photo credit: Author.

that many Ivy League graduates choose to pursue, and instead moving to China to start a nonprofit dedicated to philanthropy and social impact education—can be directly traced back to the spark from Humanities in Action that has driven me since. My education has given me the power to see beyond success as defined by society and instead to follow my calling to pursue a non-traditional path that aligns my work with my life's values. It took me away from the comforts of Hong Kong to work in the challenging environment of mainland China. Humanities in Action awoke in me my desire to create positive change, but also made me see that it was possible—that *I* can be the one leading the change.

While I found a lot of meaning and purpose in the path that I chose, four years into my nonprofit career, I was burned out. My fire was rekindled through an inner work retreat in Montana that I was invited to by chance. It was there that I rediscovered my spiritual self that I had suppressed after high school, and made up my mind to reconnect with my body, mind, and heart. Not long after, I caught up with Mr. Schmidt and he shared with me he had started incorporating spiritual practices like meditation and approaches like the Enneagram into his curriculum. It felt uncanny—his evolution as a teacher and my evolution of what I needed. I have since then taken parts of his high school curriculum to build my own spiritual practice.

True education should help individuals find wisdom that is timeless and universal. Looking back, I believe Mr. Schmidt's classes did so, and many years after I graduated, these lessons continue to reverberate and guide my life's decisions.

JENNIFER WU (2008)

I wouldn't be who I am today without meeting Dr. Schmidt 14 years ago, half my life ago! He revolutionized education for me. He was the first who prompted me to contemplate the meaning of life and the possibility that we all have a personal calling. He *believes* that each student has boundless talent and resources yet to be discovered. He is there to help us uncover and walk the journey with us even after we have all graduated. He *believes* in soul care and *cares* more about our personal and spiritual well-being than our achievements. He would take time off to lead us to a quiet place just so we can be in touch with ourselves and nature. It is then that he opened our mind to social conscience. His lessons *moved* us to take actions. He instilled a genuine belief in us that we are capable of making a difference in the world. He is the reason why my friends and I started a scholarship program which has now provided over 500 underprivileged students in a rural area of China with a high school education. For 12 years in a row, we have organized an English & Leadership Camp in rural China with the purpose of empowering the scholarship recipients to make a social impact in their own sphere of influence. As a result, a few scholarship recipients have even established their own local NGO in China to assist the needy. This all started with one teacher—Dr. Schmidt—believing in the power of education and the value of service.

JODIE CHAN (2012)

I first worked with Mr. Schmidt at age 16 on two week-long (Interim) volunteer trips to Yaowawit School—established for tsunami survivors after the 2004 calamity—in Thailand. I hadn't had the pleasure of taking his Humanities in Action class, but I did share and engage with core parts of the curriculum on those trips and over regular conversations in the years to come. What I struggled with more than anything was the absence of concrete answers of how best to "give." In putting names, stories, and faces to statistics of students who did not have the same access to education that we had, I feared I was taking more from them than I was able to give in the ways that counted and could last.

While these questions still tug at my heart, what experiences like those in Thailand taught me was to embrace the tension that should exist when we think critically about how to impact people and the world around us. That tension never left, and still inspires me to grow and seek answers. It was because of this tension that I felt on my first visit to Yaowawit that I went back for several months the following year, sought a degree in political science and global health to understand

Sonia, Jodie, and Maggie Performing on Our Last Night at Yaowawit School, Thailand During Our Interim Trip in March, 2012. Photo credit: Author

inequality and systems, worked with a human rights clinic, visited the UNHCR summit as a student rapporteur, joined a social media start-up for charities, and now work in the tech field.

What those first trips taught me is that all of us have our own unique spheres of influence, regardless of age and experience. As a result, we have a responsibility to think critically about our words, action, and impact we have, no matter the context. Being challenged to think about my purpose and place in the world is the reason I strive now to find ways where I can—in my expertise—feel empowered to give back.

An education system that expects its students to do more than study but to grow mentally, physically, and spiritually, gives students the chance to step up to that challenge. I see this year after year when I return to HKIS to present workshops at the annual Service Summit for Humanities in Action students. I see the opportunity that they're given to begin to work on my question of how to give back.

Conscious, tension-filled, critical thinking-sensitive empathy is a gift that keeps on giving. This is the best gift a Wisdom educator can give students on their journey of life.

JONATHAN CHUNG (2018)

As a first-year college student, I can say that Humanities I in Action has been the most impactful educational experience I've had so far. I entered freshman year off the back of a social awareness "Take Action" summer camp run by the Canadian social enterprise ME to WE. A particular activity we did during the program shocked me, as it made me honestly consider, for the first time, my motivations for doing service and "making a difference." Humanities in Action took the flame that ME to WE lit and kindled it, lighting in me a passion to create positive change built on a new bedrock of personal purpose and meaning. The course took the previously banal minutiae of everyday experience and charged them with narrative significance, as no situation was too small or inconsequential to avoid the big questions: what do the actions myself and others take right now say about our worldview? How is this particular moment connected to the broader worldview questions and issues we're discussing in class? What's the right thing to do, considering the different worldviews of everyone involved? I left Humanities in Action yearning for more. I longed for the sense of relevance and purpose that the course had inspired in me, the way it allowed me to see how my life was connected to a greater human story.

After finishing my sophomore year, I felt that that desire had gone unfulfilled, and entered junior year having decided that I wanted to do something to expand social conscience education at HKIS. I was joined by several classmates who were similarly inspired by Humanities in Action, and after a year of gathering ideas from teachers and students, we decided to pursue the creation of a Humanities II in Action course. We spent the summer following junior year designing a curriculum, spending days working at school and coffee shops and meeting with Humanities teachers for feedback. After continuing to revise the curriculum for the first few months of senior year, we proposed Humanities II in Action to the Humanities Department. It was approved by both the department and the school administration, and is now a part of the Humanities curriculum. This effort was born out of the lasting inspiration that social conscience education has imbued us with, and we are proud to have played a part in its continued growth and expansion.

JUSTIN LAM (2007)

The first thing which struck me deeply in Humanities I in Action was that the world is not perfect. In fact, it is full of difficult and deep-rooted problems, such as (just to name a few) the exploitation and silencing of the powerless, the supremacy of greed and profit-maximization in modern capitalism, and the disappearance of local culture in the face of globalization. All these macro socio-economic issues might have appeared to be irrelevant and out of reach to a normal 9th grader in high school, who seemed powerless to bring about any real change. However, what Dr. Schmidt has taught me is that precisely since the world is not perfect, we should have a sense of conscience, empathy, compassion, understanding, integrity and fairness. Our actions should not be driven only by our own desires and self-interests. Each of us can do something to make the world a better place.

Both in Humanities I in Action and Service, Society and the Sacred, Dr. Schmidt regularly involved us in service initiatives, including trips to an orphanage in Jungsing. Through these direct personal experiences, I was able to develop my own awareness of some of the problems affecting the less fortunate in the world. It is one thing to read about these problems from the news or textbooks, but another to experience them first-hand on a personal level. It brings home, in an intense manner, the realization that I could have been in the same position as the orphan in my arms but for the accident of birth. All this serves to reinforce Dr. Schmidt's teaching of the importance of being an empathetic and conscientious person in the modern day world.

Picture Celebrating A Successful Senior Project Presentation About Humanities II in Action by Jonathan Chung (center left), Matthea Najberg (center), and Nicole Lim (center right) in May, 2018. Humanities teachers Mike Kersten (far left), Brian Oliver (center right), and the author (far right) supported the students through this process.

I would not have thought that Dr. Schmidt had expected all of his students to make an immediate difference in the world after taking his classes. However, I think he has at least successfully sown the seeds in his students, including myself, with a desire to contribute to society in the long run, whether in a big or small way, and to affect those around them to do the same thing.

KRIS HAO (2020)

Ever since I was a child I would inevitably have dreams and aspirations. Although these goals have adapted throughout the years, as I don't exactly want to be an astronaut or professional racecar driver anymore, getting into a presumably "good" college has always been kept as a constant. I have grown up in quite a lenient household with parents who don't obsess over my grades or status. Ironically, this only causes me to consistently push myself in all aspects more, no matter the impact on my mental, social, and physical wellbeing.

Due to this, I was in very bad shape; my insomnia grew worse and worse, my coaches repeatedly questioned my poor performance, and my friends and family worried about my standoffish attitude. To my dismay, loved ones from all corners of my life said I wasn't the "Kris I used to be." Although I was terrified, I coped by focusing on the end goal in my life, college. However, when I saw Dr. Schmidt's SSS class available last year, I decided to give it a try. To my surprise, what I eventually encountered was a class that acknowledged the body, mind, and heart centers, a concept that was completely foreign to me. I didn't know what to think.

Drawing from that experience, I can now confidently say that that course changed my life, since it opened my eyes to how I had tried to go through this process alone when I needed to have loving support systems instead. Throughout the years I have consistently obsessed over college and my education, and in the process, I had completely forgotten about myself and what mattered most to me. Ironically, what I forgot to value—my friends, family, and my mental and physical health—was the key to my success in the future and ultimately being happy in life. Dr. Schmidt and his class enabled me to pinpoint this problem and even gave me solutions to bring myself back to my values. By executing various spiritual practices that acknowledged my mind, body, and heart with a loving class support system, I slowly remembered what happiness felt like and practiced how to integrate this into my future. Now, after this course and Dr. Schmidt's unwavering support, I understand that my journey to success shouldn't be alone and that I need to remember to acknowledge myself and my support system to truly succeed in life.

NATASHA KHAN (2003)

I first joined HKIS in 1999 as a freshman in high school, and was lucky enough to be in Mr. Schmidt's homeroom. He—and the school—placed a huge emphasis on service and we were all encouraged to participate in a wide range of service activities. In my four years there I attended numerous Service on Saturday sessions; participated and led initiatives through Interact, a service-oriented student group; and traveled to orphanages in Mongolia, Thailand and Vietnam on annual Interim trips.

While the school gave us the very best academic education possible and pushed us to excel in whatever endeavors we chose to pursue, when I look back on my time at HKIS I am most grateful for those experiences because they showed me a different side of society. They widened my worldview and perspective at an age when I was still searching, questioning and seeking purpose. To have seen inequality, poverty and hopelessness; and yet observe how hope, fortitude and strength still live on in those situations was perhaps the most valuable lesson I learned then.

It opened up my eyes to the world as it is, taking me out of the cozy bubble I grew up in. It made me question global forces and their foundations; it fueled a desire to understand humanity in its ambitions, actions and legacies; this reminded me that as someone who has been given so much in life, I should always be thinking about how to give back.

One of my most enduring memories as a teenager was visiting Vietnam with Mr. Schmidt in my junior year of high school. We visited the Vietnamese countryside and went to an orphanage there, accompanied by some local students. At the evening debrief, Mr. Schmidt asked us, "What did you do today that was service?" Everyone answered, "Oh, we played with orphans and brought them gifts!" He asked us whether our interactions with the students constituted "service." Most of us hesitated and didn't really know what the "right" answer was. I remember we had a long discussion that service doesn't necessarily mean solely helping the least fortunate in our communities, but involves encouraging everyone you find around you, speaking up for them, and extending kindness and compassion wherever you go.

Twenty years on, I often think back on my years at HKIS and that trip. I still carry with me so many lessons from my time at the school, which inform the way I approach my work as a reporter. I will always be thankful for that.

NIKKI KWAN (2014)

Over a decade ago, I enrolled in the Humanities I in Action course and the very first concept introduced to us on day one—defining our personal worldview—has become a lifelong habit of determining the right values to guide my life decisions with. From that first day and through each subsequent unit we tackled, I felt the explosive expansion of my consciousness. Having lived a sheltered life like many of my peers, exposure to global systemic issues and perspectives alternate to the ones we had been taught our whole lives was a deeply shocking and enlightening experience. The process of crystallizing my worldview—developing a clear set of values and beliefs—as I studied in Humanities I in Action and SSS has empowered me with the tools to combat common societal pressures, defeat cognitive dissonance, and live true to my values. Navigating business school and selecting my first post-grad job has been the clearest examples of the long-lasting effectiveness of Dr. Schmidt's programs. Facing immense pressure and competitiveness to choose a prestigious, high-paying, and mainstream career path, I saw the effects of stress my peers faced as we all easily and understandably got caught up in the mad rush to land one of these sought-after positions. While many found themselves overwhelmed by this choice, I returned to the exercises I had learned almost a decade ago to find clarity and peace in following my own goals, knowing that they are based on the personal values and priorities I identified with Dr Schmidt. Understanding my "why" has led to a conviction that has helped me overcome the self-doubt, uncertainty, and other unique challenges of blazing my

Nikki Meditating on the HKIS Field During SSS Class

own trail in the rapidly developing but still relatively niche "impact investing" space. Having exposure to worldviews that embrace spirituality and alternative values has prompted me to explore career options outside of the mainstream and to think critically about the systems we exist in. Applying Dr Schmidt's teachings to the real world has immensely benefited my mental, emotional, and spiritual health as well as long-term job satisfaction. By helping me develop my worldview and empowering me to act on that worldview, Dr. Schmidt's programs have given me a head start in the universal quest to live a fulfilling life. In striving for a more equitable and sustainable world, my hope is that his work is shared and replicated globally to provide future students with the tools to live a life of integrity and fulfilment.

CHAPTER 19

MY WISDOM WAY OF TEACHING PHILOSOPHY

To be tethered between two realms, mediating the visible to the invisible, is supremely a wisdom function; in fact . . . it is the quintessential description of Holy Wisdom herself.

—*Cynthia Bourgeault (2010, p. 168)*

Being in Humanities I in Action and Spiritual Exploration I think I now have a grasp of what I want my life to be like. I used to be very ungrateful, selfish, and full of hate. Learning from Humanities I in Action, I don't want to live in the horizontal world. In my eyes, it is filled with greed, envy, hate, materialism, and competition. I used to only be in the horizontal world. In my eyes, the vertical world is loving, accepting, and full of forgiveness. I think that learning about spirituality and the real world has helped me in rebuilding my life. I now want to do service, make others happy, and be a forgiving person.

—*Quynh, grade 9 female student*

The Wisdom Way of Teaching: Educating for Social Conscience and Inner Awakening in the High School Classroom, pages 219–229.
Copyright © 2022 by Information Age Publishing
www.infoagepub.com
All rights of reproduction in any form reserved.

INTRODUCTION

When I look back on what inspired me to write this book, I recall a one-off conversation I had with a life coach, a meeting set up by a mutual friend. I was initially skeptical of any benefit from the discussion, but as it proceeded, I realized that my gentle inquisitor had a knack for asking incisive questions, and he seemed genuinely interested in my teaching journey. Well-into our session, he asked, "How would you feel if all that you have learned about teaching never left your classroom?" I paused and answered candidly, "That would be tragic." The unequivocal response cued me to my deep need to offer what is in this book more broadly.

In this final chapter I reflect on what I have learned about social conscience and inner awakening in terms of my personal journey, which began more than thirty years ago as a search for power in education. Although it took many years for me to discover what I have shared in these chapters, the takeaways themselves are not inherently complex. In fact, whatever power they have rests to some degree in their relative simplicity. My experience implementing courses which aim to develop students' social conscience and inner awakening suggests to me that all of us are in fact hard-wired to understand and integrate these learnings and their attendant practices into our lives. Bringing this to a close, then, I would like to return to my primary worldview coordinates within the Christian tradition and offer insights from my journey in this heritage to inform the larger Wisdom perspective.

JESUS' POLITICS OF COMPASSION

First, I've come to see that a powerful teaching pedagogy needs to match our response to the perennial question of human existence: what does it mean to live the good life? My starting point is that the good life requires satisfaction of our deepest human needs, which can be broadly conceived of as a yin-yang orientation: we need a healthy relationship both within (yin), and beyond (yang), the self. Through many years of trial and error we have come to structure aspects of our HKIS humanities program in accordance with this principle. Coming into grade 9, students may choose to take Humanities I in Action, which foregrounds service to humanity as a fundamental element in a life well-lived, prioritizing global understanding, purpose, care, and positive impact as the highest goals. Drawing upon Gurdjieff's "three-centered knowing" (Bourgeault, 2003, p. 27) as a short-hand definition of the human person, Humanities I in Action asks students to use their minds for critical thinking, their hearts for empathy, and their bodies for action on behalf of the world. Turning one's awareness towards others diminishes the innate self-focus of the human condition, leading students to experience the paradoxical joy of self-emptying. This head-heart-body integration is captured in the journey of social conscience model cited throughout the book:

My Wisdom Way of Teaching Philosophy • 221

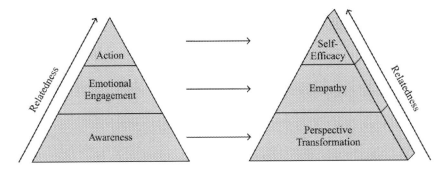

FIGURE 19.1. The Short-Term and Long-Term Impact of Social Conscience Education

Seeking how to operationalize social conscience education occupied the first 20 years of my career and was matched within my own Christian imagination by a socially conscious Jesus, the center point of my faith life. In my early years of service learning I came across historical Jesus scholar Marcus Borg's (1987) book *Jesus: A New Vision* and subsequently read his other works, including *Meeting Jesus Again for the First Time* (Borg, 1994). Borg revolutionized my thinking about Jesus, helping me to perceive him as a sociopolitical critic of the Roman Empire and the complicit Jewish religious authorities. I thrilled to read of Jesus as a Spirit-filled charismatic prophet who taught a politics of compassion—accepting the outcasts of his day—as a code superior to the conventional politics of holiness, which privileged males over females, rich over poor, able-bodied over handicapped, and Jews over Gentiles. My service work at HKIS—taking care of orphans, creating scholarship programs, working with special needs kids and the elderly—was a totally congruent living out of this image of Jesus. The deep resonance between my lived profession—in contemporary Asia—and the locus of my spiritual imagination—1st century Palestine—was animating and rewarding. I remain grateful to HKIS and the Lutheran church for giving me the opportunity to engage in such deeply purposeful and spiritually enriching work.

Meanwhile, many students, too, readily took to this "new vision," which they found deeply meaningful and even life-altering. The journey of social conscience that I came to understand through my doctoral research helped me conceptualize and implement a transformative path for 21st century schools that Jesus intuitively lived out in his 1st century public ministry. This yang of social conscience education awakens students to the reality of suffering and helps them develop self-efficacy in addressing societal pain and dysfunction. In so doing, it brings forth for many a qualitatively more meaningful and satisfying experience in students' lives than the competitive, survivalist mentality of high-stakes academics. The purpose, joy, and energy of these service experiences are undeniable; this, I have come to conclude, is what we should be doing with our lives. I assumed that I would be doing this for the rest of my life, and with great satisfaction.

JESUS' WISDOM PATH OF CONSCIOUS LOVE

Yet something was amiss. My students and I seemed dependent on doing dramatic acts of service to feel good about ourselves. We needed to be moved by the tragic conditions of the poor—usually in neighboring countries that required exciting school trips—to get that feeling of "making a difference." Meanwhile, our day-to-day lives were by comparison dull, routine, and seemingly unfulfilling. My students asked, "How do I keep the fire burning?" when the enthusiasm fueled by service decayed over time. I didn't know for sure; but meanwhile, I was leading and enjoying so many service outings myself that I personally felt inspired to continue. Undoubtedly, I reasoned, service was the best transformative show in town. And yet somehow, it didn't engender the wholeness that my students and I sought.

The crystalizing moment, as I shared in Chapter 9, was when one of our "in Action" luminaries, Janice, confessed in a school gathering that she had been so busy "saving the world" that she was ice-cold towards her own grandfather before his death. Something wasn't right.

However, I really couldn't identify the missing piece until I met Cynthia in Hong Kong about six months after I completed my doctorate. She shared insights from her newest book on Mary Magdalene (Bourgeault, 2010) at the Anglican Cathedral in Hong Kong, and from that first meeting I knew that she was the "real deal." A year and a half later I traveled to Assisi to attend my first multi-day retreat with her. After the very first teaching session, I turned to my HKIS traveling companion Richard Friedericks (see his reflection in Chapter 17) and asked, "Have you ever heard anything like this?" He simply shook his head.

The last decade has been a deep study of Cynthia's work and by extension into a global network of Wisdom tradition teachings and teachers. I had somehow missed something that now seems so obvious, which in retrospect I realize I had recognized in my dissertation in a discussion on Chinese culture:

> This focus on personal manners is a manifestation of what is known as self-cultivation (自我培養) in Chinese culture. From a traditional Chinese point of view, education for social conscience begins with self-cultivation. A Chinese saying captures the essence of this concept, "Refine oneself, establish a family, govern the nation, bring peace to the world" (修身齊家治國平天下). This traditional expression outlines a developmental path for individuals to fulfill their social responsibilities: first, manage the self; second, take care of family; third, contribute to the needs of the country; fourth, care for the world (Schmidt, 2009, p. 178).

Unwittingly overreaching by trying to change the world without any deep attention to developing the inner self, I had overlooked a fundamental insight that appears in traditions across the globe: the good life begins with self-cultivation. Stated more pointedly, I had come to agree with spiritual teacher David Hawkins

My Wisdom Way of Teaching Philosophy • 223

(2007) that "the attraction of 'changing the world' . . . appeals to the naive idealism of the inner spiritual adolescent and is transcended with maturity" (p. 200).

Reading interpretations of the classic Chinese text *Tao Te Ching* (Martin, 2018) in recent years, too, has reinforced the essential importance of inner work:

> If you truly want to leave the world a better place,
> you must release your need to do so.
> Dedicate your remaining years
> to seeing the world as a better place,
> rather than making it better.
> When you see it so,
> you begin to make it so (Chapter 49).

And so it was meeting Cynthia in 2010 that initiated me consciously and wholeheartedly into the art and practice of self-cultivation, which I have called the yin of inner awakening. Once again, Gurdjieff's "three-centered awareness" comes to the fore, but this time, in keeping with the Wisdom tradition proper, the definitions are altered. The body, mind, and heart need to be sensitized and integrated into the fullness of a human being. Specifically, the body needs to be given conscious attention and seen as an ally in the quest for inner awakening; the overly active mind needs to be reined in and trained; and the heart needs to be purified of its self-referential emotional programs for happiness (Keating, 1992). The yin of inner awakening occurs mainly through subtraction, or pruning the excesses of the body-mind-heart selves, a contrast to the yang of "learn more," "feel more," "do more" tendencies of social conscience instruction. Juxtaposing these two approaches highlights their contrasting functions in one's development (Table 19.1). These concepts can be portrayed graphically in Figure 19.2.

Understood properly, the short- and long-term yang of social conscience trains the body-mind-heart self to focus outward, attempting to identify and address the world's injustices, while the yin of inner awakening lets go of the conventional self's inherent egoic attachments and offers in its place greater internal sensitiv-

TABLE 19.1. A Comparison of the Yang of Social Conscience and the Yin of Inner Awakening

	Short-Term Yang of Social Conscience	Long-Term Yang of Social Conscience	Yin of Inner Awakening
Mind	Critical thinking becomes →	Perspective transformation	Letting go of the mind's grasping for input
Heart	Emotional engagement becomes →	Empathy	Purifying the heart's excessive attachments
Body	Compassionate action becomes →	Self-efficacy	Sensing bodily reactions and being aware in the present moment

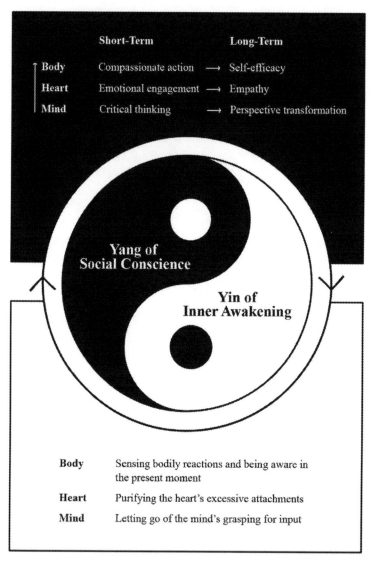

FIGURE 19.2. A Comparison of the Yang of Social Conscience and the Yin of Inner Awakening

ity, equanimity, and coherence. Put into curricular terms, while Humanities I in Action continues to serve its "yang" function, over the last five years I have enhanced the more "yin"-focused inner awakening curriculum in Service, Society, and the Sacred, some of the ideas and practices of which have now been included in our Spiritual Explorations program.

Whereas Borg served as my interpretive historical Jesus lens for social conscience education, Cynthia catalyzed my Wisdom understanding of Jesus as a teacher of inner awakening. As she compellingly argues in her book *The Wisdom Jesus* (2008), Jesus' signature phrase the "kingdom of heaven" wasn't primarily about life in the hereafter, nor about an earthly utopia through social justice, but about self-transformation through present-moment awareness. This provocative claim called into question aspects of my many years of service work: was it true that Jesus' fundamental task was inner awakening rather than creating more equitable social structures?

While I still deeply value and teach Borg's perspective of Jesus as a prophet of social change, I have become convinced that Jesus, like other world-renowned spiritual teachers, was not focused predominantly on social justice, even if relieving temporal suffering was an essential part of his vision. More fundamentally, however, I have come to believe that Jesus set his sights on something more comprehensive: the Wisdom of inner transformation. As Cynthia points out in the *Wisdom Jesus*, Jesus' message following his 40 days in the desert was "repent, for the Kingdom of heaven is at hand" (Matthew 4:17). As mentioned earlier, the word "repent" comes from the Greek word *metanoia,* which should be better translated, she explains, as going "beyond the mind" or "into the larger mind" (Bourgeault, 2008, p. 37). Entrance into God's kingdom is not primarily, as may be presumed, confessing sins to get into heaven, but more expansively the transformative change that occurs in an awakened and integrated body-mind-heart self. I have become persuaded through Cynthia's teachings, their resonance with my own deepest introspective sense, and the substantive changes in my students who implement "three-centered awareness" practices into their lives, that her assertion is correct. Thus, the Bible becomes a record of how Jesus taught and lived out this balanced wholeness in service to his 1st century world.

This larger "mind of Christ," in the final analysis, can be described as love, which Jesus referred to in some of the greatest one-liners in our planetary history: "Love your neighbor as yourself," "love your enemies and pray for those who persecute you," and "greater love has no one than this: to lay down one's life for one's friends." Such love emerges from an abundant worldview in which surrender is not capitulation, but rather an opening of space for "impulses of spirit" (London, 2016, p. 109): water can be turned into wine, a few loaves and fish can feed a multitude, and crucifixion at the hands of Roman soldiers can catalyze the emergence of the world's largest religion. Cynthia asserts that this way of Jesus, then, should actually be called the "path of conscious love" (Bourgeault, 2010, p. 112), which can be lived out in all kinds of relationships. The key touchstones are trust, yearning, and vulnerability, which Cynthia explains find their highest expression in lovers of the divine who also find themselves deeply in love with the other, and who use their shadow work for mutual inner transformation: "With honesty, trust, a huge amount of inner witnessing, and the mysterious alchemy of love itself, the two beloveds may finally set each other free" (Bourgeault, 2010, p. 123).

The power of education, then, is the power of transforming love. What drives the yang of social conscience—to make the world more just and compassionate—and the yin of inner awakening —to purify the sacred center of the self—is an all-embracing love for the universe and its inhabitants. No wonder the most powerful experiences contained in these pages are visits to orphanages, where love prompted students, such as Bethany and Tiffany respectively, to write profoundly, "Service scars you in the most beautiful way possible" and "it was a slow stirring of my soul, an insistent urging to go further out, to see more, to do more, feel more, give more, empathize more with the rest of the world." Likewise, the most powerful spiritual practice available to religion teachers seems to be the Loving Kindness Meditation (LKM), which Nana poignantly reflected on: "After the first [LKM] meditation, I felt a change in my energy and my soul. I felt my old character revived; it was amazing . . . It really hit me how life-changing this meditation can be." The power of education is love within and love without. As the Beatles shared with their global audience, all you need is love.

A FUTURE WISDOM PATH

With this final comment on the "path of conscious love" in place, then, the core philosophy of my Wisdom Way of Teaching can be stated most fully. In the context of cosmic generosity and divine compassion, the outwardly-focused yang of social conscience engages students in suffering beyond their bubbles of ignorance and affluence, resulting in an awakened life of purpose that inspires students to transcend self-oriented and career-motivated priorities in order to meet the real needs of others. At the same time, the yin of inner awakening employs Wisdom teachings and spiritual practices to cultivate within students the ability to let go of their busy minds, emotional dramas, and personal agendas. The good life is really the work of becoming a more complete human being, and this occurs most satisfyingly when the yang of social transformation meets the yin of self-cultivation. Jesus' enigmatic conclusion at the end of the Gospel of Thomas now makes sense to me: "When you make the two into one, and when you make the inner as the outer, and the upper as the lower . . . then you will enter the kingdom." This is the harmonious yin-yang interplay of an integrated life.

From the very start of my teaching career, I wanted to find the power of education. This, my experience strongly suggests, needs to speak to the full spectrum of our humanity—the physical, mental, emotional and spiritual aspects of the self. And it must extend, too, beyond our personal concerns to include the social sphere, the earth, and from a spiritual standpoint even the cosmos in its visible and invisible dimensions. The remarkable synergy that is expressed and experienced through this yin-yang integration is the template to enact such a life.

Having shared my integrated yin-yang vision of transformative education through a Christian interpretative lens, permit me one application to the development of global Christianity. In the context of Cynthia's remark quoted in the introduction that "Wisdom lost its charter in the Christian West [in the late 5th century CE]" (Bourgeault, 2003, p. 18), I take seriously the claim made by Catholic monk Bruno Barnhardt (2007) in his book *The Future of Wisdom* that Christianity is in dire need of a Wisdom path movement. Drawing from the Hindu tradition, Barnhardt writes that Christianity in the last 100 years has had a rebirth in three of the four traditional paths:

- Path of devotion (*bhakti yoga*)—Pentecostal Movement
- Path of service (*karma yoga*)—Liberation Theology
- Path of contemplation (*raja yoga*)—Centering Prayer

However, the fourth path, the path of Wisdom (*jnana yoga*), has not manifested itself as a full-fledged movement in Christianity. Barnhardt's work is a call for such an initiative.

I believe that HKIS as a Christian school in a multi-cultural context is humbly pioneering efforts towards such a path. The approaches used in SPEX and other religion courses are bringing the yin of inner awakening to success-oriented, secular-minded students. The essential broad strokes of such a yin path are now apparent: interspiritual approaches that combine a working cosmological orientation, inspiring teachings, and an array of practices that students choose themselves for the purpose of self-cultivation. I find myself in deep agreement with brother Wayne Teasdale (1999), who lived for years at Benedictine monk Bede Griffiths' Christian ashram in south India, "The human family is now much more open to receiving what I believe is so essential: a practical, mystical, and universal understanding of spirituality" (p. 4). This path needs to be *psychospiritual*, which means that it aims to benefit students' holistic health, while asking them non-coercively to consider the possibility of a vertical dimension. For those who are concerned that in SPEX Christianity has lost its distinctiveness, I invite them to speak to our students, Christian and non-Christian, many of whom are spiritually invigorated by this approach. "By their fruits you shall know them," Jesus taught.

"LONGEST STRIDE OF SOUL"

I would like to bring my reflections to a close with the poem "A Sleep of Prisoners" by the British playwright Christopher Fry (1907–2005). This poem in its own way speaks powerfully to my experience of the Wisdom journey:

> The human heart can go the lengths of God . . .
> Dark and cold we may be, but this
> Is no winter now. The frozen misery
> Of centuries breaks, cracks, begins to move;
> The thunder is the thunder of the floes,
> The thaw, the flood, the upstart Spring.
> Thank God our time is now when wrong

> Comes up to face us everywhere,
> Never to leave us till we take
> The longest stride of soul we ever took.
> Affairs are now soul size.
> The enterprise
> Is exploration into God.
> Where are you making for? It takes
> So many thousand years to wake,
> But will you wake for pity's sake!

As I reflect on the last decade of my search for power in education, I see that the joy and meaning of service wasn't enough. It didn't take into account our desire, as Huston Smith (1991) observes in his study of Hinduism, for satchitananda—for ever-expanding explorations of being, consciousness, and joy. Only when we wake up internally can we take this longest stride of soul possible. An education that leaves no room for such spiritual awakening cannot manifest our deepest inner wellsprings.

This is why education needs to draw upon the visionary Wisdom tradition, which I hope I have demonstrated is not some empty phrase, but is rather—again invoking Cynthia's understanding—a "precise and comprehensive science of spiritual transformation that has existed since the headwaters of the great world religions and is in fact their common ground" (Bourgeault, 2003, pp. xvi–xvii). Put simply, we are three-centered beings—our own personal holy trinity. We yearn to be energized and resonant, joining the dance of creation that is occurring just beyond our veil. I have had glimpses myself in which just for the briefest of moments I recognized that a love for my newborn daughter was a universal experience across time and space; that a kinship existed between myself and the green hills that surround our campus; that birds glide and I walk co-existently. I still remember these vignettes from many years ago because for a brief second the veil parted and I saw what saints and sages have said is our underlying reality: interconnectivity with what exists beyond the small self's preoccupations.

While rare individually, collectively such moments are plentiful in the human story and should be included in the process of educating students in the 21st century. For education to demonstrate its innate power, it should draw upon our most enlivened moments of connectivity to self, others, and the natural world, which I have called the yang of social conscience and the yin of inner awakening. The curricular canvas needs to be large enough to explore paths that can simultaneously lead to changing the world *and* the self. It is here that a new spirit of life—the "thunder of the floes"—emerges from the integration of yin and yang forces.

CONCLUSION

In closing, let us not ask if the great Wisdom task of teaching for transformation is possible. It is immensely doable, as the extensive accounts from teachers and students have attested. Our students' intrinsic capacities are vast, but to realize their potential requires educational experiences to match. The real question, then, is priorities and will among educational institutions: can we as leaders in education take "the longest stride of soul" and wake up to the immeasurably rich gifts bequeathed to us in our human heritage for the sake of the next generation of students? Do we have the prophetic gravitas to say that life—and therefore education—should be about engaging the biggest ideas we can imagine: wisdom, compassion, service, authenticity, purpose, aliveness, and seeking the divine? This is a vision of our most inspiring ideals and our greatest human potential. This, then, is the calling of the Wisdom teacher: to take these high ideals and look deeply within in search of integrated, holistic and spiritually nourishing learning experiences that skillfully employ yin and yang approaches. We need to state boldly in a myriad of ways through our curricula that "affairs are now soul size" involving even exploration into the divine. Acknowledging with gratitude the contributions of Wisdom masters throughout the ages, the time for us to respond is now: to realize the Wisdom way of teaching in our classrooms.

A Final Word With My SSS class in 2011 as We Finish a Deeply Introspective Labyrinth Walk as a Spiritual Practice. Photo Credit: Hong Kong International School

APPENDIX A

INTERVIEW ABOUT HUMANITIES I IN ACTION

While I was doing my doctoral research on social conscience education, I came across only one other work which specifically addressed secondary school classroom use of Mezirow's (2000) adult transformative learning theory, Amy Bintliff's (2016) *Re-Engaging Disconnected Youth: Transformative Learning Through Restorative and Social Justice Education.* Amy and I corresponded several times, and when her book went to a second edition, she asked me to write an interview about Humanities I in Action, an edited version of which now appears in her text. This appendix offers a slightly revised version of that original interview shared with Amy.

INTERVIEW RESPONSES ABOUT HUMANITIES I IN ACTION

After more than a decade of teaching Humanities I in Action, my colleagues and I remain excited to welcome students into our classrooms every August, knowing that from day one they begin a journey that challenges and expands their minds and hearts, and leads many of them to live differently as a result. This kind of transformational instruction seems to be the kind of education that is needed in our schools today.

The Wisdom Way of Teaching: Educating for Social Conscience and Inner Awakening in the High School Classroom, pages 231–234.
Copyright © 2022 by Information Age Publishing
www.infoagepub.com
All rights of reproduction in any form reserved.

1. Can you introduce the Humanities I in Action course and what you think makes it work?

I've been teaching Humanities I in Action to grade 9 students at Hong Kong International School since 2003. What makes it so powerful is a combination of factors:

- Total curricular freedom in a core interdisciplinary course with high academic expectations
- Immense amount of time in the classroom: 75 minutes/day for 180 school days
- Six or more experiential or service outings, including a weekend trip to an orphanage in China
- High achieving bilingual and bicultural students who choose to be in the class.

Beyond these factors, I think that what makes the course successful is that the teachers listen carefully to student input into the curriculum. We hold on to the most impactful materials and weed out those that may be interesting but are not transformative.

Probably the most powerful unit is the one on genocide, and the idea for this came from students. Ask students about the Rwandan Genocide, especially the film *Shooting Dogs*, and you will see how deeply they have been impacted by that unit.

2. In what ways do your students undergo the transformative learning process?

From day one when we do a free vs. fair trade chocolate social experiment, students are challenged to come to terms with many things, including the fact that many people lack the privileges they have; suffering exists on a scale they have never contemplated before; and their consumer choices play a role in the plight of others around the world.

In my dissertation research findings, I described the *journey of social conscience*, an 18-step model in which students move from self-absorption to care for the community. For many students the knowledge and experiences in the class shatter their self-prioritizing orientation, as the plight of others is considered both academically and personally. For a good number of students, the weekend experience in a Chinese orphanage brings them to the understanding, as one of my students said some years ago, that "all the things we study are true." Holding a baby girl who is a victim of the one-child policy verifies for them that every issue we study in class happens to real people who suffer. It turns their world upside down. In terms of adult transformative learning theory, this is Mezirow's (2000) "disorienting dilemma." They also experience, as Mezirow predicted, a range of painful emotions—such as fear, guilt, helplessness and hopefulness. It seems there is no other way to gain a social conscience than the painful stripping away of rosy illusions about the state of the world.

Following this difficult coming-to-terms process, we offer students ways to act on their burgeoning social conscience. During the second semester each student chooses an Elixir Project, which involves mostly off-campus, self-generated activities in which students try to make some difference in the community. Some activities seem quite humble—holding a whiffle ball training activity at a local Hong Kong School, teaching kindergarteners English, or singing at an elderly home—while a few are dramatic—establishing a health clinic on an isolated island in the Philippines, spending a week with orangutans in Malaysia, donating money on site to a special needs school in India. Regardless of the scale, what is of most importance is the sense of self-efficacy that develops within these young students to help them realize not only that they are capable of positively influencing society, but that there is joy in the experience. Even a simple smile on the face of a child can be enough to reverse the downward spiral of fear and guilt of their disorienting dilemmas. This is the power of student-initiated action projects.

3. **What would you say to researchers who doubt that transformative learning can occur with young people?**

I have had so many students speak of how the course has changed them—whether it be in conversations and essays during the class, or emails years later from alumni. One of the striking aspects of teaching these courses is just how predictable student responses are. Every year I know that many of my students will go through a journey of transformation— and certainly for some of these students, it is irreversible. How many? I don't really know— and that's what I would like to investigate at some point: how many students can point to lasting change ten years down the line? My sense is that a significant number of students were deeply influenced by the course in that their values were fundamentally re-aligned and their perspectives deeply expanded. However, this is anecdotal evidence; I'd like to see a longitudinal study done on our students to get a better sense of the long-term impact of our courses.

4. **What's your pitch to students?**

My pitch is that simply repeating "business as usual" in our world is a recipe for disaster . . . and students know this. Few question that climate change is real, that income inequality results in some winners but more losers, that gross injustice occurs globally on a daily basis. But they feel powerless to effect change. I'm reminded of the documentary *Scared Sacred* (NFB, 2017) in which the director Velcrow Ripper (yes, his real name) has a recurring nightmare of being on a train to a concentration camp. And in the dream a woman riding in the train says, "I never thought that they would come for me." Ripper explains that in making the film he decided to do the opposite of his instinct: instead of running from his fear, he decided to run directly into it. Over the next several years he visited many of the "ground zeroes" on the planet—Bhopal, Cambodia, Hiroshima—in search of hope.

Ideally, this is the mindset of students who choose Humanities I in Action. It is uncomfortable to watch a film on genocide, to contemplate the disadvantage of an orphan one is holding, to consider the consequences of a world with melting ice caps, but in opting for this course, they collectively choose to run into their fear rather than continue business-as-usual. When the future of the planet is at stake, studying urgent global issues seems far more relevant than polishing one's resume. Of course, we as both teachers and students know this is all a heady gamble. Staring into the face of an orphan might mean making oneself vulnerable to suffering. Yet what they don't know is that beneath the fear are layers of resilience that can emerge. Oftentimes the hope comes from the close-knit relationships that develop in a class that's driven by a mission to make the world a better place. We see this every year.

5. **What is your advice to teachers who want to teach for transformation?**

The bottom line is: in order to teach for transformation, you need to be willing to go on your own journey of personal change. Here are some questions worthy of reflection for potential social conscience teachers:

- Are you willing to enter into the dark side of human nature with yourself and your students?
- Is your great joy seeing a student grow into a more aware and compassionate human being?
- Do you enjoy "getting your hands dirty" with students on field trips and outings?
- Are you open to dealing with students beyond the academic expectations of the course, delving into the personal and emotional?
- Are you willing to apply the class materials to your own life?

It's obvious that teaching a social conscience course is not for everyone. This is one of the reasons the course is optional for students; both students and teachers can choose a more conventional academic experience. But for those teachers and students who believe that education fundamentally must involve transformation, Humanities I in Action offers a powerful combination of in-class study and out-of-class experiences. I believe that this kind of course is needed to shift students from an instrumental view of education—what's in it for me? —to one that calls on them to participate in the quest to sustain life on the planet. This is a high calling, and one that many students of the 21st century are eager to hear.

APPENDIX B

EXEMPLARY "SERVICE, SOCIETY, AND THE SACRED" FINAL ESSAYS

What does it look like when the yang of social conscience, typified by study of Humanities I in Action, comes together with the yin of inner awakening, as experienced in a religion class? The following two essays were written at the end of two students' HKIS careers who both took Humanities I in Action as freshmen and Service, Society, and the Sacred as seniors. They exemplify in a sense of culmination the deep level of personal integration of social conscience and inner awakening that is possible by high school students.

AMAR (2016)

My Journey to Living Deeply

I stand at a monumental transition in my life. In under a week, I will be a high school graduate, and in exactly three months a freshman in college. I face an ambiguous future, one defined by countless decisions, trials, and tribulations. However, I look to the next step with a sense of confidence and assuredness. The wisdom I have gained through Humanities I in Action and Service, Society, and the Sacred will afford me the clarity and depth of outlook I need to meaningfully navigate my path through life.

Humanities I in Action

I came to Hong Kong in 9th grade, and entered Humanities I in Action shallow and narrow-minded. I had never heard of the term "worldview," much less considered my place and meaning in this world. I was largely unaware of humanity's greatest issues; learning about child labor in the chocolate industry and the Stolen Generations of Aboriginal Australians was a swift kick in the teeth directly from the outset. I was completely knocked off balance by each lesson as I tried to make sense of the ugly reality with which I was being confronted. The course shattered my sheltered perception of the world and expanded my awareness immensely, making me think critically in ways I never had.

Being bombarded lesson after lesson by the seemingly hopeless host of problems with which the world is plagued, it is no surprise I became somewhat demoralized. But Humanities I in Action went further than simple identification of problems. The course stimulated deep contemplation on the nature of humanity, the intricacies of morality, the existence of evil, and my purpose in this convoluted world. These discussions broadened my way of thinking about myself and my surroundings, and fostered in me a more comprehensive understanding of reality. I realized I was born into a position of tremendous opportunity to help solve our most pressing issues. No longer demoralized, I was awakened and empowered to dedicate my potential for the benefit of humanity.

As I entered the second semester of the course, I was invigorated by this realization and primed to discover exactly what form my dedication to humanity would take. My answer came when we studied *Ishmael* by Daniel Quinn. I did not simply read that book; I turned each page in an idealistic fit of intellectual wonderment and concern. Chapter after chapter revealed how distressing it is that humans have a fundamentally twisted and narcissistic relationship with the environment. If we continue to see ourselves as conquerors instead of caretakers, the place we call home will soon no longer be able to sustain us.

Absorbing and discussing the ideas presented in *Ishmael* invoked my passion to the fullest. It astonished me to see how selfish and short-sighted the earth's "intelligent" species acted in its relationship with our home that has nurtured us so lovingly. Through this unit, I developed the passionate conviction that environmental issues were the most grave and imminent we face, and I identified the cause to which I have resolved to devote my life.

I wasted no time dedicating myself to this cause. My Elixir Project at the end of Humanities I in Action was in glass recycling, and I continued to develop my efforts in this cause for the next three years, eventually making it my Senior Project as I concluded my high school career with glass recycling. In addition, I became involved in the leadership of environmental groups at HKIS, and in the summer after my junior year travelled to the US to conduct environmental science research

Amar's Elixir Project in Grade 9, Which Continued to evolve Throughout His Four Years of High School. Amar is now pursuing a Ph.D. at Stanford University in Chemical Engineering with the aim of developing technologies for low-carbon fuels. Photo credit: Monica Bhardwaj

on invasive plants in a lake ecosystem. This array of pursuits that I undertook for the environment has served to affirm my freshman year commitment to further my enthusiasm for my chosen cause, and to set the stage for even more impactful efforts in the future.

After my profound awakening in Humanities I in Action, I felt I had finally figured life out. I had a clear idea of how I wanted to impact the world in a way that was meaningful to me, and now it was simply a matter of working towards an environmentally sustainable society in my education and subsequent career. Although this state remained intact for the next three years, in the second semester of my senior year I entered Service, Society, and the Sacred. As has become commonplace in these "living deeply" courses, SSS transformed my perspective once again, introducing me to an entirely new dimension and approach to life.

SERVICE, SOCIETY, AND THE SACRED

SSS was an unconventional course, even from the first lesson. We started the semester in a circle, listening to Mr. Schmidt read out a list of words as he invited us to do nothing but observe our bodily reactions. In the context of a typical HKIS course, this activity was starkly out of place, but as I delved further into SSS, I began to understand its significance.

Body-Mind-Heart Framework

The course operated under the framework of furthering the pursuit of wisdom through an integration of the body, mind, and heart. By finding a balance between the three centers, we can draw from the strengths and purposes of each, allowing us to experience an enhanced, integrated, multi-dimensional, and holistic awareness of our world, and giving us clearer direction in our path through life.

Relevance of the Framework

Throughout the past 18 years, I had not been exposed to nor given any consideration to these ideas. As such, the very premise of SSS was both foreign and elucidating to me. I realized that—shocking as it seemed—I did not have life figured out. In Humanities I in Action and the vast majority of my schooling, the focus had always been on studying the world around me and maximizing my impact on it. At the outset of SSS, my attention was entirely outward. However, the course turned this model on its head, taking me on a profound inward journey unlike any I have ever experienced. I examined all aspects of my inner self, identifying their respective merits, and reflecting on how I could better manage and utilize their value.

Though at first it seemed difficult to draw a connection between my outward efforts and the inner self that SSS maintained as important, a concept explained in the introduction of the course has remained with me throughout the semester. When we perform work to make any impact in our society, we are simply projecting our self onto the outside world. Therefore, it is of utmost importance for the efficacy and beneficence of this outward work that the inward self is first pure and fulfilled. In this way, I have come to understand more clearly the application of body-mind-heart cohesiveness to my mission for the environment and to my future path on the whole. Nurturing a healthy balance between the three centers will ensure that the effect I have on the world will be positive, and will help provide clarity and guidance in my pursuits.

Lessons in Practice

Seeing the relevance of these lessons to my seemingly unrelated outward journey, I can now put in practice my learning from the semester. First and foremost, I have corrected my one-sided view of the mind as the sole source of intelligence. I will attribute more effort to nurturing my body and heart, while still maintaining wellness of the mind. I have learned that a healthy body is essential to full wisdom—if you don't have your health, you have nothing. I have studied a range of health techniques in SSS, from proper nutrition to alternative health practices, and I hope to employ this learning to elevate my bodily self. I was also given the opportunity to engage in spiritual practices for integration of the heart. I found prostrations to be surprisingly effective, grounding me in the heart and bringing greater humility and peace. Practices of this nature will help significantly in achieving full three-centered cohesiveness.

I experienced a powerful example of bodily intelligence in making one of the biggest decisions of my life to this point. When Paul Saltzman visited our class, he advised that in deciding on a university one should meditate, envisioning oneself living life on each campus, and observe which university felt "right." So, in my college decision, I underwent Saltzman's meditation and surrendered the expanse of information I had gathered on each university to raw, simple feeling. When I completed the meditation, I could feel which school was right for me, and assuredly made my decision. The level of intuition I employed in this anecdote couldn't have arisen from the logic-driven mind—it was a tangible testament to the body-mind-heart framework of wisdom. I will continue to utilize this wisdom in the future to guide my most consequential moments.

In an even broader view of wisdom, I was worried early on in the semester when I read on Mr. Schmidt's blog about the pitfalls of passion, as I had based my entire life plan on my passion for the environment. However, when Buddhist monk Rabten visited our class, he explained that passion can be a phenomenal positive force, but only if it is pure. Purifying passion is eliminating oneself from the equation—passion must be wholly in the service and love of others, and never for personal benefit. Through Rabten's wisdom, I learned to maintain "pure" motivation in benefiting the earth and the people who inhabit it, and if desire for personal recognition develops, I now know to identify and remove it. With this understanding, I can be assured that my career efforts will be righteously motivated and as beneficial as possible to my cause.

IVY (2015)

My Humanities I in Action and Service, Society, and the Sacred courses have been integral in my process of internal and external awakening. Through Humanities I in Action, I was exposed to the big problems of society, including genocide, eugenics, sex slavery in Thailand, and injustice at the cage dwellings literally in our backyard. Although it was disorienting, broadening and deepening my worldview as such allowed me to break out of the self-concerned bubble I had inadvertently trapped myself within. Humanities I sparked in me a passion for service. In addition to opening my eyes to the world's problems, the course fostered in me a genuine will to help. Studying our compassionate instinct gave me hope in combating the darker sides of our nature. Engaging in real-life service experiences proved that acts of compassion are both personally rewarding and powerful means of making positive change. In this way, I was freed from the unawareness and apathy associated with an underdeveloped social conscience.

Yet, as I advanced to my sophomore and junior years of high school, our adventures in Humanities I in Action felt like a distant dream . . . I found myself reverting back to the fast-paced, achievement-oriented lifestyle that is the norm at HKIS. The cultural influence of my family and community was just too overpowering. As I got older, I also became less idealistic. Trying not to disturb the status quo, I excused my inaction by thinking that I should live simply without making a fuss. This is not to say my insights and energy from Humanities I in Action stopped affecting me. My perspective of the world had been permanently imbued with the color and fire within me that seeks a greater purpose irreversibly ignited. But as I fell back to the rhythm of hectic teenager schedules, I felt like a robot again—practical and efficient, yet lacking a distinctly human quality . . .

The problem for me is that I saw the world of Humanities I in Action in Action and the "real" world as separate and closed off from each other. The course allowed me to visit a transcendental world through which I felt as if I had completed my heroic journey. After I brought back my elixir through Kids4Kids [a local NGO] advocacy, I didn't know how to continue to channel my experiences into ordinary life, to transcend but include. SSS is the course that taught me how to do so.

SSS taught me to pay attention. I realized that in order to impact the larger world, we must deal with the immediate distractions at home. After all, at the roots of big problems are often smaller ones that we can control. That's why rather than attempting to end genocide, we should tackle our technology addiction, which arguably facilitates the lack of empathy that underlies evil. Likewise, in order to truly be of service to orphaned children, we need to strengthen our own filial relationships. In order to help others, we must first take care of ourselves.

As we explored issues relevant to our lives, I became more in tune with myself and my surroundings. I started paying attention to my mind, body, and spirit and to those of others. I notice my subtle bodily sensations. I notice when I deliver bad news through a technological medium instead of in person. I notice my emotion-driven behavior and the hours I spend cooped up at home instead of outside enjoying the fresh air . . .

In addition to paying attention, this course pushed me to open up. Both in and outside of class, I've shared personal stories that I had always kept to myself, such as the transformative experience that brought me closer to [name]. The communal nature of the course encouraged me: hearing my classmate's stories or perspectives has exposed me to new outlooks or ensured me that others understand what I've been through. And because that's been rewarding to me, I feel that in turn, I must share pieces of myself also. It delights me to have been able to open up as such. After all, in addition to personal observations, I've found that collective reflections are key to making sense of our common experience—the experience of being human.

But the greatest value of the course lies in that after we recognize our situation, we're empowered to initiate change. Narrowing our focus on issues closer to home has enabled me to take small, concrete steps to improve my life, in essence seeking micro-solutions to macro-problems. My efforts to make little changes have definitely had a positive impact, at least on a personal level. Increasingly, I initiate intimate conversations with others instead of hiding behind screens. I feel less guilty when I sing or take long walks, activities that nourish my body and spirit but that I thought were "unproductive." I keep my emotions in check, making a conscious effort not to think too much or behave rashly, such as lying in bed idly when I'm stressed . . .

There is no doubt that I have had an incredible journey. Humanities I in Action challenged me to step outside my bubble and instilled in me a passion for service. SSS guided me in integrating that energy in a way that is cognizant of my immediate surroundings. As I work on my gratitude project and think about how to make the best out of my remaining time here, I feel myself radiate with life. Throughout my journey, I've learned how to live.

Yejee (l), Ivy (center), and Michelle (r) Preparing for their Refugee Run Simulation at Crossroads, a Local NGO Run by an HKIS Family. Photo credit: Author

APPENDIX C

MY WORLDVIEW

Do I Believe in a Vertical Dimension?

Directions: Religion and spirituality involve considering the possibility of a spiritual dimension of existence. In religion classes we use the terms **horizontal** (visible, material, life in time/finite) and **vertical** (invisible, metaphysical, life outside of time/infinite) to explore our beliefs and assumptions about reality. The following set of questions will help you uncover your worldview assumptions with regard to the possibility of a vertical dimension. Read over the statements in each of the categories below. Decide which statements you **agree** with (whether strongly or somewhat) and which statements you **disagree** with.

Committed Horizontal

1. I only believe in what I experience with my five senses; I don't believe that any kind of invisible world exists.
2. Nobody in my family is very religious, so for me to become religious would seem rather odd. It's just not what our family takes an interest in.
3. As people modernize, they become less religious. Eventually, I think religion will fade away.

4. When I die, I'll just decompose like everything else. Game over.
5. God up in sky? Obviously, that's a very unscientific idea. Australians are pointing one way and Chinese the other!
6. To be a good person today does not require being religious. I think religious people cause as much harm, and maybe more, than non-religious people.
7. People who say they have had an NDE (near-death experience) had hallucinations caused by a lack of oxygen. Science can explain these things.
8. I have no problem with all the different religions. I respect them, even if I don't think they have a true picture of reality.

Agnostic Horizontal

1. While I generally trust in only my five senses, there may be an invisible world. No one can say for sure.
2. It's not that our family doesn't care at all about religion; it just seems that it's far down our list of priorities. We focus on the practical.
3. Religion seems to be what you're born with. I didn't have much religion growing up and we seem to get along fine without it.
4. Who knows what will happen when I die? I guess I'll find out when I get there.
5. God seems to have left us alone. I like the God as Watchmaker concept—wound up the world like a clock and let it go.
6. Religion is mostly about teaching good values. In the past, religion was the best way to teach these values, but now as modern people, we can be good without God.
7. I'm not sure what to make of NDEs (near-death experiences), but I don't know anyone who has ever experienced anything like that, so it's hard to believe.
8. While I'm not religious, it does make me wonder that every traditional culture had religion until modern times. Are we missing something? Maybe . . .

Traditional Vertical

1. My family believes that the Bible/other religious texts are true and I haven't really had any reason to question this belief up until this point.
2. Religion is part of my family heritage; it would be odd for me to object to my family's beliefs. Besides, it helps keep us together as a family.
3. Being religious is part of my family and my culture, and if it were removed, we would lose something pretty fundamental to who we are.
4. I believe that there is another world, like a heaven or maybe reincarnation. I'm not so sure about hell, but I definitely think we live on.

5. When I pray, I think of God in heaven. I don't know if he's really up or not, but he's above and beyond the here and now.
6. God stands for what is good and right in the world. Of course, people are more moral when they believe in God rather than when they don't.
7. People had all kinds of experiences with God in the Bible, so while NDEs (near-death experiences) sound a bit 'out there,' I'm certainly open to learn more.
8. I wouldn't say this out loud very often, but while I respect other religions, deep down (sh!!) I really do think my religion is truer than other faiths.

Fading Vertical

1. I used to believe in a religion when I was a kid, but now as I've grown up science just raises too many questions for me to believe in religion.
2. We used to go to religious services when I was young and it seems part of our family values, but as we've gotten older, we've just gotten too busy.
3. My grandparents were quite religious and my parents lost some of that. Since attending HKIS, I've become even less religious.
4. When I was young I was concerned about life after death, but as I've gotten older, I've lost my fear and questioning. What comes will just come.
5. I prayed as a kid, but I just never felt anything happened, so I eventually stopped believing there was anything up there.
6. I used to be "good" because I was afraid as a kid what God would do. But obeying out of fear isn't a good motivator. God is playing less of a role in my moral values.
7. NDEs (near-death experiences) are hard to prove scientifically, so I think they only speak to people who have had them or believe in that kind of thing.
8. I used to believe in the religion I was raised with, but when I got exposed to how many different faiths there are, it made me doubt that any of them are true.

Progressive Vertical

1. Jesus may be the "way" for some people, but I don't think he's the only way. I think Muslims and Hindus and Buddhists can also go to heaven or be accepted by God.
2. Whether Jesus was really born of a virgin or whether he really walked on water doesn't matter to me as much as the meaning of the stories.

3. I've become more interested in religion. There's so much mystery that science can't explain, and religion gives me a chance to explore that mystery.
4. I do believe that there is life after death, and some people even experience the vertical dimension in the here and now. Eternity begins now, not only when you die.
5. I think NDEs (near-death experiences) are authentic experiences. Could so many people all be crazy or seeking fame or trying to get on Oprah? Don't think so.
6. I think of myself as spiritual, but different than traditional religious people. God in my view is more like Star Wars: "Luke, use the force." God is not a man up in the sky, but a force in the universe.
7. God isn't up there, and certainly isn't male or female! God is everywhere, and my morality is inspired by the idea that God is in everyone and everything.
8. So many world religions show that every culture has a spiritual side. I think it's natural for every culture and every person to search for the infinite.

APPENDIX D

OVERVIEW OF THE SPEX CURRICULUM

Over the last five years religion teachers in the Humanities Department have created a four-year Spiritual Explorations (SPEX) curriculum. The following summaries provide an overview of each course in the program. Those lessons marked with an asterisk indicate that a summative, or major assignment, was handed in or assessed during that class period.

Having now completed implementation of the curriculum for the first time this year, we are very pleased with not only the overall outcome, but also with what we feel is its basic stability. Certainly adjustments will be made, but we expect that such amendments will mostly be in making the lessons more streamlined and impactful rather than any large-scale curricular changes.

SPEX 9 COURSE OVERVIEW—"WAKE UP"

Course Overview: This introductory course sets the foundation for the four-year Spiritual Explorations (SPEX) program. Students in grade 9 explore the material and spiritual dimensions of life, teachings from the world's spiritual traditions, and practices aimed at awakening to a more enlivened sense of self.

Unit 1—"It's Time to Wake Up!"—The Vertical Dimension of Life

Essential Question: How can spiritual exploration help me live a better life?

Enduring Understanding: Learning to be present in my life leads to a greater sense of happiness, meaning, and purpose, and contributes to a better world.

Unit 2: "What Makes for a Meaningful Life?"—My Spiritual Journey

Essential Questions:

1. What guidance can teachings from the world's great religions offer us with regards to living a meaningful life?
2. How do I live a spiritual life?

Enduring Understandings:

1. The world's great religions offer many stories of individuals who have awakened to meaningful lives and are models for us to follow.
2. One can live a spiritual life by loving God, one's neighbor and oneself. This can be done through experiences such as communal worship, meditation, prayer, song, and service to others.

Overview of the SPEX Curriculum • 249

TABLE D.1. SPEX 9 Course Overview—Unit 1

#	Theme	Essential Question
1	This Matters—"This is Water"	Why will this course be valuable to me?
2	You Matter—Kintsukuroi,[1] "Butterfly Circus"	Why am I valuable?
3	Introduction to the Vertical Dimension—Awe Walk	What is the vertical dimension and why is it worth exploring?
4	Horizontal and Vertical Dimensions (see Appendix C)	What do I believe about the vertical dimension and why?
5	Religious vs. Spiritual	What is the difference between religion and spirituality?
6	My Spiritual DNA	What are my family's religious or spiritual traditions?
7	*Summative #1: "My Spiritual Identity" reflective essay	What is my spiritual identity and what have I taken away from this course so far?
8	Begin With the End in Mind	What's the difference between living for the resume self vs. living for the eulogy self?
9	Dying To Live	What regrets can I burn to lighten my load?

TABLE D.2. SPEX 9 Course Overview—Unit 2

#	Theme	Essential Question
10	*Summative #2: Interview Project Sharing (Pre-COVID-19: Visit to a Holy Site in Hong Kong)	What can I learn from religious or spiritual people? (Pre-COVID-19: What did I learn from my field trip?)
11	Documentary: A Multitude of Religious Perspectives	What do I believe?
12	Hinduism—Just Do It! (Introduction to the Spiritual Practices Project)	Which spiritual path is the right approach for me?
13	Buddhism—Just Do It, But Not Too Much	How can I learn to let go of my achievements?
14	Judaism—Life is Beautiful	How do I find meaning in life's difficult circumstances?
15	Christianity— Love Wins	What does it mean to love someone unconditionally?
16	Islam—We Are Family	How can communal worship bring me closer to God?
17	*Summative #3: Spiritual Practices Shared Reflection	How did my chosen spiritual practice impact me?
18	Introduce Summative #4 and work time	What did I learn about myself, religion, and spirituality this year in SPEX?
19	*Summative #4: SPEX 9 Video Sharing	How did my spiritual journey go this year?

---

[1] Kintsukuroi is the Japanese art of restoring broken pottery. This concept serves as a powerful spiritual metaphor for students, which is why we introduce it early in SPEX 9. We have two lessons built around this pottery practice in SPEX 12.

SPEX 10 COURSE OVERVIEW—"GROW UP"

Course Overview: This grade 10 course builds upon the foundation of SPEX 9 by exploring the themes of personal identity and a sense of purpose by considering the open, hidden, blind, and unknown dimensions of the self. These unknown aspects are explored from the perspective of the world's religious traditions, asking students to consider a self that is conscious, connected, infinite, and of inherent value. Students will engage in two Spiritual Practices projects, including a Loving Kindness project, to help them discover more about their identity and purpose.

Unit 1—"Who Am I?"- Exploring My Identity

Essential Question:
How can explorations of various aspects of myself—open, blind, hidden, and unknown—impact my self-understanding and sense of purpose?

Enduring Understanding:
1. I have a unique combination of strengths, weaknesses, and beliefs, some of which are known to myself and others, while others are hidden.
2. The world's religious traditions offer a provocative array of interpretations about the unknown self that challenge our conventional perceptions.
3. Loving myself and others reveals new insights into my identity and purpose.

Unit 2: "What is My Purpose?"—Exploring My Purpose

Essential Question:
Given who I am, what is my purpose?

Enduring Understandings:
My sense of purpose may be better understood by employing archetypal metaphors from the world's Wisdom traditions. These metaphors can help explain underlying motivations for my decisions, and guide me in connecting my identity to the world's needs.

Overview of the SPEX Curriculum • 251

TABLE D.3. SPEX 10 Course Overview—Unit 1

#	Theme	Essential Question
1	Grow Up! (Introduction to the Loving Kindness Spiritual Practices Project)	Who am I and what is my purpose?
2	Who am I really?	Is the self that I show the real self I know?
3	Investigating the Self using Johari's Cube	What aspects of myself are open, hidden, blind, or unknown?
4	The Unknown Self of Atman	Am I connected to everything in a deep and fundamental way? Could consciousness be more primary to the universe than matter?
5	*Summative #1: Shared Reflection on Loving Kindness Spiritual Practices Project	What have I learned about my identity and purpose through intentional acts of loving others and myself?
6	The Unknown Infinite Self	What happens when I die?
7	The Unknown Self of Incomprehensible Value	Is it possible I have inherent value beyond my personality and my achievements?
8	The Unknown Self as a Holon	Is it possible to be simultaneously unique and part of the whole?
9	*Summative #2: Letter to my Future Self	What kind of person do I want to be five months from now?[1]

TABLE D.4. SPEX 10 Course Overview—Unit 2

#	Theme	Essential Question
10	What's the Point? Essentialism vs. Existentialism	Is life random or purposeful?
11	The Purpose-Driven Life	How do you see your life's purpose?
12	Spiritual Metaphors of Transformation	Which of Metzner's (1998) spiritual metaphors speaks to your life at this moment?
13	Purpose and Decision-Making (Introduction of the Spiritual Practices Project)	How can I use body-based techniques to destress myself as I face decisions?
14	Tightening My Focus: Minimalism	What could I leave out of my life to make it more fulfilling?
15	Spirituality and Minimalism	Do I accept the conventional HKIS narrative of an achievement-based sense of self?
16	Life Purpose Statement	What do I understand now to be the purpose of my life?
17	*Summative #3: Spiritual Practices Project Sharing	How did my chosen spiritual practice impact me and my sense of purpose?
18	Introduce Summative #4 and work time	What did I learn about myself, religion, and spirituality this year in SPEX?
19	*Summative #4: SPEX 10 Video Reflection	What have I learned in my spiritual journey this year?

[1] Distinct among the SPEX courses, SPEX 10 has a five-month break between October and March. This is why the letter to the future self asks what kind of person students would like to be when they return for the second half of the course.

SPEX 11 COURSE OVERVIEW—"CLEAN UP"

Course Overview: The grade 11 course focuses on "cleaning up" our lives through teachings and practices related to reconciliation and forgiveness. Throughout the semester students explore different views about good, evil, suffering, injustice, and how damaged relationships can be restored. The primary objective is that through personal reflection on class materials and spiritual practices students will develop and be able to articulate their own spiritual journey of self-realization.

Unit 1—"Restore Yourself"—Fill Up the Tank

Essential Questions:

1. Why does suffering exist?
2. What in my body, mind, and heart need to be cleansed?

Enduring Understandings:

1. The nature, meaning, and purpose of suffering is reflected upon through various religious, spiritual, and philosophical belief systems.
2. "Cleaning up" my life brings integrity, which means a person's actions match his or her values.

Unit 2: "Let it Go!"—A Spirit of Reconciliation

Essential Questions:

1. How do I mend and restore my broken relationships with others?
2. How can I mend myself?

Enduring Understandings:

1. A spirit of reconciliation and a heart for forgiveness can mend and restore broken relationships.
2. Forgiveness can be assisted by letting go with the use of spiritual practices.

Overview of the SPEX Curriculum • 253

TABLE D.5. SPEX 11 Course Overview—Unit 1

#	Theme	Essential Question
1	Time to Clean Up!	What does it mean to restore myself?
2	Cleansing the Mind	What is my relationship to my thoughts?
3	From iPhone to MYPhone	How do I take control of my phone (and my mind)?
4	Deliver Us From Evil	What is evil?
5	We're Only Human	Why does evil exist?
6	Lemonade From Lemons	How do I respond to evil/suffering?
7	*Summative #1: Shared Reflection	What is your thinking about our unit's two essential questions?

TABLE D.6. SPEX 11 Course Overview—Unit 2

#	Theme	Essential Question
8	The Cost of Making Mistakes	Does everyone deserve a second chance?
9	Another Form of Justice (Restorative Justice)	How can I restore my relationships?
10	*Summative #2: Restorative Justice Simulation	How can I empathize with others?
11	The Courage to Be Honest	How can I overcome shame and vulnerabilities?
12	Understanding Intimacy	What is the relationship between spirituality and sexuality?
13	Communicating with Love (Introduction of the Spiritual Practices Project)	What are my love languages?
14	Acceptance Precedes Change	How can I love my neighbor as myself?
14	Forgive Us Our Trespasses	What is forgiveness?
15	The Power of Forgiveness	Why forgive?
16	*Summative #3: Spiritual Practices Shared Reflection	How did my chosen spiritual practice impact me?
17	Introduce Summative #4 and work time	What did I learn about myself, religion, and spirituality this year in SPEX?
18	*Summative #4: SPEX 11 Video Reflection	What have I learned in my spiritual journey this year?

SPEX 12 COURSE OVERVIEW—"MOVE UP"

Course Overview: The fourth year of the Spiritual Explorations program culminates students' journey through high school and looks to their future beyond HKIS. Unit I of SPEX 12 assists students to cope with the stress of the college admissions process and, accordingly, to let go of attachment to specific outcomes. Unit II uses the Enneagram as a tool for greater self-understanding and for strengthening relationships. Throughout the course, students will not only implement spiritual practices in their own lives, but will also lead their peers in such practices in order to balance the body-mind-heart self.

Unit 1: Coping with and Letting Go During the College Process

Essential Questions:

1. How can I employ spiritual teachings and practices to cope with and accept the college process?
2. What have I learned about myself through dealing with the college process in SPEX?

Enduring Understandings:

1. Students will consider spiritual approaches to making major life decisions and will be challenged to let go of their desire to control the outcome of the college process and accept the results.
2. Students will reflect on their personal experience with the college process and share these reflections with their peers.

Overview of the SPEX Curriculum • 255

TABLE D.7. SPEX 12 Course Overview—Unit 1

#	Theme	Essential Question
1	Move Up! Revisiting "This is Water"	How can I think differently about my senior year and beyond?
2	Considering the Broken Self	What's gotten broken in me during the college process?
3	Golden Seams: How do I Repair the Cracks?[1]	How can I begin the process of repair?
4	Opening to Yin and Yang: Visit by a Tai Chi Master	How can the universal principles of yin and yang help me think differently about the college admissions process?
5	The Yin-Yang of Everyday Life (Introducing the Spiritual Practices Project)	What practice can I do that will help balance my body, mind and heart?
6	The Yin of Letting Go (Rock-Stacking as a Spiritual Practice)	How can I stay present and live in the moment?
7	Letting Go through Vibrations[2]	How can sound vibrations help me relax deeply?
8	Letting Go through the Welcoming Prayer	How can I welcome those aspects of my life that are uncomfortable or disappointing?
9	*Summative #1: Sharing of Spiritual Practices Project	Have I been able to repair myself through spiritual practices?

[1] We purchase a Chinese-style bowl for each student, have them break the bowls in class to symbolize their own sense of brokenness, and then repair the bowls using glue and gold markers. This is an application of the Japanese art of repairing broken pottery called *kintsukuroi*.

[2] This year one of our teachers became trained to play a gong as a tool of relaxation and meditation. Most students totally enjoyed this experience.

Unit II: Understanding the Self and Leaving Well

Essential Questions:

1. What new aspect of my self-understanding can I learn through the Enneagram and how can I rebalance my body-mind-heart self?
2. Can I lead a personally meaningful spiritual practice with my peers?
3. How can I leave HKIS well and transition to the future?

Enduring Understandings:

1. The Enneagram enables students to gain greater self-understanding and suggests areas that need rebalancing through spiritual practices.
2. Students will implement various practices in their own lives and share these with their peers.
3. Students will make a list of their own personal "best practices" to take to college with them.

TABLE D.8. SPEX 12 Course Overview—Unit 2

#	Theme	Essential Question
10	Who am I? Introduction to the Enneagram[3]	What is my personality type?
11	Who am I? Further Enneagram exploration	Which spiritual practices can help me bring out the positive aspects of my personality type?
12	Enneagram Type/Spiritual Practice Finalization	Which spiritual practices can help me bring out the positive aspects of my personality type?
13	The Enneagram and My Relationships	How can the understanding that comes from the Enneagram improve a significant relationship in my life?
14	*Summative #2: Sharing of Type and Spiritual Practices in Small Groups	Have I been able to become a better version of myself?
15	Horizontal vs. Vertical Worldview Revisited	Has my worldview regarding the vertical dimension changed over the past four years?
16	Do Not Fear	What practices can I adopt to help me leave well?
17	Preparation for Final SPEX Video (reviewing SPEX artifacts from the last four years)	What have I learned and how have I grown through my four years of Spiritual Explorations?
18	*Summative #3: Final Sharing of Video	What have I learned and how have I grown through my four years of Spiritual Explorations?

---

[3] We first began teaching the Enneagram in SPEX 12 in January, 2021 during the height of COVID-19. Since we were teaching online, I made a series of videos for students' home study. I have posted these videos and representative student examples by type on my "Social Conscience and Inner Awakening" blog in an entry entitled, "Matching Your Enneagram Type with a Spiritual Practice: Exemplars from the Class of 2021" (April 7, 2021).

REFERENCES

Adyashanti. (2012). *The way of liberation: A practical guide to spiritual enlightenment.* Open Gate Sangha.

Allen, J. (1999). A community of critique, hope, and action. In J. Allen (Ed.), *Class actions: Teaching for social justice in elementary and middle school* (pp. 1–17). Teachers College.

Armstrong, K. (2019). *The lost art of scripture: Rescuing the sacred texts.* Alfred A. Knopf.

Banks, J. A. (2006). *Cultural diversity and education: Foundation, curriculum, and teaching.* Pearson.

Barnhardt, B. (2007). *The future of wisdom: Toward a rebirth of sapiential Christianity.* Continuum.

Batchelor, S. (2015). *After Buddhism: Re-thinking the dharma for a secular age.* Yale University Press.

Beah, I. (2007). *A long way gone: Memoirs of a boy soldier.* Farrar, Straus, and Giroux.

Berry, W. (1981). *"Solving for pattern." The gift of the good land.* North Point Press.

Bertolucci, B. (Director). (1993). *Little Buddha.* [Film]. Miramax Films.

Bintliff, A. (2016). *Re-engaging disconnected youth: Transformative learning through restorative and social justice education* (2nd ed.). Peter Lang.

Borg, M. (1987). *Jesus: A new vision: Spirit, culture, and the life of discipleship.* Harper San Francisco.

Borg, M. (1994). *Meeting Jesus again for the first time: The historical Jesus & the heart of contemporary faith.* HarperCollins.

Bourgeault, C. (n.d.). *Frequently asked questions about wisdom schools.* The Wisdom Way of Knowing. https://wisdomwayofknowing.org/resourcedirectory/frequently-asked-questions- about-wisdom-schools/

Bourgeault, C. (2003). *The wisdom way of knowing: Reclaiming an ancient tradition to awaken the heart.* Jossey-Bass.

Bourgeault, C. (2004). *Centering prayer and inner awakening.* Cowley.

Bourgeault, C. (2008). *The wisdom Jesus: Transforming heart and mind: a new perspective on Christ and his message.* Shambhala.

Bourgeault, C. (2010). *The meaning of Mary Magdalene: Discovering the woman at the heart of Christianity.* Shambhala.

Bourgeault, C. (2011). Through Holy Week with Mary Magdalene. *The Contemplative Society.* Audio recording at Pender Island, British Columbia, Canada. https://www.contemplative.org/product/through-holy-week-with-mary-magdalene/

Bourgeault, C. (2013). *The holy trinity and the law of three: Discovering the radical truth at the heart of Christianity.* Shambhala.

Bourgeault, C. (2014). *Spiritual practices from the Gurdjieff work.* Online course available from "Spirituality and Practice website. https://www.spiritualityandpractice.com/ecourses/course/view/181/spiritual- practices-from-the-gurdjieff-work

Bracher, M. (2006). *Radical pedagogy: Identity, generativity, and social transformation.* Palgrave Macmillan.

Brahmamuni, A. (2012, February 14). *The burdened heart.* Buddhism Now. https://buddhismnow.com/2012/02/14/the-burdened-heart-by-ajahn-brahmamuni/

Braskamp, L. (2007). Three "central" questions worth asking. *Journal of College and Character, IX*(1), 1–7.

Bregman, R. (2020). *Humankind: A hopeful history.* Bloomsbury.

Brown, M. (2010). *The presence process: A journey into present moment awareness.* (Revised Edition). Namaste.

Buchanan, M. (2015). *Chocolate: The bitter truth. 1 of 5 Child Trafficking. BBC Panorama Investigation* [Video]. Dailymotion. https://www.dailymotion.com/video/x2mo7g4

Buchbinder, A. (2013, April). Out of our heads: Philip Shepherd on the brain in the belly. *The Sun, 448*, 1–10.

Campbell, J. (2008). *Hero with a thousand faces* (3rd ed.). New World Library.

Cobb, E. F., McClintock, C. H., & Miller, L. J. (2016). Mindfulness and spirituality in positive youth development. In I. Ivtzan & T. Lomas (Eds.), *Mindfulness in positive psychology: The science of meditation and well-being* (pp. 245–264). Routledge.

Cohen, A. (2003). The challenge of our moment: A round-table discussion with Don Beck, Brian Swimme, and Peter Senge, moderated by Andrew Cohen. *What is Enlightenment?, 23*, 42–56.

Cook-Sather, A. (2006). Newly betwixt and between: Revising liminality in the context of a teacher preparation program. *Anthropology and Education Quarterly, 37*(2), 110–127.

Davies, L. (2006). Global citizenship: Abstraction or framework for action? *Educational Review, 58*(1), 5–25.

Deng, M. D. (n.d.). *The spiritual value of repetition.* Spirituality and Practice. https://www.spiritualityandpractice.com/explorations/teachers/deng-ming-dao/quotes

Diessner, R., Rust, T., Solom, R. C., Frost, N., & Parsons, L. (2006). Beauty and hope: A moral beauty intervention. *Journal of Moral Education, 35*(3), 301–317.

Earley, J., & Weiss, B. (2013). *Freedom from your inner critic: A self-therapy approach.* Sounds True.

Edmundson, M. (1997, September). On the uses of liberal education. *Harper's Magazine, 295*, 39–59.

Eiseley, L. (1978). *The star thrower.* Harvest.

Elliott, J. (2007). A curriculum for the study of human affairs: The contribution of Lawrence Stenhouse. In I. Westbury & G. Milburn (Eds.), *Rethinking schools: Twenty-five years of the journal of curriculum studies* (pp. 281–298). Routledge.

Ellsworth, J. (1999). Today's adolescent: Addressing existential dread. *Adolescence, 34*(134), 403–408.

Eves, H. W. (2003). *Mathematical circles adieu and return to mathematical circles.* Mathematical Association of America.

Eyler, J., & Giles, D. (1999). *Where's the learning in service-learning?* Jossey-Bass.

Ferrer, J. (2008). What does it mean to live a fully embodied spiritual life? *The International Journal of Transpersonal Studies, 27*(1), 1–11.

Fruehauf, R. (1999). *Chinese medicine in crisis: Science, politics, and the making of 'TCM'.* ClassicalChineseMedicine.org.

Gardner, H. (1999). *The disciplined mind.* Simon & Schuster.

Gardner, H. (2011). *Frames of mind: The theory of multiple intelligences.* Basic Books.

Gladwell, M. (2008). *Outliers.* Little, Brown.

Glanzer, P. L., Hill, J. P., & Johnston, B. R. (2017). *The quest for purpose: The collegiate search for a meaningful life.* State University of NY.

Golding, W. (1954). *Lord of the flies.* The Berkeley Publishing Group.

Handley, G. B. (2001). The humanities and citizenship: A challenge for service-learning. *Michigan Journal of Community Service Learning, 8*(1), 52–61.

Haste, H. (2004). Constructing the citizen. *Political Psychology, 25*(3), 413–439.

Hawkins, D. R. (2007). *Discovery of the presence of God: Devotional nonduality.* Veritas.

HeartMath Institute. (2012, August 20). *Heart-focused breathing.* Retrieved from https://www.heartmath.org/articles-of-the-heart/the-math-of-heartmath/heart-focused-breathing/

Heifetz, R. A., & Linsky, M. (2002). *Leadership on the line: Staying alive through the dangers of leading.* Harvard Business School Press.

Helminski, K. (1992). *Living presence: A Sufi way to mindfulness and the essential self.* Penguin/Tarcher.

Hicks, D. (2007). Responding to the world. In D. Hicks & C. Holden (Eds.), *Teaching the global dimension: Key principles and effective practice* (pp. 3–13). Routledge.

Huberman, A. (2021, March 22). *How to increase motivation and drive. Huberman podcast #12* [Video]. YouTube. https://www.youtube.com/watch?v=vA50EK70whE

Hudson, J. R. (2019). *Spiritual direction and dream work training in the Jungian Mystical Christian tradition.* https://www.thelightclinic.org/dream-work-spiritual-direction.html

Ilibagiza, I., & Irwin, S. (2006). *Left to tell: Discovering God amidst the Rwandan holocaust.* Hay House.

Jennings, B., & Prewitt, K. (1985). The humanities and the social sciences: Reconstructing a public philosophy. In D. Callahan, A.L. Caplan, & B. Jennings (Eds.), *Applying the humanities* (pp. 125–143). Plenum.

Johnston, D. K. (2006). *Education for a caring society: Classroom relationships and moral action*. Teachers College Press.

Keating, T. (1992). *Invitation to love: The way of Christian contemplation*. Continuum Publishing.

Keltner, D., & Haidt, J. (2003). Approaching awe, a moral, spiritual, and aesthetic emotion. *Cognition and Emotion, 17*(2), 297–314.

Kennedy, K. J. (2005). *Changing schools for changing times: New directions for the school curriculum in Hong Kong*. Chinese University Press.

Kielburger, C., & Major, K. (1998). *Free the children: A young man fights against child labor and proves that children can change the world*. HarperPerennial.

King, U. (1996). *Spirit of fire: The life and vision of Teilhard de Chardin*. Orbis.

King, U. (1999). *Pierre Teilhard de Chardin: Writings selected with an introduction*. Modern spiritual masters series. Orbis.

Ko, T. Y. (2016a). *Mindfulness meditation befriending* [Video]. YouTube. https://www.youtube.com/watch?v=pLt-E4YNVHU.

Ko, T. Y. (2016b). *Mindfulness meditation body scan* [Video]. YouTube. https://www.youtube.com/watch?v=CyKhfUdOEgs.

Larson, K. (2017). *Adolescents' self-described transformations and their alignment with transformative learning theory*. (Unpublished doctoral dissertation.) Antioch University.

Lee, W. O. (2002). The emergence of new citizenship: Looking into the self and beyond the nation. In G. Steiner-Khamsi, J. Torney-Purta, & J. Schwille (Eds.), *New paradigms and recurring paradoxes in education for citizenship: An international comparison* (pp. 37–60). JAI.

Leung, Y. W. (2006). How do they become socially/politically active? Case studies of Hong Kong secondary students' political socialisation. *Citizenship Teaching and Learning, 2(*2) 51–67.

Levine, S. (2013). *Becoming Kuan Yin: The evolution of compassion*. Weiser.

London, R. (2016). The Enneagram: A spiritual perspective for addressing significant problems through research. In J. Lin, R. L. Oxford, & T. Culham (Eds.), *Towards a spiritual paradigm: Exploring new ways of knowing, researching, and being*. Information Age Publishing.

Lothstein, A. S. (2008). Teaching for lustres: An essay on the Emersonian teacher. In A. S. Lothstein & Brodrick, M. (Eds.), *New morning: Emerson in the twenty-first century* (pp. 67–98). State University of New York.

Loung, U. (2006). *First they killed my father: A daughter of Cambodia remembers*. HarperPerennial.

Mam, S. (2009). *The road to lost innocence. The story of a Cambodian heroine*. Spiegel & Grau.

Marshall, H. (2005). Developing the global gaze in citizenship education: Exploring the perspectives of global education NGO workers in England. *International Journal of Citizenship and Teacher Education, 1*(2), 76–92.

Martin, W. (2018). *The Tao te Ching as a path and practice*. Online course available from Spirituality and Practice. https://www.spiritualityandpractice.com/ecourses/course/view/121/the-tao-te-ching- as-a-path-and-a-practice

Maxwell, T. P. (2003). Considering spirituality: Integral spirituality, deep science, and ecological awareness. *Zygon, 38,* 257–276.

McGonigal, K. (2014, November 16). *Kelly McGonigal flow yoga practice* [Video]. YouTube. https://www.youtube.com/watch?v=j2tV8zi_TvQ

McMahon, E. M., & Campbell, P. A. (2010). *Rediscovering the lost body-connection within Christian spirituality: The missing link for experiencing yourself in the body of the whole Christ is a changing relationship to your own body*. Tasora.

Merlin's Diary Podcast. (2015, December 7). *What piece of advice would you give the 16 year old you?* [Video]. YouTube. https://www.youtube.com/watch?v=3h-maz3f4jM

Merryfield, M., Lo, J. T. Y., Po, S. C., & Kasai, M. (2008). Worldmindedness: Taking off the blinders. *Journal of Curriculum and Instruction, 1*(2), 6–20.

Metzner, R. (1998). *The unfolding self: Varieties of transformative experiences*. Origin.

Mezirow, J. (2000). Learning to think like an adult: Core concepts of transformation theory. In J. Mezirow & Associates (Eds.), *Learning as transformation: Critical perspectives on a theory in progress* (pp. 3–34). Jossey-Bass.

Miller, J. P. (2007). *The holistic curriculum* (2nd Ed.). University of Toronto Press.

Mosley, C. (2014). *THIS IS WATER! by David Foster-Wallace* [Video]. YouTube. https://www.youtube.com/watch?v=eC7xzavzEKY

Mustakova-Possardt, E. (2004, December 16–19). *Critical consciousness—Motivation for service to humanity*. Keynote plenary address at the Baha'i Conference on Social and Economic Development for the Americas, Orlando, FL.

Myers, A. (Director). (2004). *China's lost girls* [film]. National Geographic.

Nazer, M., & Lewis, D. (2010). *Slave: My true story*. Virago.

Needleman, J. (1999). In search of the miraculous. A synopsis by Jacob Needleman. *Gurdjieff International Review 2*(2). https://www.gurdjieff.org/needleman1.htm

Neff, K. (2011). *Self-compassion: The proven path of being kind to yourself*. HarperCollins.

NFB. (2017, June 22). *Scared sacred* [Video]. YouTube. https://www.youtube.com/watch?v=nYuqAGC1X2w

Nino, A. G. (2000). Spiritual quest among young adults. In V. H. Kazanjian & P. L. Lawrence (Eds.), *Education as transformation: Religious pluralism, spirituality, and a new vision for higher education in America* (pp. 45–57). Peter Lang.

Noble, C. (1994). *Bridge across my sorrows: The Christina Noble story*. John Murray.

Noddings, N. (2002). *Educating moral people: A caring alternative to character education*. Teachers College Press.

Nottingham, R. (2018). *The work: Esotericism and Christian psychology*. CreateSpace Independent Publishing Platform.

Ouspensky, P. D. (2001). *In search of the miraculous*. Mariner.

Oxfam. (2018). *Teaching controversial issues: A guide for teachers*. Oxfam. https://oxfamilibrary.openrepository.com/handle/10546/620473

Oyler, C. (2012). *Actions speak louder than words: Community activism as curriculum*. Routledge.

Palmer, P. (1983). *To know as we are known*. HarperCollins.

Palmer, P. (1998). *The courage to teach: Exploring the inner landscape of a teacher's life*. Jossey-Bass.

Palmer, P. (1999). The grace of great things: Reclaiming the sacred in knowing, teaching, and learning. In S. Glazer (Ed.), *The heart of learning: Spirituality in education*. Tarcher/Penguin.

Palmer, P. J., Zajonc, A., & Scribner, M. (2010). *The heart of higher education: A call to renewal: transforming the academy through collegial conversations.* Jossey- Bass.

Panksepp, J. (2004). *Affective neuroscience: The foundations of human and animal emotions.* Oxford University Press.

Park, Y., & Vollers, M. (2015). *In order to live: A North Korean girl's journey to freedom.* Penguin House.

Parks, S. D. (2000). *Big questions, worthy dreams: Mentoring young people in their search for meaning, purpose, and faith.* Jossey-Bass.

Parks, S. D. (2005). How then shall we live? Suffering and wonder in the new commons. In S. M. Intrator (Ed.), *Living the questions: Essays inspired by the work and life of Parker J. Palmer* (pp. 298–320). Jossey-Bass.

Pinker, S. (2018). *Enlightenment now: The case for reason, science, humanism, and progress.* Viking.

Plotkin, B. (2003). *Soulcraft: Crossing into the mysteries of nature and psyche.* New World Library.

Powers, W. (2008, September). Future Zarahs. *The Sun, 393,* 12–15.

Pryce, P. (2018). *The monk's cell: Ritual and knowledge in American contemplative Christianity.* Oxford University Press.

Purpel, D. E. (2004). A curriculum for social justice and compassion. In D. E. Purpel & W. M. McLaurin, Jr. (Eds.), *Reflections on the moral and spiritual crisis in education* (pp. 226–260). Peter Lang.

Quinn, D. (1992). *Ishmael: An adventure of the mind and spirit.* Bantam/Turner.

Real Stories. (2017, November 16). *Slavery: A global investigation (modern slavery documentary).* [Video]. YouTube. https://www.youtube.com/watch?v=WfdibtC4RYg

Riso, D. R., & Hudson, R. (1996). *Personality types: Using the enneagram for self-discovery* (Revised Edition). Houghton Mifflin.

Riso, D. R., & Hudson, R. (1999). *The wisdom of the enneagram: The complete guide to psychological and spiritual growth for the nine personality types.* Bantam.

Rohr, R. (2016, October 10). The inner witness. *Center for Action and Contemplation.* https://cac.org/the-inner-witness-2016-10-10/

Rosling, H. (2018). *Factfulness: Ten reasons you are wrong about the world—And why things are better than you think.* Flatiron.

Salzberg, S. (2015). "The self-hatred in all of us." *On Being.* https://onbeing.org/blog/the-self-hatred-within-us/

Sandel, M. J. (2010). *Justice: What's the right thing to do.* Farrar, Straus and Giroux.

Schmidt, M. E. (2009). *Teaching for social conscience in Hong Kong secondary schools.* (Unpublished doctoral dissertation). University of Western Australia, Perth, Australia.

Selby, D. (2001). The signature of the whole: Radical interconnectedness and its implications for global and environmental education. *Encounter: Education for Meaning and Social Justice, 14(*4), 5–16.

Senge, P., Scharmer, C. O., Jaworski, J., & Flowers, B. S. (2004). *Presence: Human purpose and the field of the future.* The Society for Organizational Learning.

Seppälä, E. (2014, September 15). 18 Science-backed reasons to try loving-kindness meditation. *Psychology Today.* https://www.psychologytoday.com/intl/blog/feeling-it/201409/18-science-backed-reasons-try-loving-kindness-meditation

Shapiro, H. S. (2006). *Losing heart: The moral and spiritual miseducation of American children*. Lawrence Erlbaum.

Shea, P. (2015). *Alchemy of the extraordinary: A journey into the heart of the meridian matrix*. Soul Pivot.

Shusterman, N. (2018). *Scythe*. Walker.

Smith, H. (1991). *The world's religions*. HarperCollins.

Tappan, M. B. (2006). Moral functioning as mediated action. *Journal of Moral Education, 35*(1), 1–18.

Taylor, C. (1991). *The ethics of authenticity*. Harvard University Press.

Teasdale, W. (1999). *The mystic heart: Discovering a universal spirituality in the world's religions*. New World Library.

Teasdale, W. (2002). *A monk in the world: Cultivating a spiritual life*. New World Library.

TED. (2009, October 8). *The danger of a single story. Chimamanda Ngozi Adichie* [Video]. YouTube. https://www.youtube.com/watch?v=D9Ihs241zeg

TEDx Talks. (2013, February 7). *The space between self-esteem and self-compassion: Kristin Neff at TEDxCentennialParkWomen* [Video]. YouTube. https://www.youtube.com/watch?v=IvtZBUSplr4

Twenge, J. M. (2017, September). Have smartphones destroyed a generation? *The Atlantic*. www.theatlantic.com/magazine/archive/2017/09/has-the-smartphone-destroyed-a-generation/534198/

WE Movement. (2017, February 7). *Craig Kielburger—It takes a child—A journey into child labour* [Video]. YouTube. https://www.youtube.com/watch?v=-7fnOhwJm2k

Welwood, J. (2000). *Towards a psychology of awakening: Buddhism, psychotherapy, and the path of personal and spiritual transformation*. Shambhala.

Whitmont, E. (1979). *The symbolic quest: Basic concepts of analytic psychology*. Princeton University Press.

Williams, M., & Penman, D. (2011). *Mindfulness: A practical guide to finding peace in a frantic world*. Little, Brown.

Wright, R. (2001). *Non-zero: The logic of human destiny*. Vintage.

Yu, H. (1993). *To live*. Random House.

Printed in the United States
by Baker & Taylor Publisher Services